EVOLVING

SOULFULLY

Copyright © 2014 by Dave Wali Waugh, RPC. All Rights Reserved, including the right of reproduction in whole or part form, or by any means. This book is the proprietary work of Dave Wali Waugh, RPC. Any unauthorized use of this copyrighted material or the titles, diagrams and details contained in this book in relation to goods and/or services (including seminars, workshops, training programs, etc.) is prohibited without the express written permission of the Author. Every reasonable care has been taken to acknowledge ownership of copyrighted material in this book; however, the Author and Publishers will gladly receive any information that would enable them to rectify any reference or credit line in subsequent editions. Names and identifying characteristics of people in the book have been changed where necessary to protect the privacy of the individuals.

This publication expresses the ideas, opinions and suggestions of its Author and is intended to provide useful information with regard to the subject matter at hand. It is not the intention of the Author to replace relevant professional advice, and readers are advised to consult a competent professional in all instances. The Author and Publishers expressly disclaim any responsibility for any liability, loss, or risk, personal or otherwise, which is incurred either directly or indirectly, or as a consequence of, the use and application of any of the contents of this book.

Canadian Cataloguing First Publication Date: October 2014

ISBN 978-0-9939771-0-7

Dave Wali Waugh, RPC

EVOLVING SOULFULLY

1. Spirituality   2. Psychology

Layout, design, typography and cover design by Lee Johnson

Book enabled by Lee Johnson: Literary Consultant, Ghostwriter and Editor

EVOLVING SOULFULLY

Cultivating Natural Vitality, Deep Presence,
Intimacy, Meaning and Purpose

Dave Wali Waugh, RPC

PRAISE FOR 'EVOLVING SOULFULLY'

"*Evolving Soulfully* is an enjoyable weave of story, poetry, philosophy, psychology and ancient wisdom!" ——*Christine J. Elsay, PhD; Associate Professor of anthropology and sociology and author of The Poetics of Land & Identity among British Columbia Indigenous Peoples*

"Reading *Evolving Soulfully* felt like a soulful conversation with a wonderful friend who is sharing from his heart the wisdom gathered on his journey. Dave's naturalness is his unique gold. His writing invited me to deeply relax and open to some soul soothing insights that feel so approachable. The examples he shares from his life resonate with our essential human experiences so that we immediately recognize we are on a shared journey." ——*Thomas Atum O'Kane PhD; is a senior teacher in the Sufi Order International and the Founder of the Spiritual Guidance Wisdom School*

"Dave is a wise, inspiring, good-hearted person, and with such a creative approach that his new book, *Evolving Soulfully*, promises to follow suit with those personal qualities I have known him to have. —*David Roomy, Author of Inner Journey To Sacred Places*

"Dave offers up this contribution from his own travels in depth exploration. Within it is a sacred call to embrace a framework, a sequential map and clear steps for the journey of soulful living. This is clearly well written; it offers both information, and very practical guidance in the movement from our sense of individual separation to the interpersonal and the sacred. A gentle and substantial contribution to the field of psychological healing and spiritual transformation. Well worth both its initial reading and as an ongoing reference and practice guide through time." ——*Ian Macnaughton Ph.D., is a registered clinical counsellor and editor of Embodying the Mind & Minding the Body*

DEDICATION

"The planet does not need more successful people. The planet desperately needs more peacemakers, healers, restorers, storytellers and lovers of all kinds."

- Dalai Lama

I would like to dedicate this book to my parents Ron and Edna Waugh for the love and gifts they have given me. I also would like to wholeheartedly thank my mentors and guides for their kind encouragement and wise, soulful guidance. Many of their names are sprinkled throughout this book.

I am especially grateful to my wife Sue, for the wonderful dance of this great love.

CONTENTS

	Page
INTRODUCTION:	
A WHOLISTIC MAP TO THE INNER TREASURE	9
CHAPTER 1:	
THE ORDINARY LIFE OF SEPARATION	39
CHAPTER 2:	
THE CALL TO THE INNER WORLD OF PSYCHE	67
CHAPTER 3:	
ALLIES, MENTORS AND ELDERS ON THE PATH	89
CHAPTER 4:	
HOME OF THE SOUL AND SOULFUL RELATIONSHIPS	111
CHAPTER 5:	
TRANSFORMATION—OUR UNFOLDING SOUL	137
CHAPTER 6:	
THE GIFTS OF SOULFUL MEANING AND PURPOSE	167
CHAPTER 7:	
SOUL OF THE WORLD—LIVING THE SOULFUL LIFE	195
APPENDIX	231
PRACTICE THE PATH—MATURATION ATTAINMENT PATH OF WHOLISTIC AWAKENING YOGA	244
ACKNOWLEDGMENTS	280
ABOUT THE AUTHOR	281

INTRODUCTION: A WHOLISTIC MAP TO THE INNER TREASURE

"Where your treasure is, there will your heart be also."

- Anonymous, Holy Bible: King James Version

"Science is, at least in part, informed worship!"

— Carl Sagan

"Let the beauty you love be what you do, there are hundreds of ways to kneel and kiss the ground!"

— Rumi, translated by Coleman Barks

REMEMBRANCE DAY

Have you found your Inner Treasure? Is it true that where your treasure is, there your heart is also? Is science partly informed worship for you? Have you found your unique ways to kneel and kiss the ground? Do you wake up with a sense of adventure or are you feeling burnt out, heartbroken or lost?

Today is Remembrance Day in Canada and Veteran's Day in the USA. Remembrance Day is important to me for many reasons. Today I am embarking on a nine-month adventure of awakening and I invite you to join me on the journey. Remembrance Day has become an important reminder for me to learn from the past, awaken in the present and look for inspiration in the future.

When I reflect on the past, I feel grateful for the selfless service of those who gave their lives so that we may live with greater freedom and choice in our lives.

Remembrance Day also reminds me to remember what matters most to me in the present moment. If I uncover my Inner Treasure it can lead me to manifesting the three facets of true prosperity: personal, relational and vocational vitality. This orientation gives me a healthy balance of meaning and prosperity that helps me to transform and evolve soulfully.

My hope in writing this book is for any of my family members, clients or others who feel stuck in a major transition to receive greater understanding into why they get caught in habitual patterns that lead to deep suffering. Throughout these pages and in the appendix I offer you practices and resources that can lead you to lasting relief from suffering and can help you thrive with personal, relational and vocational vitality.

We may need to dig deep inside so we can identify our Inner Treasure as Inner Resources and Gifts. With these inner resources we can cultivate wellness in body, mind, heart, soul and spirit for personal vitality. Inner Treasure can manifest as more awareness, love and wisdom for cultivating deep intimacy and greater relationship vitality. If we give our Inner Treasure as Gifts to a meaningful need, we feel the joy and fulfillment of vocational vitality as a deep sense of meaning and purpose.

When I see the incredible potential in our children, I am inspired to cultivate a soulful life of integrity while leaving a legacy to ensure their future is also meaningful and prosperous.

This is very challenging at times. I often fall far short of my intentions and goals, but this orientation does give me a sense of adventure and meaningful and purposeful direction in life.

Today is also the anniversary of the day my wife Sue and I met twelve years ago. I feel so blessed to journey with a life partner who is also dedicated to cultivating a soulful life of natural vitality, deep presence, intimacy, meaning and purpose. We have come to see our relationship as a soulful path that guides us toward uncovering the Inner Treasure that can help us heal and transform whatever remains unresolved in each other, so we can continue evolving.

For many years, I have made it a practice on Remembrance Day to dig for Inner Treasure. I begin by reflecting on the past so that I can harvest the experiences and lessons of my life. This time of reflection allows me to understand more deeply all that I've learned and to make the issues that are arising in the present more visible. With this mirroring I am better able to work with whatever emerging and long-standing challenges are present, and to treat them as invitations to continue to heal, transform and evolve soulfully.

In the following pages, I will share some of what I have learned to be helpful for me, and express some of what I have witnessed to be beneficial for others in their journey of healing and transforming to evolve soulfully.

What nine months does for the embryo,

forty early mornings will do

for your growing awareness.

—Rumi

Inspired by this quote from the 13th-century mystic poet and Sufi teacher, Jelaluddin Rumi, I set the intention to dedicate the following nine months of daily practice to catalyze my own transformation and evolution into my next stage of my development. It is no accident that the timeframe I chose is linked to the gestation period of the human. Like birthing a child into the world, this text is both an offering and an invitation.

It is simultaneously my most intimate and vulnerable act of sharing, and, a sincere invitation for you to join me in the deliberate, deep dive into healing, transforming and evolving to the next stage of your soul's unfolding. In the appendix you will find practices and possibilities to assist you on your journey of cultivating your soulful life.

I am attempting to write two books in the next nine months that honour the richness of soul and the purposeful meaning that comes from impassioned living. The first is a collaborative book for the Natural Gifts Society, a nonprofit that I co-founded (*www.naturalgiftssociety.org.*) The first book is entitled *Awakening Your Inner Gifts—A Map for Living with Greater Wellness, Joy, Fulfillment, Meaning and Purpose*.

The purpose of that collective work is to offer readers a map that helps them to begin uncovering their unique gifts and Inner Treasure for manifesting more soulful work that is uniquely meaningful and purposeful.

> *The meaning of life is to find your gift.*
>
> *The purpose of life is to give it away.*
>
> — Pablo Picasso

Expressed as an equation, the map is:

$$MAP = TN + EQ + NG - PR + MN$$

For greater wellness, joy, fulfillment and MAP (Meaning and Purpose), rest into your (TN) True Nature, remember your (EQ) Essential Qualities and (NG) Natural Gifts; clear your (PR) Personality Resistances, and give your Inner Gifts to a (MN) Meaningful Need you see in the world.

In this book, *Evolving Soulfully—Cultivating Natural Vitality, Deep Presence, Intimacy, Meaning and Purpose—* I share more theory and methods for how to heal and work through personality resistance that block your Inner Gifts.

I'll also be expanding upon the Natural Gifts Society (NGS) map and process to show how to apply this teaching to heal, transform and evolve for personal vitality and to cultivate relationship vitality as well.

Many of the world's wisdom traditions teach that there is great Treasure hidden within each of us. They offer direction and guidance with a kind of map and process to help us uncover our True Nature and Inner Gifts so we are able to thrive with natural vitality, deep presence, intimacy, meaning and purpose.

Sometimes in childhood we get a glimpse of this Treasure but then we lose sight of it again for many years. There is a Grimm's Folk Tale called The Golden Key that captures the essence of this golden time of childhood. I will intersperse this story with my own observations and comments:

One winter's day, when the ground lay deep in snow, a poor boy was sent to the forest with a sled to bring back some wood.

(When I was a young boy, growing up in rural Nova Scotia in the early sixties, my parents were not afraid to send me off into our twenty-five-acres of woods that led to the wild Atlantic Ocean. Usually, I went with my sisters and friends, but often I went alone. Yet I was not really alone because my loyal companion, my dog King, was always there to play with and protect me.)

After gathering the wood and loading it onto the sled, he was so cold that instead of going straight home, he thought he'd make a fire and warm himself a bit.

(At eight years old I was in Boy Scouts and was proud of my fire making ability. I had even earned a badge for fire making and basic survival skills.)

He cleared a space, and as he was scraping away the snow, he found a little golden key.

(In my boyhood, I was fascinated with chasing swallows and the adventure of tracking rabbits with my dog. Later I learned to orient with map and compass and had fun hunting for lost treasure.)

"Where there's a key," he said to himself, "there's sure to be a lock."

(What is the key to unlock your Inner Treasure?)

So he dug down into the ground and found an iron box. "There must be precious things in it," he thought. "If only the key fits!"

At first he couldn't find a keyhole.

(How many of us find the key, but can't find the box or the keyhole?)

Then at last he found one; though it was so small he could hardly see it. He tried the key and it fitted perfectly.

(If you found a golden key, did it fit? What did you discover inside?)

He began to turn the key....

Now we will have to wait until he turns it all the way and opens the lid. Then we will know what treasure is in the box...

At eight years of age I had a glimpse of that key and what was in that mysterious box, but then I lost sight of them. I was forced to say farewell to Nova Scotia and leave behind my innocence, my beloved dog, my friends, and a great adventure in nature.

Those times stayed with me, faithfully held in some deep recesses that I could retrieve years later. Today, most parents would not think of sending their eight-year-old out in the woods by himself. Instead, many children spend their spare time parked in front of the TV, computer or video game. This skewed environment and socialization might be part of the reason we are seeing so many children with symptoms that were unheard of fifty years ago.

Author Richard Louv, in his compelling 2005 book *Last Child in the Woods—Saving Our Children From Nature-Deficit Disorder*, explores how adults and children are spending less time in the woods and suffering from what he calls 'nature-deficit disorder'. Although not recognized by the medical diagnostic manuals yet, he believes that nature-deficit disorder results in a wide range of behavioural problems.

It was not until I was in my mid-thirties and suffered a painful midlife crisis that I was called to embark on an adventure of healing so I could search for the Inner Treasure again.

The trouble began with a quarter life crisis at age twenty-five when my father died painfully of lung cancer. I was in shock at the loss of such a prominent figure in my life. Having no capacity to grieve such a significant loss, my habitual response was to self-medicate the pain with addictive substances, and then get busy, so I did not have to stop long enough to feel the loss.

However, my avoidant strategies caught up to me in midlife when my marriage broke apart. Through all the heartache, I realized that the business that I had worked so hard to build, no longer felt meaningful. This led me on a quest of healing and exploring what my heart was really yearning for.

After much soul searching, I eventually sold my business and went back to school to train as a wilderness leader and guide. I was excited to explore the beautiful forests, mountains and ocean on the West Coast of Canada. Exploring the vast wilderness of British Columbia brought me back in touch with my early love for the wilderness that I had first experienced as a young boy in Nova Scotia.

I've always been drawn to the adventure of orienteering with map and compass, so I was thrilled to pick up the adventure again where I left off at eight years of age, almost thirty years earlier.

In midlife, as I reconnected with my joy, the pain I had been repressing for decades also began surfacing—there is no telling what event will be the cause for the wall of the emotional dam to start cracking.

I remember when I first went back to school to brush up on my writing skills. The teacher asked us to choose a simple topic to write about, such as a childhood pet or a family vacation.

My family had many cats over the years, and I vaguely remembered having a dog when I was a boy, so I decided to write about the dog. When I tried to access these distant memories, my recollections suddenly got more clouded and I experienced a sleepy exhaustion. In this state, I felt helpless against the turbulent bombardment of waves of buried emotion that began welling up within me. Unable to contain the storm, the tears started to flow.

Here I was, thirty-five years old and crying like a child in the back of the class. I tried to stop the tears and pull myself back together, but I could not help but fall apart.

I felt an overwhelming urge, like *The Hobbit*'s Bilbo Baggins, to put on the ring of invisibility when faced with danger. I had even chosen to sit in the back of the class to minimize my exposure. I knew my attempt to turn invisible did not work when the teacher asked me to share my essay with the class. I shook my head side-to-side and nervously said, "I'll pass, thanks!" I was thankful she went quickly on to someone else, but I felt flushed with shame thinking everyone in the class knew exactly how I felt and that I was coming unglued.

That was one of the clues that led me to realizing that I was carrying a lot of trauma. I had repressed the memories of losing my dog and of my father's death because they were so painful. The floodgates were opening, and I was powerless to stop them. This crack in my armour helped me see just how emotionally blocked I had become and how much this had been impacting all of my relationships.

The journey of discovery and healing is rarely a straight line;

rather, it is a journey of peaks and valleys. I spiraled through periods of gaining clarity and insight and then got out of balance again, both physically and psychologically. Over time, I started to heal and became fascinated with the exploration of the inner wilderness as well as the outer wilderness and how they are naturally connected.

The adventure into the inner wilderness became a long initiation and apprenticeship in personal healing that led me to training in my present vocation as a mentor and psychotherapist.

I like the term mentor and psychotherapist because it is an acronym for map. "Maturation Awakening Path," "Meaning and Purpose" and "Midlife Awakening Process" can also be abbreviated to the letters MAP.

In this vocation, as a mentor and psychotherapist, I often meet people when they are in a state of great suffering that has become overwhelming. They are seeking some therapeutic support that acts like a safe cocoon for part of their journey.

For others, there is a yearning for something more in life. They may be searching for something precious that seems missing. This is often a longing for their Inner Treasure. They want a mentor as a catalyst in their path of awakening. Some people want both, therapeutic support and mentoring.

I prefer the term wholistic instead of holistic in the sense of treating the whole person who has a desire to evolve in greater wholeness. For evolving wholeness and maturation, we can confront our dragons and uncover our Inner Treasure to heal, transform and evolve physically, emotionally, cognitively, relationally, vocationally, soulfully and spiritually.

Quite often a person is undergoing a major life transition of some kind. They may be looking for meaningful and purposeful work, searching for a life partner, starting a family, going through separation or divorce, mourning the loss a loved one, feeling lost or stuck in Quarter Life Crisis or Midlife Crisis or are feeling confused about the transition to retirement. They may be experiencing unusual symptoms like exhaustion, burnout, anxiety, Adrenal Fatigue, allergies, Chronic Fatigue, Anorexia, Bulimia, Migraines, Depression, overwhelming stress, negative self-talk or similar ailments.

In order to soothe their pain, perhaps they have reached for substances or activities to self-medicate. Those strategies may have become addictive and gotten out of control, like using alcohol, cigarettes, cocaine, marijuana, work, constant busyness, gambling, binge eating, shopping, power, affairs, promiscuous sex, the Internet, porn, or other high-risk activities to numb out.

When our inner dragons take over, the old life does not work anymore, and the new life has not yet arrived.

It often feels excruciating to be caught in this in-between time blocked from our Inner Treasure because something inside us feels like it wants to die—and yet something else wants to be born. This causes a great tension inside of us, and it's normal to want to reach for whatever 'quick fix' will ease the pain.

Many of the strategies we try to employ for easing our pain do provide some temporary relief, but then the suffering or longing calls us to begin anesthetizing or searching again.

I believe this tension is not only happening for individuals but also couples, groups, and nations—in fact, for all of humanity. It's like we have become trapped in a story that is too small for us, and the only choice seems to be to collapse in despair or to expand our story by soulfully transforming and evolving.

To be clear, I am not against taking the appropriate medication to ease a splitting headache. Or, if someone needs his or her gallstones removed, I am not against taking advantage of modern medical treatment when needed. Some symptoms can be caused by allergies or a poor diet. It is wise to take a wholistic approach and consult the appropriate health professionals.

When people come to see me though, they have likely exhausted their attempts at getting the kind of relief they are looking for from the conventional medical model of treatment.

Often, they have been looking in the wrong place!

DREAMS OF INNER TREASURE

Previously I mentioned that in 1989, I was thirty-five and suffering from a painful midlife crisis. One night I had a powerful dream that eventually led me on the journey of healing and quest for Inner Treasure.

In my dream, I was visiting a wise old man and I began asking him a lot of questions. He looked like a sage with long hair and a flowing robe. He seemed very loving, kind, patient and peaceful. He listened to me intently and then he looked deeply into my eyes and said to me gently, 'All you need to do is relax!' His words sparked a tremendous energy surge that coursed through my body. This was followed by the thought, 'This is more than a dream; I'm actually feeling this powerful energy!'

At this thought I woke up. It was pitch dark in my bedroom and about 3am. I lived alone then and was so energized by the dream that I couldn't get back to sleep. My mind started obsessing about what the dream meant. Finally I said to myself, 'Just relax!' When I thought this, the energy began to surge up my spine and then lit me up like a Christmas tree in the dark. This time it was much more intense! I started getting scared wondering if I was possessed.

I had worked in the electrical field for over a decade and had been shocked by high voltage many times, but I had never experienced anything like this! I didn't think of myself as the least bit religious back then, but in that moment I started to pray to be protected, fearful that this power flow could be something detrimental to my wellbeing. I had never paid much attention to dreams before, so I tried to just write it off as a strange experience. Then things seemed to stabilize so I quit praying and felt relieved and grateful.

Later that year, in the fall of 1989, I went to my first soulful men's retreat with Archetypal Psychotherapist and author of *The Soul's Code* James Hillman and Mythologist Michael Meade, author of *Fate And Destiny —The Two Agreements of the Soul*. They introduced me to the heart of soulful ritual, storytelling, poetry and dream work. At the end of the retreat I joined my first soulful men's group and have been deeply involved with evolutionary men's work ever since.

I had rejected the Christian Religion as a boy reasoning that it was judgmental of me and of other traditions and unscientific because it did not seem to include evolution. In my electrical work, objective reason and science were what mattered to me. James Hillman's work introduced me to a more subjective way of knowing, which led me to realize that I had been living a polarized life. In his book *Re-visioning Psychology* he says, "Loving is a way of knowing and for love to know, it must personify... Personifying is thus the heart's mode of knowing. It's not a lesser, primitive way of apprehending, but a finer one. To enter myth, we must personify. To personify carries us into myth."

Through Hillman and Meade, I learned that the word *myth* could be used in different ways. On the one hand, the objective part of me can logically say that Bilbo Baggins, the Hobbit, is not real. He is a fictional character. *The Lord of the Rings* is 'just a myth', a fantasy! On the other hand, The Lord of the Rings as a 'myth' is a symbolic personification of a subjective truth, like a subjective map of the Inner World of the Psyche. Bilbo has to face his inner dragons to discover his Inner Treasure of courage and resourcefulness to foster natural vitality, deep presence, intimacy, meaning and purpose.

I realized that the world's religions are also symbolic personifications of subjective truths, like maps to the Inner Treasure as well. I did not have to polarize and choose Science or Spirituality; I could choose both as long as I did not confuse the literal with the symbolic. I could embrace both: reason and love, the objective and the subjective, thinking and feeling.

This opened the world's mystical traditions to me as mythic metaphors for the deep reality of subjective experience.

I was particularly entranced with hearing the mystical poetry of Rumi for the first time. Jelaluddin Rumi (1207-1273) was a 13th Century Sufi mystic and spiritual teacher. I was drawn to his rowdy, ecstatic teaching and felt like I had come home! Just as in Rumi's poem, I realized there are "hundreds of ways to kneel and kiss the ground." I simply needed to, "Let the beauty I love, be what I do!" This ignited my quest with the parallel questions; 'What is love? What do I really love?'

It was humbling to admit that at thirty-five I was very confused about love. In many ways I had enjoyed my career but I could not really say that I loved it. When someone says, 'I love my work!' it is usually an indication that his or her work feels meaningful and purposeful and they are experiencing a sense of destiny. I felt trapped in fate and longed to discover my destiny.

Armed with these compelling questions, I began the quest to learn the ways to balance the subjective and objective, heart and head, love and reason. Since Rumi spoke so deeply about love, I yearned to meet a living Sufi guide who could help me to mature and evolve soulfully.

Then in 1992, I read an article about the midlife passage, by Sufi Teacher and Transpersonal Psychotherapist, Thomas Atum O'Kane, PhD. Still held in the turbulence of my own midlife crisis, Atum's words spoke deeply to my heart and Soul. He spoke wisely of the difference between a transition and a transformation. Sometimes we make a transition from one job or relationship to another and nothing much changes. Midlife crisis can be an opportunity to enter into a deep metamorphosis, a passage of transformation to our Self, Soul and Spirit. It is like a death of the old life and a birth of the new. He used metaphors like the transformation a mother undergoes in the nine months it takes to birth a child or how the caterpillar needs to enter the cocoon for a deep metamorphosis. Like Rumi, this Sufi teacher was resonating with my deep heart and soul's longing.

That summer, when I went to my first retreat with Atum, I instinctively knew I was in the right place. I admired how inclusive he was of all the World's Traditions. He said that he was not interested in acquiring students or followers; his intention was to help awaken the teacher within the student!

I have the same intention for this book, to help awaken the teacher within you. It was like a dream come true for me to meet a soulful teacher like Atum—one who holds such a deep connection between many Wisdom Traditions and Transpersonal Psychology.

As mentioned earlier, I was raised in the Catholic Tradition but as soon as I saw the first pictures of the Earth from space at age ten, I knew that Catholicism and indeed Christianity was not the only way. I also knew instinctively that Christianity, as a whole, had not kept up with the truth Science was revealing.

Atum introduced me to a deep interspiritual and psychospiritual dialogue and appreciation. One of his central teachings was that it is important to know what you serve. He serves Love, and therefore studies all the great teachers of Love from many traditions. He described the Sufi path as a path of Love. This inspired me to explore many mystical traditions.

He is a masterful storyteller and soulful guide. One of the stories he shared resonated deeply with my dream of the wise old man who guided me to relax to uncover my Inner Treasure. This was my first glimpse of the 'wise teacher within.'

ISAAC'S DREAM OF TREASURE

There is an ancient Jewish folktale about a man named Isaac who was very poor. He was so poor that many nights he would go to bed hungry.

One night he had an amazing dream. A guide spoke to him in the dream and told him of a great Treasure that was buried near the bridge leading to the Royal Palace in the capital city. He was instructed by the guide to make the journey to the capital city where he would find a great treasure.

When Isaac awoke the next morning and realized that it was just a dream, he felt even more depressed. The next night the same dream visited him, and the same guide insisted that he make the journey to the capital city to find the Treasure. When he awoke the next morning, he shared his dream with some friends and family.

The answer he got was basically what he expected: "Don't be foolish, Isaac—it's only a dream—go back home!"

Then the third night, the dream came again. When Isaac awoke in the morning, he kept the dream to himself. He packed his shovel, a light bag and what little food he had left, and set out on a journey toward the capital city.

As he walked, he could hear different voices in the back of his head. One of the voices sounded much like those of his friends and family: "Don't be foolish, Isaac—go back home!"

Another part of him was quite worried about his food not lasting very long, and also that he would be a stranger in the capital city. How would he survive?

On Isaac's journey he walked through the dark forest and over the mountains. Occasionally he got a lift from a kind stranger, but most of the way he walked.

When he arrived at the capital city, it was getting close to nightfall. It turned out there had been a lot of crime of late, and the palace guards were on high alert. They had been instructed to imprison anyone who was out wandering the streets late at night.

Isaac managed to make his way to the heart of the city close to the Royal Palace without being spotted. Just like in the dream he saw a small bridge that went across the river to the Royal Palace. He felt confused as to where to start. The guide had only told him the Treasure was buried near the palace bridge.

As he paced back and forth wondering what to do next, the captain of the guards spotted him. Isaac was so lost and confused that he didn't notice the captain rush up to him. The captain held his rifle firmly pointed at Isaac's chest. He commanded, "You there, what are you doing? What are you doing with that shovel?"

Isaac was so shocked and stunned to see the captain standing there with a rifle pointed at his chest that he began to cry out, "Please sir, don't arrest me, I'm an honest man, I'm from the country, I'm not here to steal anything or hurt anyone!"

Then Isaac told the Captain the whole story, about the dream and about the buried Treasure that he was guided to find there.

Hearing Isaac's sincere grief pour out like this touched something in the captain and he softened, then he said, "Somehow I believe that you are harmless and honest, but I also think you're a fool. I once had a dream just like this one, where I was told to go to a particular street in a particular village and dig under the hearth of a man named Isaac to uncover great Treasure. Don't be a fool—they are just dreams!"

Suddenly Isaac's spirit brightened. He hadn't told the captain his name, what village he was from, or what street he lived on—and yet the captain had described it all perfectly.

Isaac bowed humbly to the captain and implored him to allow him to go back home. The captain warned him sternly to leave immediately before he changed his mind.

Isaac turned gratefully and began the long journey home. All the way he contemplated his good fortune. He walked over mountains and through dark forests. Most of the way he walked, but occasionally he got a ride from a kind stranger.

Once he arrived back home he immediately went to work digging under his hearth. Before long he uncovered a wonderful Treasure.

In gratitude, he sent a large ruby to the captain of the guards. Then he renovated his house and turned it into a temple in appreciation to the divine guidance that the dream had revealed to him.

From that day forth, he invited all his friends and neighbours to his home to celebrate the divine and share their dreams and support for each other.

FALSE GOLD AND REAL GOLD

When Atum shared a version of this story it felt like synchronicity! The Swiss Psychotherapist, Carl Jung, taught that synchronicity means meaningful chance and Atum taught me that synchronicity could be the modern word for Grace.

Unlike Isaac in this story, I was not literally poor when my dream of Inner Treasure came to me, but like him I was impoverished from living alone and feeling spiritually bereft from a lack vitality, intimacy, meaning and purpose.

Rumi teaches about the difference between 'false gold' and 'real gold.' Gold has value to us because we give it value. I had gotten out of balance because I placed greater value in acquiring the outer gold of possessions and pleasure while neglecting the inner gold of my deepest values. This resulted in a tremendous cost to my health, relationships and direction in life.

The wisdom of my dream guided me to seek for the source of true happiness within for living with a greater balance of being and becoming, rest and activity, love and reason!

As I grieved my losses, some of my habitual rigidity started melting and I began humbly calling out for help. Then the soulful guidance came in my dream. My inner guide suggested that all I needed to do is to relax in order to uncover a glimpse of the Inner Treasure of Being!

"We shall not cease from exploration, and the end of all our exploring will be to arrive where we started and know the place for the first time."

— T.S. Elliot

Have you ever had a dream that transformed your life? It might have been a dream that came in the middle of the night, or perhaps you've held a vision for a better life for yourself, your family, and your community, or for the world?

Did you tell others about the dream? Were they supportive, or critical? Are there some parts of you that have doubted or criticized your dream?

This story of Isaac's Dream is close to my heart for many reasons.

Firstly, it reminds me of how I too was living in a state of inner poverty from not appreciating the Inner Gifts or Inner Treasure that I had inherited.

Secondly, I am still learning to honour my dreams and visions.

Thirdly, I feel blessed to have received soulful guidance from my dreams and my mentors.

Finally, this story of forgetting and remembering—losing and finding—false gold and real gold—represents for me the collective conundrum that humanity is in at the present time.

A variation of this story showed up for me again within the pages of Michael Meade's exquisite book, *Fate and Destiny—The Two Agreements of the Soul*. In the story, 'Eisik's Dream', Meade articulates the difference between getting stuck in an unhappy fate, or following the golden thread of our purpose until it unfolds into our unique destiny.

The original Jewish story of The Treasure is found in a book by Jewish teacher Martin Buber, called, *Tales of the Hasidism: The Later Masters*. In this version Eisik is a Rabbi.

He, too, waits until the dream comes a third time before he overcomes his inner dragons of doubts and follows his dream's guidance. After going on the long journey he returns home and finds the Inner Treasure by digging beneath his stove.

Another word for stove is hearth, and some teachers emphasize that we must do the inner work of digging into our deepest heart. After all, 'Home is where the heart is'—the home of our greatest Treasure, our Soul.

'I-IT' AND 'I-THOU'

Martin Buber is famous for pointing out the need to shift from an 'I-it' experience to an 'I-Thou' relationship in life. If we get caught in the polarization of 'I-it' then we objectify life, each other and nature. In this mode, we can justify unsustainable practices that rob the earth of its precious resources like mining gold, oil, diamonds, and so on.

If we only identify with our rational objective side, we can justify turning the earth into a huge lumberyard or open pit mine.

On the other hand, if we have an 'I-Thou' relationship to the Earth, then we are in relationship to the Great Web and we experience meaningful and purposeful connection to life. We feel a desire to honour the Earth, as our Home.

This doesn't have to be a polarization between Science and Soul. We can practice clear thinking and warm-hearted loving. We can bring soul to science and science to soul, as long as we honour that each has its own language and rules of engagement.

All these wonderful mentors have helped me to break through the spells and curses of my habitual forgetfulness and to keep practicing the art of remembering the Inner Treasure.

This story of the Inner Treasure is a great example of the 'wisdom stories' shared by many mystical traditions. There is another story that resonates deeply with my personal journey through the midlife passage, which I'd like to share.

THE LOST RING

The Sufis tell many stories that orient us in the direction of discovering our hidden Inner Treasure. One of my favourites is about Mullah Nasruddin, a foolish (yet sometimes wise) character in many of the teaching stories. He reminds me of the trickster Coyote in the First Nations teaching stories.

One dark night Mullah was searching around in the grass for something that he had lost. He searched for a long time but had no success. Along came a neighbour on his way home, and he saw Mullah frantically looking in the grass.

The neighbour called out to Mullah and asked him what he was searching for. Mullah replied, "I'm looking for my wedding ring." The neighbour offered to help, and took up the search along with Mullah.

After quite a bit of time the neighbour said to Mullah, "Do you remember when you last saw the ring?"

Mullah replied, "Oh yes, the last time I saw it was when I dropped it in the basement of my house."

The neighbour looked confused. "I don't understand. If you dropped the ring in the basement, why are you looking for it here outside?"

Mullah replied, "Well, it's too dark in the basement, and the light is much brighter out here by the street light!"

We can imagine Mullah's neighbour shaking his head in frustration. How many of us are like Mullah, spending a lot of time, effort and resources searching outside for something we lost inside? In order to heal, transform and evolve soulfully, we need to search thoroughly inside for what we have lost before venturing outside.

A ring is often a symbol for our wholeness. Many of us have been taught to look outside toward the light for all of our answers. The story tells us, however, that we have to journey into the darkness in the basement below the ground to recover some essential aspect of our wholeness.

These ancient teaching stories often show what is there and hint at what is missing. In Mullah's case, what we can see is two men searching for a missing wedding ring outside by a streetlight.

In some versions of this story, it simply states that Mullah lost his ring. In other versions, the ring he lost is his wedding ring. The storyteller has some discretion in this.

I'm emphasizing the wedding ring version for several reasons—first, it implies there is someone Mullah is (or was) wedded to. For the Sufis, there can be many levels to this teaching. Mullah may be wedded to a partner we don't see.

Second, I relate to the story on a personal level because there was many losses I needed to grieve in my own midlife crisis. One was losing my marriage and my wedding ring, but I also lost some of my primary identities. I was identified with being a husband, father, business owner, and so on.

When the dust settled from my midlife crisis, all these identities were gone. For quite a while, I searched frantically 'outside' for my missing identities and the ring of wholeness, but eventually I learned that I needed to search inside for the Inner Treasure.

> *"Lovers don't finally meet somewhere.*
> *They're in each other all along."*
>
> — Rumi

DIE BEFORE YOU DIE

In mysticism the soul is often depicted as feminine. In Sufism and other mystical traditions a core teaching is to 'Die before you die!' This means to shift from an egocentric identification with your limited self, and rest into a more soulful perspective that draws from your unlimited Self, Soul and Spirit.

In Christian mysticism, to 'Die before you die!' is practiced by taking on the metaphorical cross. We are instructed to symbolically nail one hand into one side of the horizontal plane of a pair of opposites, and then nail the other hand in the other. Then we need to hold the tension of the opposites until a third vertical perspective is birthed.

At this point, there is a transformational change of heart that Christian mystics call metanoia.

Anyone who has quit an addiction will know what I'm talking about. To heal, we are asked to die to the old pattern and be reborn into a new life. It is not a one-time event though. There will be many temptations. Each day we are asked to shift from an egocentric perspective to a soulful perspective.

When a Sufi dies, it is said to be his or her true, 'Wedding Day'. This is the day he or she is finally reunited with their True Nature, known by many names—the Friend, Source, Reality, Oneness, Great Mystery, Creator, Great Web, Love, or Beloved.

There is usually a great celebration on a Sufi's wedding day, like seen in an Irish wake. As a result of practicing this orientation of 'Die before you die', there isn't so much fear of death when we practice surrendering daily to the little deaths.

EMBRACING OPPOSITES

There are many splits these days between light and dark, head and heart, mind and body, masculine and feminine, science and soul, and so forth. In this book, I will attempt to point the way toward a path of healing these splits so we can recover our wholeness and evolve towards even greater wholeness. I will be drawing from many of the world's wisdom traditions, popular culture, from the frontiers of psychology and neuroscience, and using examples of clients I have worked with and my own personal experience.

In order to transform and evolve soulfully we need to watch out for getting too polarized with either/or thinking, yet honour specific differences. As Einstein astutely noted, "We can't solve a problem with the same level of consciousness that created the problem in the first place." To transform and evolve soulfully, we need greater awareness to embrace different perspectives or ways of being that appear to be opposites, like science and soul.

Individuals, couples, groups and even Nations are experiencing great turbulence and crisis in these dark times. It is tempting to want to escape or bypass that which does not feel good and ascend towards the light, but it is important to remember that there is great potential in the dark places, such as within the fecund earth, the womb and the cocoon. These are the dark, moist places traditionally considered to be part of the feminine territory that the soul loves and is the birthplace of all transformation. A seed must first be planted in the dark earth!

In all three of these stories, we only see the masculine landscape, if we are just looking for the obvious. We may not notice that the feminine seems missing. If we look deeper, we see that there is a play of light and dark, outside and inside. For wholeness, we need to include both. It is time to invite the feminine and masculine into a dance of equality, in conscious, soulful partnership.

For wholeness we need to see what is missing, what appears to be invisible! Many creative individuals are awakening by giving space to what appears in the outer world, and also honouring what seems invisible. They are going beyond either/or thinking to embrace both/and, masculine and feminine, Soul and Spirit, the Form and the Formless.

The great mythologist, Joseph Campbell, taught that the disease of our time is literalism. When our story is too small for whom we really are, we get stuck in a limited imagination. If we imagine our transformational cross again, we need to shift from the horizontal to the vertical for imagination of Spirit, and then back down to earth again to manifest our soulful creativity. There is a one-dimensional poverty that comes from getting too identified with either the worldly horizontality or the other-worldly verticality. To transform, we need to embrace both.

In his amazing video series *The Power of Myth*, Campbell brought postmodern people insight into how indigenous cultures from different times and places have helped their young people to transform and evolve soulfully.

In his 1949 book, *The Hero with a Thousand Faces*, Campbell outlines three major stages of what he calls the 'Monomyth'. Some refer to this as the Hero's (or Heroine's) Journey—a journey of Separation, Initiation and Return. At some point in our lives, we are called to separate from what is familiar, enter a trial period of ordeals, and then hopefully return with the 'gold' or Inner Treasure of greater maturity, love and wisdom. This helps us re-orient to living our soul's destiny.

Campbell and other scholars such as Erich Neumann, describe narratives of Gautama Buddha, Moses, and Christ in terms of the 'Monomyth', and Campbell argues that classic myths, and modern myths such as the *Star Wars* Trilogy or the *Lord of the Rings*, follow this same basic pattern.

Family therapist, educational consultant, and writer Maureen Murdock outlines a uniquely similar map of the journey for women in her book *The Heroine's Journey —Women's Quest for Wholeness*.

As noted earlier, we have been taught that a "myth" means an untruth, as in, "It's just a myth!" The original meaning, however, was to point toward a mystery that is profoundly true, yet hard to put in ordinary language.

Used in this context, we could say that the world's religions are great myths that point toward great mysteries and truths.

MATURATION AWAKENING PATH

My root mentor for cultivating a more soulful life is Atum O'Kane Ph.D. He teaches that one of the simplest maps of human maturation is the journey from innocence to wisdom.

Atum also teaches that there are four worlds of soul—The Home of The Soul, The Unfolding Soul, The Inner World of Psyche, and The Soul of the World. We will be exploring these four subjective worlds with our soulful map.

Many years ago I attended an international conference of spiritual guides with Atum. At the conference, one of Atum's mentors, co-founder and the first president of the Association for Transpersonal Psychology, Francis Vaughn Ph.D., a Transpersonal Psychotherapist and author of *Shadows of the Sacred—Seeing Through Spiritual Illusions* laid out four-life stages of human maturation. She called these life stages: Magic, Mastery, Meaning and Mystery.

These four life stages have been expanded upon in this book to create maps of the four major life stages, or life maps of maturation:

STAGE

Childhood	**Youth**	**Adult**	**Elder**

LIFE MAP

Magic	Mastery	Meaning	Mystery
And	And	And	And
Play	Proactivity	Purpose	Presence

Of course, we can experience magic, mastery, meaning and mystery at any stage of life, but the question is: where is our present centre of gravity? Are there elements from earlier stages that we need to heal or integrate so that we are able to fully step into the next stage of our life?

To navigate from one-life stage to another, we must traverse the territory of soulful initiation. I have mapped seven evolutionary phases of the initiatory journey.

We will cover one of these evolutionary phases in each of the chapters of this book.

1. The Ordinary Life of Separation

2. The Call to the Inner World of Psyche

3. Allies, Mentors and Elders on the Path

4. Home of the Soul & Soulful Relationships

5. Transformation—Our Unfolding Soul

6. Soulful Meaning and Purpose

7. Soul of the World—Living the Soulful Life

When someone first contacts me for support, they are usually in phase two of answering the call to the Inner World of the Psyche. When they commit to their process and engage me as a mentor and psychotherapist, this catalyzes phase three of their journey.

Our journey together is about weaving the cocoon of transformation for deep healing and intimacy in phase four; uncovering inner resources in phase five; identifying inner gifts and purpose in phase six; and giving their inner gifts to a meaningful need in phase seven for living with natural vitality, deep presence, intimacy, meaning and purpose.

THE BODY AS A MAP

I find it useful to use my body as my primary map and compass for healing, transformation and evolution.

We will be exploring these four stages of life, seven evolutionary phases, and three life areas (natural vitality, deep intimacy, meaning and purpose) in detail in the rest of the book. I like to use the number seven as a reference because there are seven directions, seven days of the week, seven colours of the rainbow, seven major energy centres in the human body and seven elements.

It is easy to get stuck in any one of the major life stages. For example, at eight years of age I suffered from an incomplete life passage when I could not grieve my losses.

Then at twenty-five, I suffered a quarter life crisis for the same reason.

Finally, at thirty-five, I suffered a major midlife crisis because the losses became overwhelming. I lacked wise mentors in my previous initiatory passages to help my evolving maturation.

Fortunately, I found helpful mentors in my late thirties.

Many people these days get overwhelmed and stuck in midlife without mentors. They need help to transform their midlife crisis into a midlife awakening process.

In the following pages I'll share some of my journey spanning my 'quarter life crisis' to 'midlife crisis' and finally toward my 'midlife awakening process'.

These maps help orient us, but it's important to remember that the map itself isn't the territory or the journey. I recommend that you keep a journal of your experience so it can become your own custom map of your journey. Whenever you stray from your path, you can pick up your journal and retrace your steps to find the fork in the trail along your path where you were sidetracked. Your detour might be an opportunity for deepening into soulfulness!

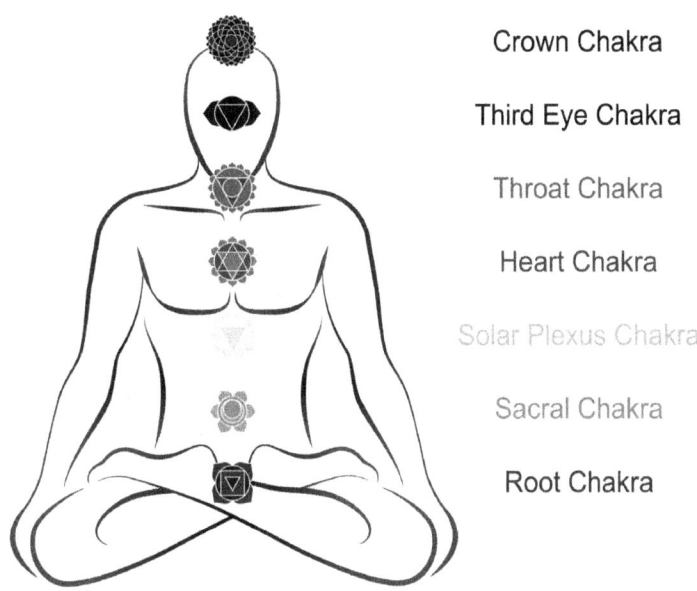

SEVEN CHAKRAS

Chakras are energy centres in our subtle body. When they are open and vital we have access to the unique Inner Treasure they contain. When they are closed or blocked they become barriers to our Inner Treasure. Imagine a car that is only operating on four of its six cylinders! Our vehicle will operate poorly because it is blocked from accessing its full potential. In each chapter we will focus on one of the chakras.

CHAKRAS AND THE ELEMENTS

The elements, the building blocks of the natural world, are an essential part of who we are. Many traditions, such as the 5-element system of Traditional Chinese Medicine, use the elements as a kind of map of transformation.

Many years ago I was teaching a series of classes in a local Sufi Meditation Centre, entitled Living Your Purpose, which used the elements as a map to manifest one's life purpose. The lessons relied heavily on Atum's teaching and the wisdom of Sufi teacher Hazrat

Inayat Khan. In this branch of Universal Sufism, originating in India, the Yogic teaching around integrating the elements of earth, water, fire, air and ether and the seven major energy centres, or chakras, is emphasized as essential to cultivating a soulful life.

This orientation to the elements is like a map from the ancient Sanskrit that shows the ascending and descending paths of creation. We ascend the elements and chakras for inspiration and descend the elements and chakras for manifesting our soulful creativity.

Rumi also points towards an evolution through the elements when he teaches; "God slept in the mineral kingdom, dreamed in the vegetable, became conscious in the animal, and realized Himself (Herself) in the human being."

In other teachings he describes that the elements, "Fire, water, air, and earth are God's servants!" This points to the possibility of a subjective experience of the elements and an objective experience of the elements. When we cultivate the subjective experience we feel more connected to nature because our body is made up of the elements.

Since there are seven chakras, I like to use seven elements:

1. Earth 2. Water 3. Fire 4. Air 5. Ether 6. Mineral 7. Nature.

ADDICTIVE TENDENCIES

Another influence on my thinking around the elements, especially with respect to addiction theory, is Therapist and yoga teacher Anodea Judith, author of many books including *Eastern Body Western Mind*, within which she uses the seven chakras as a comprehensive map of healing, transformation and evolution.

Anodea Judith suggests that certain addictions are related to particular chakras (energy centres):

7. Religion, Spiritual Practices

6. Hallucinogens, Marijuana

5. Opiates, Marijuana

4. Tobacco (Smoking), Sugar, Love, Marijuana

3. Amphetamines, Cocaine, Caffeine, Work, Anger

2. Alcohol, Sex, Heroin

1. Foods, Gambling, Shopping, Work

These addictive tendencies can be compensations for the pain of living without access to our Inner Treasure. They can be ways that we self-soothe the pain of not living with natural vitality, deep presence, intimacy, meaning and purpose. These addictive tendencies can provide temporary relief but can create more suffering for us because they don't address the root causes of our pain. In each chapter we will be looking at the addictive tendencies that correspond with that particular chakra or energy centre.

PRACTICE THE PATH

In order to embark on a quest it is helpful to know what your questions are. Ancient wisdom teaches us to, "Know thyself!" There are universal questions that often arise when someone is undergoing a major life transition—questions like:

- Who am I really?
- Who am I becoming?
- What is love?
- What do I love to do?
- What is meaningful?
- What is my soul's purpose?
- Who is going with me?

There are also specific questions we can contemplate that support the clearing of barriers to accessing our Inner Treasure for living a soulful life of natural vitality, deep presence, intimacy, meaning and purpose.

In the following chapters we will explore these questions:

- How can we clear our barriers to living with deeper physical vitality?
- How can we clear our barriers to living with deeper emotional vitality?
- How can we clear barriers to accomplishing our goals in life?
- How can we clear barriers to living with deeper intimacy for relational vitality?
- How can we clear barriers to uncovering our inner resources?
- How can we clear barriers to uncovering and giving our inner gifts so we can live with deeper meaning and purpose?
- How can we clear barriers in our thinking so we can heal, transform and evolve soulfully?

And so, let's begin our journey!

CHAPTER 1: THE ORDINARY LIFE OF SEPARATION

"Listen to the story told by the reed, of being separated. Since I was cut from the reed bed, I have made this crying sound. Anyone apart from someone he or she loves understands what I say. Anyone pulled from a source longs to go back."

—Rumi; Translation by Coleman Barks

One: How can we clear our barriers to living with deeper physical vitality?

PREPARATION FOR THE JOURNEY

In the first stage of the hero or heroine's journey, we usually feel ordinary and separate. In the opening of the story of *The Golden Key*, the boy is poor. In *Isaac's Dream*, Isaac is also living in poverty. Mullah is searching for a wedding ring that he lost. In all three stories the Inner Treasure seems to be missing.

Rumi teaches that "separation" is the root cause of our yearning and our suffering. In his poem above, cutting the reed from the swamp is a metaphor for being cut off from our Self, Soul and Spirit, often symbolized by the moment when our umbilical cord was cut in childbirth.

If all our needs were met in the womb, we felt secure and connected. As soon as our umbilical cord is cut, however, we enter a new world where we are highly dependent on others for our survival.

For some of us the transition into the family nest went well if we were embraced into loving arms. For others, our connection was tentative or even perilous when our essential needs were not met.

In the ordinary life of separation, many of us might identify with being literally poor or feel a kind of poverty in our health, relationships, career or spirituality. All of these facets are important for cultivating a soulful life of meaning and prosperity.

In myths, the hero or heroine may be under a spell or a curse. Similarly, we might be experiencing symptoms that are robbing us of our physical vitality.

In this chapter we will look at some of the causes for lack of physical aliveness and some ways to clear barriers to our physical vitality.

"You do not have to walk on your knees for a hundred miles through the desert, repenting. You only have to let the soft animal of your body love what it loves. "

—Mary Oliver

If you are reading this book, you are likely undergoing a major life transition or perhaps are about to undergo one. Before we go on a journey it is essential to know where we are now.

Some maps have a locator that says, 'You are here!' Where are you? Are you in a major life transition now? What stage of life are you in now? Are you feeling separate and disconnected?

According to Anodea Judith, the addictive tendencies of the first chakra are "food, shopping, gambling, and work".

Jungian Psychotherapist Marion Woodman brings a profound depth of wisdom when working with addictive tendencies and eating disorders like Anorexia or Bulimia. In her insightful book, *Addiction to Perfection* she skillfully uses mythology to show how we can use creative imagination and creative expression to heal, transform and evolve soulfully from these kinds of symptoms.

At the root of many addictive tendencies is an attempt to be perfect. This activates an inner critic that says that we will never be good enough no matter how perfect we are! Woodman is a great example of a wise healer who invites us into the wound until it becomes a womb to birth the Inner Treasure of new life.

In my experience, the attempt to be 'perfect' is a way to compensate for some deep wounds we received earlier in life and for feeling cut off from Self, Soul and Spirit. These core wounds become like a cloudy lens that colours our reality. Even if we do not remember the event or events, they often they take the form of overwhelming feelings and negative limiting beliefs like:

- 'There is something wrong with me!'
- 'I'll never be good enough!'
- 'I'm a mistake!'
- 'I'm a failure!'
- 'I'm bad!'
- 'I'm fundamentally flawed!'
- 'I'm unlovable!'

- 'I hate food!'
- 'I hate my body!'
- 'I don't trust myself!'
- 'I don't trust people!' —and so on.

On a physical level these beliefs may manifest as addictive tendencies, an obsession with how we look, poor eating habits, mindless shopping or gambling, or workaholism.

THE POWER OF CRAVINGS AND ADDICTIONS

According to the American Society of Addiction Medicine (ASAM), the short definition of addiction is: "a primary, chronic disease of brain reward, motivation, memory and related circuitry. Dysfunction in these circuits leads to characteristic biological, psychological, social and spiritual manifestations."

Before 2011, the focus was on distinct addictive substances or behaviours, but the field of addictions is seeing a common denominator in the functioning of the reward circuitry of the brain. Some people it seems do not produce enough dopamine in their brain, and addictive substances help produce dopamine. The ASAM goes on to say:

"This is reflected in an individual pathologically pursuing reward and/or relief by substance use and other behaviours. Addiction is characterized by an inability to consistently abstain, impairment in behaviour control, and craving, diminished recognition of significant problems with one's behaviours and interpersonal relationships, and a dysfunctional emotional response.

"Like other chronic diseases, addiction often involves cycles of relapse and remission. Without treatment or engagement in recovery activities, addiction is progressive and can result in disability or premature death."

Evolutionary Psychology is also shedding some light on our addictive tendencies. 'Supernormal stimuli' was a term coined by ethnologist and ornithologist Niko Tinbergen. In an article by Integral Spirituality teacher Terry Patten, the author believed that Niko, "had discovered that by enhancing key stimuli he could trigger unnatural behaviours in animals and insects." For example, "he discovered that butterflies could be duped into being attracted to imitation cardboard butterflies that were colourfully painted. This applies to humans too! We see grown men being duped by Internet porn as if it were real."

An authority on supernormal stimuli is Harvard psychologist Deidre Barrett, author of *Supernormal Stimuli: How Primal Urges Overran Their Evolutionary Purpose*. She says, "You can't trust your instincts in the modern world. This is because the very structures of our brains and nervous systems are fitted to the original circumstances in which they evolved, not to the present conditions of the modern world, which have themselves evolved in order to appeal ever more powerfully to our instincts."

This poor matching of our instincts and our modern environment is causing us tremendous problems. As Barrett says: "The most dangerous aspect of our modern diet arises from our ability to refine food. This is the link to drug, alcohol, and tobacco addictions.... Salt, fat, sugar and starch are not harmful in their natural contexts. It's our modern ability to concentrate things like cocaine, heroin, alcohol—and food components—that turns them into a menace that our body is hardwired to crave."

Buddhist teachers remind us that the only real power comes from living as fully as you can in the present moment. Trying to live in the past is based on guilt, and trying to live in the future is based on fear. However, in everyday life we are taught to avoid the present moment with the promise of supernormal rewards, which creates craving. It's like dangling the carrot of pleasure on a stick in front of us fostering a culture of addiction.

Evolutionary Theologian Michael Dowd teaches that evolutionary brain science has helped us understand human behaviour better. He states that, "Humans aren't motivated well by carrots or sticks." When motivation comes from reward or punishment it is seriously limited.

The first part of the brain to develop is instinctual and yearns for supernormal stimuli such as fat, sugar, salt and sex that can lead to addictive tendencies.

The second evolution of the brain is our mammalian brain, which is social in nature. Our mammalian nature is to be a social being—we are compassionate and empathic at our core. Like the Bonobo apes, dogs and some other mammals, we have evolved to be caring, kind and loyal, so that we can thrive in relationships.

We do not see reptiles like crocodiles playing!

Michael Dowd draws on the insights of modern brain research and evolutionary psychology in a TEDx talk called *Why We Struggle and Suffer*. He says that the neocortex is the third part of the brain to develop. It is the interpretive part of the brain for "meaning making and comprehending".

This part of the brain is also where our instincts for self-deception reside. We are actually programmed in an evolutionary sense to deceive ourselves!

The most recent part of the brain is our prefrontal cortex, the place where we can override our more base instincts. It's about doing the right thing. Many of the opportunities and challenges of spirituality and higher purpose reside in this part of the brain.

The good news is that by accessing the Inner Treasure we can transform and evolve our brain.

The reason we struggle is because of the mismatched instincts and supernormal allurements ubiquitous in the modern world. Barrett and Dowd's research helps explain some of our bizarre behaviour.

For example, a bag of chips is not food; they are supernormal stimuli. You will never find anything like this in the natural world. Today we are faced with a concentration of food-like items that we were evolutionarily programmed to want and want more of. Everyone will overeat if dining on supernormal stimuli… and hard liquor wasn't even invented until three hundred years ago. We also have things like Internet porn and hundred-channel television and computer games that our ancestors never had to deal with.

One way we can move beyond guilt and shame is by realizing that some of these addictive tendencies were evolutionarily programmed into us. We all have an instinctual craving for salt, sugar and fat because it helped our ancient ancestors to survive.

These substances were rare to find for our ancestors, but today they are available in abundance and we still have the craving as if they are rare. By coming out of denial and acknowledging the truth of our instinctual cravings that have led us into to addictive behaviour, we can come into right relationship with Reality.

We could even say that when substances become addictive we are under a spell. 'We are what we eat.' But how can we wake up to the 'matrix' of our social conditioning if we are numbed out? Our environment and socialization are major factors in addiction.

Marion Woodman and Robert Bly speak powerfully about how our culture is lacking in elders and is therefore descending into a "sibling society." In many indigenous cultures there were complex rituals led by the elders to help youth mature from the lower chakras to the upper ones. Instead, immature marketers are taking advantage of the hormonal changes in youth and targeting them to sell addictive products. (See the documentary *fedupmovie.com*).

THE SPELL OR CURSE

When we are in infancy our parent(s) usually make sure our physical needs are met. If all goes well there, our physical bodies become strong and flexible and we experience physical vitality. This is one of the gifts from our parents.

If our physical needs are not met, then we may have experienced trauma and lack physical energy. We could say this is a 'spell' or 'curse' from our parents and family.

Furthermore, some people did have their essential needs met in childhood but then experienced physical trauma later in life.

Like many therapists, I have been trained in numerous modalities that aim to undo the 'spell' or 'curse.' It depends on the client, the situation and the timing as to which method I will recommend.

The essence of psychological and spiritual healing that is soulful, requires fostering a clear channel for Healing Presence to emerge through the process. There must be a kind of space holding so that awareness can witness what wants to become visible, or what is trying to emerge from beneath the surface of the known world. I imagine that Healing Presence is a Third Presence that connects my client and me. It is constantly available as a resource for both of us. It is all around us and inside both of us, although we may not be aware of it.

If I am open to this possibility and curious about the wisdom of my client's unfolding process, I encourage my client to be open to it too. This Healing Presence is one way the Inner Treasure manifests as Essential Qualities (in our MAP which we explore later, we label these as EQ) such as Love, Compassion, Truth, Courage, Forgiveness, Peace, Wisdom, and so on. Have we been taught to see our body as a temple for Self, Soul and Spirit? Some traditions, like Universal Sufism, view the body as a temple of the divine.

> *"This is not my body, this is the temple of god!"*
>
> *Hazrat Inayat Khan*

One of my mentors for training in spiritual healing is Himayat Inayati. He is the Founder of the Raphaelite Work School of Healing and states that the gift of this method is that it orients both healing and evolution toward the sacred. The symbol for which this work is named after, is the archangel Raphael, the archangel of pilgrimage, healing and science. One image that Himayat describes for Healing Presence is, when you are open and curious, a child will come up to you and tell you their secrets. If you are a 'wounding presence' then others will feel diminished around you.

When a client comes to see me with a physical symptom, I find it helpful to remain open and curious about what the wisdom of their process wants to reveal to us at that particular time. If we both can be open and curious, a part of their body that is contracted may soften and unfold. Usually discharge happens in the way of tears, laughter, gas, electrical pulsations, burning, and so on, and this creates more space. In this space, Essential Qualities (EQ) begin to arise.

Our bodies speak in the language of sensations, and if we learn to understand and speak its language our body will reveal its wisdom to us. I am constantly amazed at how the very antidote to the condition we are suffering from is often contained within our own body.

Raphaelite Work uses physical touch and the spiritual connection between the healer and the one receiving the healing. It is a wholistic method of healing that includes the physical, emotional, mental, moral and spiritual domains. We often speak about these domains of human experience as if they are separate from each other, but like Russian dolls, they are contained within each other and there is communication between them.

A symptom in one domain can lead to another domain for healing. The element in the first chakra is earth, and it pertains to our physicality and sense of place. It is connected to sensation and our senses.

HELEN'S NEW HIP

Helen was in her sixties when she came to see me. Her hip operation was not healing well. She limped into my office and told me that she was worried that there was no feeling in her left leg. She lost the feeling when her hip was operated on. She said it felt like her leg had been amputated. As she lay on the massage table fully clothed, I held different energy points along the left side of her body. At one point she told me that her whole leg felt lifeless.

I invited her to be present to her leg, and told her that I would do the same. After a while she said she felt some burning in her belly. I suggested that she be present with curiosity to the burning sensation and let me know if anything changed. A couple of minutes later the burning increased, and then she exploded in anger.

She proceeded to tell me how upset she was at the surgeon who operated on her leg. He had told her there were three options for different hip replacements and there was quite a difference in cost between them. She was on a limited income but wanted good quality, so she chose the middle priced one. When she arrived for the surgery however, he told her that she was scheduled to receive the least expensive one. She said she tried to complain, but she was unable to.

After she expressed her anger with me, I could feel some energy moving in her leg. After empathizing, I asked her if she noticed any change in her leg? She said, "Yes, there's energy flowing now but it feels very strange. It feels quite different than my right leg."

I suggested that she put her attention on her right leg and then move her attention back to her left leg again. "See if you can have your healthy right leg teach your left leg how to be," I suggested to her.

She moved her attention back and forth from one leg to the other, and within a few minutes the energy in her left leg was flowing smoothly. At the end of the session she fell into a state of deep peace. She healed very rapidly after that.

In this example, Helen had physical trauma but was unable to heal because there were physical, emotional and mental barriers. As a patient undergoing surgery, we are usually given an anesthetic. This helps us endure the pain, but some part of us is still being traumatized.

If this is the case, then we can disassociate from this part of our body as a form of protection. Only when we are ready to be fully present to that part of the body can we regain full association and aliveness again. This is a form of 're-membering'—putting our lost, dissociated parts back together again.

Psychologically, Helen had been taught that she should always be nice and accommodating, resulting in an inability to assertively confront the surgeon about the change to her treatment plan. Repressing her anger created a block in her second chakra, so the energy could not flow well through her first chakra and down to her left hip and leg. By accepting her burning belly with curiosity, she regained passage into her emotional domain through the anger, and her barrier was released.

She had come to the session worried. Once she expressed her anger, she understood what had happened and experienced healing, and then she received the Inner Treasure—the Essential Quality (EQ) of deep peace. Through her journey of getting a hip replacement she was also called into a major life transition—the re-evaluation of how she identified with the belief that she should always be nice and accommodating, and how this belief no longer served her.

Her healing invited her to practice presence and discernment for breaking this particular spell, in order to transform and evolve into the next stage of her soul's development.

SPEAKING WITH WISE OWL

Another method that I use for clearing physical barriers is called Voice Dialogue—the Psychology of Selves and the Aware Ego Process. It is a psycho-spiritual (or wholistic) process co-created by Hal and Sidra Stone, PhD.

A middle-aged manager named Steve came to see me about his weight issues. He was about fifty pounds overweight. His health was getting progressively worse, resulting in a lack of energy, Diabetes and Sleep Apnea. It was negatively impacting his marriage and work life too. I suggested that I could interview some of his sub-personalities that were involved in his relationship to eating and food.

Steve said he had tried many diets and some of them would work for a while. He would lose some weight, but then it would quickly come back on again, leaving him discouraged and hopeless.

In Voice Dialogue we begin with a centre position as a home base for the multifaceted person—in this instance, the man called Steve. First, I invited him to move to another part of the room to interview one of his sub-personalities.

The first 'self' we spoke to was his 'controller.' This part of him likes to be in control. After interviewing the controller, I asked its permission to speak to another part of him. He moved over slightly and what emerged was a responsible self who was a 'workaholic'.

When he gets home, another part of Steve who likes to eat takes over. I asked to speak to this self. This part of him described himself to me as his 'reward eater'. Whenever he puts in a long day, this part rewards him with sweet junk food and 'vegging out' in front of the TV. (Interestingly, the slang 'vegging out' refers to relaxing and turning into a vegetable).

This self was completely unapologetic about how much he liked to eat and said his only responsibility is the taste. I asked this self how much it weighed and where it lived in his body. The 'reward eater' self answered that it weighed two hundred and twenty pounds and lived in his lips, chest, belly and thighs.

When I asked Steve to move back to the centre position, he reflected on the 'reward eater' and was amazed at how unapologetic it was. Usually he feels very guilty and apologetic about his over-eating.

I then invited him to move to another position in the room, and this time interviewed his 'dieter self'. This self was incredibly knowledgeable about diets and even nutrition and felt guilty about the lack of progress he was making. When I asked this self how much it weighed and where it was located in his body, it told me, "Ten pounds," and that it lived in his head.

When Steve moved back to the centre again, he felt an energetic shift. Then I shared an analogy of a teeter-totter with him. The 'reward eater' self weighs 220 pounds and is sitting on one side, and the 'dieter self' weighs only ten pounds and is sitting on the other side. Picturing this image, he could immediately see why his dieter wasn't getting any traction with his diets. In this manner, we worked energetically to create a better balance within his inner world.

I asked him if he had ever dreamed of an animal. (Sometimes I'll ask clients this to help them access their instinctual body). Steve said that he had dreamed of owls occasionally, one of his favourite birds.

I invited him to find a place in the room and become the owl. He chose a place close to the open window with a view of a tree and the vast blue sky. I asked the owl what perspective it had on this situation. The wise owl told me that his condition was eighty percent psychological and twenty percent biological.

I asked the owl to elaborate further. The owl said that when he was an infant his grandmother would reward him with sweet treats to control his behaviour. If his grandmother wanted him to be good or responsible or to stop crying, she would give him a treat.

When Steve came back to the centre position again, he was surprised by his revelations and had an epiphany around how his relationship with his grandmother was bound up in his relationship with food. He was thrilled to discover that he could access the wise owl from his dreams to guide him in making healthy food choices and decisions.

MORE INNER BARRIERS

Over time we worked with Steve's inner critic, inner perfectionist, inner pusher, and inner child to discover his core pattern for breaking the spell of his addictive tendencies. He also started seeing a Doctor of Functional Medicine to initiate a game plan for improving his overall health.

As the eldest child he was conditioned to be responsible at an early age. His parents expected high standards from him and were critical if he didn't achieve exemplary results. This attitude turned into an inner perfectionist that placed the bar unreasonably high for his success. His inner critic was never satisfied, so his inner perfectionist raised the bar higher, and the inner pusher brought forth more push to meet the demand. His vulnerability was repressed and he was exhausted as he was out of balance between doing and being, thinking and feeling.

As he learned to embrace his vulnerability and get his basic needs met, his protective voices transformed and evolved. His inner critic transformed into a voice of discernment, his inner perfectionist learned to set reasonable goals and his inner pusher gave him the energy and focus to accomplish them.

Steve's weight issue became a call to the adventure of healing his relationship with food and work. As a young boy he needed his grandmother's care while his mother was away and he was rewarded for his good behaviour with sweet food which raised his dopamine level.

After some time he learned to internalize his inner grandmother as his reward eater. His inner child was starved for a healthy diet but also for love and acceptance. No matter how much his inner dieter learned, it didn't have enough weight or 'matter' in his psyche.

The word mother is related to the word matter. The first food for most of us came from our mother's milk, so when exploring issues with weight and food it is often helpful to look at our early relationship to our mother, or in this case grandmother. What was her relationship to her body and food like? Was she under a spell?

WISE ADVICE THE OWL

Clients are often amazed at the wisdom they hold within themselves, and the answers their 'disowned selves' can provide. In Steve's case he was burnt out by working so much, identifying with the role of the responsible one. He had learned to be the provider and to put his health and relationships last. Once he integrated his Inner Treasure of wisdom from his instinctual body, his cravings (that were an attempt to manage his stress), began to subside and he learned to balance his health, relationships and work life. He became a wise coach for others.

Furthermore, to fully heal it is essential to discover the root causes of our symptoms to break our spells. What has become normal in our habits and in our culture may not be very natural for our wellbeing. In the appendix I show natural ways to increase our dopamine. Our modern industrialized society's highly processed refined substances that we try to pass off for food is causing massive physical and social problems. There is another film called *The Perfect Human Diet* that investigates this.

SOULFUL HEALING AND PSYCHOTHERAPY

These innovative therapeutic processes used with Steve and Helen are examples of a soulful approach to healing and psychotherapy oriented toward transforming and evolving. As a life-long learner, my approach to healing, mentoring and psychotherapy is constantly transforming and evolving too.

'Raphaelite Work Healing' helped me to embrace the physical, emotional, mental, moral and spiritual domains of experience by orienting both healing and evolution toward the sacred.

'Voice Dialogue' showed me a practical way of working with the inner world of the psyche.

Humanistic Psychology invited me to look beyond a pathology-based model to a positive approach to wellness by identifying what needs of highly functioning people are being met.

Jungian Psychology gave me a comprehensive map of the inner world of the psyche.

Training in the 'Clear Your Beliefs Process' provided me an elegant method of transforming core beliefs.

Family Systems therapy reminded me that we are all part of systems, such as our family system and cultural system.

The Couples Institute taught me a developmental approach to working with couples.

Transpersonal psychology and consciousness studies highlighted the importance of including my spiritual life, even if I didn't think of myself as 'Religious' at the time.

Process Psychology encouraged me to follow the wisdom of the unfolding process.

Integral Psychology taught me to integrate the body-mind-spirit connection of the individual and the collective.

Interpersonal Neurobiology (IPNB) offered me a model of psychotherapy that integrates objective domains of science and the subjective domains of human knowing.

Ecopsychology helped me to restore my connection between my human nature and nature. When I felt separate from my True Nature, I ended up objectifying nature, myself and other living beings. Ecotherapy helps me to reconnect with the Great Web.

Universal Sufism helped me to respect and embrace the essence of all Mystical Traditions.

One of my earliest influences came from Humanistic Psychology and Maslow's Hierarchy of Needs.

MASLOW'S HIERARCHY OF NEEDS

Humanistic psychologist Abraham Maslow discovered a 'Hierarchy of Needs' that became a useful way of looking at our basic human needs, starting with physiological needs like food, clean air and clean drinking water.

Maslow's next level is safety, then love and belonging, esteem and recognition, followed by self-actualization and aesthetics such as beauty, harmony, and spirituality. Maslow concluded that if we don't get our basic needs met, it is difficult to integrate the more subtle levels.

One of the reasons why the 'Hierarchy of Needs' chart has been very popular for personal growth is because Maslow's research focused on highly successful people—as opposed to most of the early psychological pioneers who tended to study people who had psychological problems. Looking at the patterns that made high functioning people so successful emphasized a more positive psychology.

Later Maslow added the need for aesthetics and spirituality to his hierarchy. At that stage of his life, the Transpersonal Psychology movement had started to become more popular and his chart became applicable to those working on the soul and spirit level. Maslow's chart is one that nurses use when learning 'Nursing Fundamentals.' In their training they are taught that in order to administer proper health care, all of our basic human needs must be considered.

Elegant in its simplicity, Maslow's 'Hierarchy of Needs' chart also soon became a practical model and tool for leadership. I first saw this play out when I was training to be a wilderness guide in a three-year training program at Capilano University in 'Wilderness Leadership.' I was in my mid-thirties—in midlife—while most of the other participants were in their early twenties.

I was in poor shape when I started. My diet consisted of eating a lot of processed food and junk food. I smoked cigarettes and the occasional joint, drank alcohol and coffee. Imagine my shock when I discovered that one of the first activities was cross-country skiing.

I had never cross-country skied in my life, and so I was soon huffing and puffing a lot, trying to keep up with the younger people. About mid-way through the training I was forced to make a decision—commit to getting healthier, or quit! I decided to focus on my health and started giving up some of my addictive tendencies. I was amazed at how quickly my health started improving!

What I noticed was that—like me—a lot of these young people would go out on a Friday night and party to all hours. Then in the morning they would arrive at the beach where we did wilderness canoeing or kayaking, and they would be hung over. Because they hadn't slept enough, they slept in as long as they could... and consequently didn't have time for breakfast, either skipping it or quickly eating some fast food. Again, the fast food raises dopamine levels. Lack of sleep raises our stress and increases cortisol, which can lead us to unhealthy cravings.

Relating this to Maslow's theory, it became apparent to the leaders that there was no point in trying to teach them anything until they rested and got some healthy nourishment.

Being a leader means you have to take self-responsibility. Then you are able to respond to what is needed in the moment. Meeting your own needs becomes essential. When you are responsible for others you have to make sure that they get enough rest and they are well fed, because they can potentially be dangerous to themselves and to others on the trip.

I remember my instructor getting frustrated because these young people were supposed to be training as leaders. However, many of them were used to their parents taking care of them, and ended up being rebellious towards the instructor. I remember smiling to myself in understanding; I could see an earlier version of my rebellious self with my addictive tendencies reflected in some of them.

That's where Maslow's Hierarchy of Needs became a very practical model and method for me. In order to have physical vitality we need to meet our physical needs for food, shelter, water, sleep, oxygen, elimination, activity, or sensory and motor stimulation, including sex, physical exercise, and rest. Our instinctual brain governs these basic needs.

This is the most ancient part of the brain and the first to develop. It can cause us to automatically go into an instinctual fight, flight, freeze, fake or fold mode if it perceives our survival is threatened.

In affluent countries we usually take it for granted that we have more than enough food to eat and water to drink. However, for people who are not getting enough to eat or drink, it's critical to address their basic survival needs before engaging in deep psychological or spiritual issues. Survival is their priority, as it would be for any of us.

In later years, as I became a trained therapist, I learned that in affluent societies poverty is usually more psychological and spiritual in nature. We can have lots of 'stuff' and yet we still feel poor. In fact, the challenge that many affluent people face is having had easy abundance that comes with being born into a privileged family and society.

It's easy to take what we are given for granted. Where I live there is an abundance of free clean water, and so it's easy for me to take it for granted. Sometimes I forget to be appreciative for this gift and that there are many people dying of thirst or hunger every day. In the wilderness, I learned how essential water is.

INTEGRATIVE PSYCHOLOGY

One of the pioneers of 'Integral Psychology' is Integral Theorist Ken Wilber. In his book of the same name Wilber writes, "Psychology means the study of the psyche, and the word psyche means mind or soul. In the Microsoft Thesaurus, for the word 'psyche' we find synonyms such as:

'self: atman, soul, spirit; subjectivity: higher self, spiritual self, spirit'. One is reminded, yet again, that the roots of psychology lie deep within the human soul and spirit." Wilber and Integral Psychology emphasize how important it is to integrate soul and science, the subjective and the objective in the individual and in groups. See the appendix for more on Integrative Maps.

INTEGRATIVE MEDICINE

Some people have been taught to consult their medical doctor for every 'problem' in their life. This can be wise for some symptoms but lacks healthy discernment in other cases. Most doctors are not trained in psychotherapy or spirituality. There are some rare exceptions that can be seen in Integral or Functional Medicine that look at the root causes of our symptoms that cause us disease and dis-ease.

In the past, our family doctor would make house visits and had much more time to spend with our whole family. During such visits he or she was able to discern the patient's physical, emotional and social environment, and factor these into the diagnosis.

These days, doctors are directed to give under ten minutes of attention to each patient. Doctors are under a lot of stress themselves, and could benefit from reflecting on what is missing in their lives to bring themselves into a healthier state of wholeness.

There are some medications that can assist one to produce more dopamine. But if it is a psychological or spiritual dilemma, they may resort to prescribe potent medication that might help, or might make things worse.

Even if he or she refers you to a conventional psychiatrist for treatment, you are likely to be treated in the medical model method of prescribing powerful medication that does not necessarily honour your soul and its resources, your Inner Treasure.

This can push people further towards a 'spiritual emergency.' Dr. Stanislav Grof, M.D. PH.D has devoted his life to bridging science and soul. Trained as a psychiatrist, he and his wife Christina speak passionately about how our modern medical system does not treat psychological and spiritual conditions very skillfully. In their audio series, *The Transpersonal Vision—The Healing Potential of non-ordinary States of Consciousness*, Dr. Grof gives an important history of psychological and spiritual development. He teaches that it is natural to yearn for transpersonal states of consciousness, and that it is harmful to treat this as pathology.

In the recent past, there has been a lot of stigma attached to going to see a 'mental health professional.' More often than not, reaching out for support was associated with having a 'mental' illness of some kind.

Of course, there are some people who could benefit from healthy allopathic medical care blended with compassionate psychotherapy. Again, it's a matter of discernment as to what your specific need is.

These days, however, the field has changed, and most of the people who visit psychotherapists do so for general psychological healing, personal growth, and to uncover their inner gifts for living a more soulful life of natural vitality, deep presence, intimacy, meaning and purpose. Not all counselors and psychotherapists, however, are trained in all three of these levels of evolution, so it is best to do some thorough research.

A COMPARISON OF CARE

It is challenging to discern what level of care and support you need. One of the most useful and comprehensive charts I've seen that educates people between the different psychological and spiritual options available to us comes from British Psychotherapist John Rowan. In his book *Healing the Male Psyche—Therapy As Initiation* he reveals an integrative 'map of care' comparing his approach with Ken Wilber's for articulating an integrative psychology.

Rowan calls his chart *A Comparison of Four Positions in Personal Development*, and he uses it to skillfully organize psychology and spirituality into four columns. (See next page)

A COMPARISON OF FOUR POSITIONS IN PERSONAL DEVELOPMENT

Wilber	Persona/Shadow	Centaur	Subtle self	Casual self
Rowan	Mental Ego	Real self	Soul	Spirit
Self	I am defined by others	I define who I am	I am defined by others	I am not defined by others
Motivation	Need	Choice	Allowing	Surrender
Personal goal	Adjustment	Self-actualization	Contacting	Union
Social goal	Socialization	Liberation	Extending	Salvation
Process	Healing Ego-building	Development Ego-extending	Opening/ Ego-reduction	Enlightenment
Traditional role of helper	Physician/ Analyst	Growth facilitator	Advanced Guide	Priest(ess) Sage
Representative approaches	Hospital treatment Chemotherapy Psychoanalysis Directive Behavior/ Modification Cognitive/ behavioral Some T A Crisis work REBT Brief Therapy	Primal Intergation Gestalt Open encounter Psychodrama Neo-Freudians Some T A Person-centerd Co-Counseling Bodywork	Psycho-synthesis Some Jungians Some pagans Transpersonal Voice Dialogue Some Wicca or magic Kabbalah Some atrology Some Tantra Shamanism	Mystical Buddhism Raja Yoga Taoism Monasticism Da Love Ananda Christian mysticism Sufi Goddess Mystics Some Judaism Advaita
Focus	Individual & Group	Group & Individual	Supportive Community	Ideal Community
Representative	Freud Ellis Meichenbaum Beck Eyesenck Skinner Lazarus Watzlawick Wessler Haley	Maslow Rogers Mahrer Perls Lowen Schutz Moreno Stevens Argyris Bugental	Jung Hillman Starhawk Assagioli Gordon-Brown Mary Watkins Jean Houston Bolen Grof Boorstein	Eckhart Shankara Dante Tauler Suso Ruysbroeck Nagarjuna Lao Tzu Fox Julian of Norwich
Research methods	Qualitative	Collaborative	Transformative	None
Questions	Dare you face the challenge of the unconscious?	Dare you face the challenge of freedom?	Dare you face the loss of your boundaries?	Dare you face the loss of your symbols?
Key Issues	Acceptability Respect	Autonomy Autheticity	Openness Vision	Devotion Commitment

Rowan's chart is based on a complex and comprehensive model, and there are whole schools of psychology that are devoted to this. He sees each of the four columns as stages of evolution. Like Russian dolls, each level is nested within the others. As we shift from one stage to another however it is often experienced like a death of the previous stage, yet we transcend and include it.

In the *Mental Ego – Persona/Shadow* Level of the first column it is the stage of being able to ply our social roles effectively, and to carry them off well enough to make us acceptable workers, spouses, parents, and so forth. This is the level at which most counselling and psychotherapy is carried out. It has to do with adjustment to consensus reality. The client at this stage is going through some unpleasant emotional experiences, and wants to get back to the status quo.

The first initiation is from column one to column two. The *Real Self—Centaur* level of the second column often starts with some crisis, such as a partner leaving, loss of a valuable job, death of a loved one, and so forth, which brings us into therapy. This is the line of personal growth, rather than problem solving; it starts the movement away from role-playing towards authenticity.

The second initiation is from column two to column three, from the *Real Self—Centaur* level to the *Soul—Subtle Self* level. This often occurs in the second half of life, though it can arise anytime. There is often a sense of experiencing a higher self, a transpersonal self, or deep self. Essentially it has a touch of the divine: it is a symbolic representation of the sacred.

Navigating from columns two to three requires soulful transformation and evolution, and this is where my main specialty resides. I have trained in some of the methods from Columns One, Two, Three and Four. I like to think of Column Three as a cocoon, resting between Column Two and Column Four.

The third initiation is the journey from column three to column four, from *Soul – Subtle self* to *Spirit – Causal self*. This is the realm of religion proper, and all the advanced forms of mysticism. If column three is the cocoon, column four is the flame.

Each of my clients is unique and some need extensive ego healing for stability, represented by column one, and then some ego growth for freedom, represented by column two, before they are ready for the soulful transformation required in column three. The process is not usually linear though.

HOW I USE THE CHART

I find this chart useful for discerning where somebody is at in his or her therapeutic need. They may need to focus on what Rowan calls 'ego repair.' After all, having an ego is just part of being a normal, healthy, functioning human.

If a potential client has what I would call a very wounded ego, then I know they need some healing as represented in column one.

This chart demonstrates that there are different appropriate approaches for different conditions, and helps me to refer a new client to the right professional or right resources. Discernment is needed to choose wisely.

Perhaps the person has suffered severe abuse or trauma of some kind, and they come to me after they have unsuccessfully explored healing through the medical system.

Rowan labels the traditional role of the helper as 'Physician/Analyst' in the first column.

In the second column, the process is about ego extending, and so personal growth is a big part of this. The role is 'growth facilitator.'

I also find it useful for mentoring young people who are suffering from a quarter-life crisis. They want greater personal development for the mastery and proactivity phase of life. Often their goals are things like, "I want a decent job, a car, a partner or my own place."

These are healthy goals at a certain stage in one's journey. This is particularly applicable to the first two columns, which are both still addressing the ego level.

SOUL WORK

The third level is where my main interest lies and where my clients do most of their transformational and evolutionary work. It is soul work. This level is about ego-reduction, or ego thinning. The first two columns are metaphorically about becoming a healthy caterpillar, and column three is about transforming into the beautiful winged butterfly.

What often happens in mid-life crisis is that someone has become successful, and by all of today's standards should have a feeling of fulfillment, of finally making it—only to find that they often feel flat, unfulfilled, empty, and lacking in their real essence of being.

Others may have taken a different path, living a life of spontaneity and freedom of expression. They may be struggling to attain some stability in their health, home, relationships or career.

Thus, when midlife hits, some people are so stable they need some shaking up, while others don't feel they have a solid foundation and are now seeking more stability in their lives. Either way, mid-life crisis is a time for integrating the opposites.

Mid-life crisis is often a time of ego reduction, but it's scary because our culture promotes ego growth—especially when you've come from a corporate background that has been feeding you on the incessant, continual success programming.

To shift into a soulful life one needs a healthy ego foundation in order to transform and evolve through ego reduction. The role of the helper is that of an "advanced guide." I call it 'mentoring'. To do this, it's useful to have training in both psychotherapy as well as broad-based spiritual guidance. By broad-based I mean incorporating practices from many different traditions—Buddhist, Christian, Jewish, Sufi, First Nations, and so on, and then also from Transpersonal, Process, Wholistic, or Integrative psychology.

When people come to see me, my role is to work with them on many levels including the soul level. On this level, it's like they're pregnant with their unique spiritual path. If I think of that state as being like a fetus, then my role is to be like a midwife. It's not up to me whether they're having a Buddhist baby, a Jewish baby or a baby that is spiritual but not religious (SBNR)—the essence of all traditions is to bring more love, kindness, compassion, honesty and your inner gifts to the world.

My role is to help them breathe this new life of Inner Treasure into the world so they manifest a vital soulful life.

In the Orient, the word for crisis is a symbol that means both danger and opportunity. If we are to go into the dark places to find what was lost, at times it will seem dangerous, and yet there is an opportunity to uncover our Inner Treasure, our true Gold, hidden in the shadows. Our wounds can lead us to our buried Treasure.

A DEEP FORM OF SUFFERING

Many years ago I went to a another talk by Michael Meade, where he helped me to see that the symptoms I was experiencing were also being experienced on a collective level, all over the world. It helped bring some perspective and meaning to my suffering.

In Meade's brilliant book, *The World Behind The World – Living at the Ends of Time*, he shares that the United Nations had conducted a study of all the major countries in the world, and the main question they asked was: "What's the greatest source of suffering in your country?"

After a great deal of research and time spent, they had it down to a list of four categories that described the most suffering in each country. Some of the words were things like "rootless, powerless, futureless and ruthless leaders", but then the authors of the study said, "Now I want you to take all those words and summarize them into just one word. Distill those four categories into one single word that represents all the suffering in the world."

And the one word that they came up with was "meaninglessness."

Meaninglessness is a deep form of suffering that I would call existential suffering. It brings up core issues that call into question our very existence. Some of the deepest questions of life can begin to arise from the depths like, 'Who am I really? What is meaningful now? Where am I going? What is my unique purpose? Who is going with me? Who am I becoming?'

That's exactly how I felt during my midlife crisis; everything was meaningless, and these were some of my deepest questions.

Some of my clients have even felt suicidal when faced with this overwhelming sense of meaninglessness. I can relate to that because early in my life I felt suicidal too. Fortunately, I followed my deep questions and they eventually invited me on a quest for healing and Inner Treasure.

DIE BEFORE YOU DIE

In a deep passage from one stage of life to another something inside of us wants to die. In the Sufi teaching mentioned earlier—'Die before you die!'—there is a profound practice for soulful transformation and evolution. In fact, this mantra is essential to the deeper practices found in all wisdom traditions.

The way we have been living needs to radically change. To some parts of us, this feels terrifying and life-threatening, so we resist the change. In soulful psychotherapy we are invited to symbolically die to the old life or pattern and be reborn into our new life.

In nature, change is the great constant. We see the tadpole transform and evolve into a frog. The tadpole is restricted to the water. The transformed frog can transit from the water to the land and back again. As infants, we all begin in the watery womb and then emerge onto the earth of our family nest. We learn gradually to venture out and then safely return to the nest.

We also see transformation happening in the journey of the caterpillar that is living on the earth, and is constantly consuming. We could call this the horizontal plane. This kind of consuming can turn addictive. Then one day the caterpillar slows down, turns inward and spins a cocoon. If there is a complete metamorphosis, the caterpillar transforms and evolves into a beautiful butterfly.

The caterpillar begins transforming into the butterfly by pausing its voracious activity of consuming. If the cocoon is tight enough, then it transforms by dissolving and navigating from the horizontal plane to a vertical plane and then back again. As the transformed butterfly, its purpose is now to engage in pollination, spreading beauty all along its path. This process is a natural symbol for our transformational cross and journey.

The word 'psychology' comes from the Greek work *psyche*, which means *soul*. The butterfly is the symbol of the soul in Depth Psychology. In fact, the word *psyche* comes from the Greek word meaning *soul*. The butterfly symbolizes our capacity to shift from an egocentric orientation in life that is constantly outwardly referenced and consuming resources, to a 'ecocentric' soulful way of living that spreads the beauty of giving our gifts in a sustainable way, while pollinating the world with our beautiful service.

In fact, we see change, transformation and evolution happening all the time. Yet, we unconsciously and stubbornly cling to the familiar for a sense of security.

This is a normal response to deep change because we don't know if our transformation will be safe or not, so our instinctual responses kick in to slam on the brakes of our soul's evolutionary progress.

THE PURSUIT OF HAPPINESS THROUGH PLEASURE

We are led to believe by the media and our governments that if only we had more 'stuff' we would be happy. The focus always seems to be on improving the economy at the expense of everything else, including our health and the health of the Earth.

It is even written in the US Constitution that US citizens have a right to pursue happiness. We saw this attitude go to ridiculous proportions when former President George W. Bush Jr. suggested that to deal with their grief around 911, US citizens should "go shopping". It was like telling them, 'Don't feel the grief—just keep busy shopping'!

This kind of advice fosters greater stress and addictive tendencies by reaching for supernormal stimuli, instead of embracing our emotions and being with them compassionately.

Hopefully, readers of this book will realize the folly of that.

To take a wholistic approach in examining our addictive tendencies we need to investigate many perspectives. It is tempting to think that one expert has the ultimate answer.

There is a story from India shared by many Wisdom Traditions that speaks to this tendency to miss the big picture. In Idries Shah's book *Tales of the Dervishes*, Rumi's version is called, "The Elephant in the Dark." He teaches about an elephant that is brought in a dark room to be exhibited. A number of men reach out in the dark to determine what is hidden before them. Depending on where they touch it, some believe the elephant to be like a water spout (trunk), a fan (ear), a pillar (leg) and a throne (back). Rumi uses this story to illuminate the limits to our perception.

Looking back at Rowan's chart on page 59 we can see that practitioners in each of the different columns would have a different perspective depending on their point of view.

And so—are you ready to answer the call to the Inner World of your Psyche?

"Where you stumble, there your treasure lies."

—Joseph Campbell

CHAPTER 2:

THE CALL TO THE INNER WORLD OF THE PSYCHE

"The illness of our time is a loss of soul...that leads to meaninglessness."

—Carl Jung

Two: How can we clear our barriers to living with deeper emotional vitality?

In the story of Isaac's Dream, Isaac has to feel the pain of living in poverty. His call for help was answered in a dream. When I was living alone in midlife, I too was suffering and called out for help. A dream came to me too.

This is one way the 'Call to the Inner World of the Psyche' comes. Rumi quotes the Prophet Mohammad who said that a true seeker must be completely empty like a lute to call out and make the sweet music. Rumi goes on say, "Tears come that dissolve our habitual stubbornness, then we become empty and call out for help". He says, "There is nothing more subtle and delightful than to make that music. Stay empty and held between those fingers, where 'Where' gets drunk with 'Nowhere'!"

The second chakra's addictive tendencies include alcohol, sex, and heroin, according to Anodea Judith.

There are many biological, environmental and social factors that contribute to healing addictions, but for a soulful perspective we need to also bring imagination to addictive tendencies. For example, alcohol is also called spirits. Therefore reaching for alcohol is also reaching for spirit. There is a thirst for spirit, and this kind of thirst can only be quenched by the Inner Treasure of true Spirit.

Rumi is pointing at our thirst for spiritual ecstasy when he says paradoxically, "Where 'Where' gets drunk with 'Nowhere'!" There is often an experience of ecstasy or spiritual bliss when one embraces the opposites. Rumi is using poetic language to point toward the form (Where) and the formless (Nowhere).

Sufis tended to hide their realizations in metaphor and poetry of drunkenness, because the literal-minded authorities of the time would write them off as drunks and not persecute them. You have to develop a subjective consciousness to understand the kind of Truth they are pointing to.

Alcohol can be used medicinally. It can also be used to numb out our feelings or to get access to them. Some use it as a downer to relax or get some sleep. Unfortunately, their quality of sleep usually suffers. It can also be used to knock out our shyness, seriousness or workaholic tendencies so we can loosen up and enjoy the dance.

It can make one more spirited, but we pay the price later with a hangover. According to Sara Gottfried M.D., more than three drinks per week can raise cortisol levels and clog our liver.

Furthermore, it is used in the ritual of the Christian Eucharist to represent the blood of Christ. In Greek Mythology, Dionysus was known as the god of wine and ecstasy. Jungian Psychology sees Dionysus as an archetype of the collective unconscious. Symbolically, when a culture becomes overly rational, it is like they have identified with Apollo, the

Greek God of objective reason—then Dionysus (subjective feeling) is needed for balance. Reaching for the spirit of alcohol could be an unconscious attempt to balance objective and subjective reality.

THE JUNGIAN PERSPECTIVE

One of the early pioneers of bringing more imagination and soul to working with alcohol addiction was Carl Gustav Jung.

Jung is often referred to as 'the doctor of the soul' and he offered us a comprehensive map of the human psyche. In Jung's experience, the Inner World of the Psyche is populated by our persona, shadow, anima, animus and archetypes. Our Ego is the centre of our personal consciousness. Our Self is the centre of our personal wholeness. In Jung's view, the purpose of life is to individuate toward greater wholeness. Many respected psychotherapists like James Hillman, Hal & Sidra Stone, Arnold & Amy Mindell, Marion Woodman, Thomas Moore, Helen Luke and others have been influenced by the soulful ideas of Jung.

Jung traveled widely to cultures like Africa and noticed that some of the indigenous people he encountered had a glazed look in their eyes. The healers and shaman explained to him that these people were suffering from a 'loss of soul'. They lacked connection to their essential Self, Soul and Spirit, and weren't fully present. The trauma they had experienced was so great that in order to protect themselves they disassociated from the essence of themselves.

We see evidence of this locally in people who seem lost, confused, overly distracted or extremely righteous. They often struggle with a deep sense of inadequacy or inflated self-importance. There can be lack of meaning and confusion about who they really are and what their unique purpose is. If terribly wounded, they are sometimes drawn to extreme behaviour or to habitual self-medicating with addictive substances to ease this pain and elevate their dopamine.

In order to understand our present relationships, we need to understand our earliest relationships through a wholistic lens that includes all parts of us. Jung taught that individuals and couples get stuck because they need to work through the psychological dynamics in their relationship that are the result of early childhood conditioning and spiritual disconnection.

He believed that we each have an essential religious instinct but need to address our shadow first. He said: "Filling the conscious mind with ideal conceptions is a characteristic of Western theosophy, but not a confrontation with the shadow and the world of darkness. One does not become enlightened by imagining figures of light, but by making the darkness conscious."

Jung's contribution to psychology has had a profound practical influence on people suffering from addictions and alcohol abuse. One of Jung's patients who suffered from alcoholism was Roland H., and it was after guidance from Jung that he was inspired to join a spiritual group for his deeper recovery.

Jung told him, "I can only recommend that you place yourself in the religious atmosphere of your own choice, that you recognize your own hopelessness, and that you cast yourself upon whatever God you think there is. The lightning of the transforming experience may then strike you.... The only cure for addiction to spirits is Spirit."

Jung's astute advice worked where no psychological, religious, or medical therapy had. Later Roland shared this insight with Bill W, the famous co-founder of Alcoholics Anonymous. In A.A., the gift of healing comes from the grace of surrendering to a Higher Power and from the gift of community. When someone receives the gift of recovery, they often become sponsors to help mentor others in recovery. This forms an essential gift economy of giving. Jung, therefore, indirectly influenced the beginning of A.A. and many other addiction recovery groups.

It has been a very successful model of recovery and now there are many associated groups, like Adult Children of Alcoholics (A.C.O.A.), Codependents Anonymous (Coda), Overeaters Anonymous, Debtors Anonymous, Gamblers Anonymous, Workaholics Anonymous, Sex Addicts Anonymous, Drugs Anonymous, and more.

We saw in the first chapter how the latest addictions research is showing that there is common brain physiology at work in the brain's reward circuitry. There are still great benefits to the emotional, psychological and spiritual support someone receives by being with others who empathize with their suffering.

The shadow side of narrowly focusing on one particular substance or behaviour, is becoming blind to how they are all interlinked. In A.A. groups for example, we often see someone quit drinking but not be so aware of their other addictive tendencies. To compensate from self-soothing with alcohol there is often an increase in binge eating, excess coffee drinking, smoking, co-dependency or spiritual addiction. We need to address all the root causes that lead to all the addictive tendencies. Ernie Larson, a pioneer in the field of recovery taught, "Quitting drinking is just the first step—learning to love our self and others is the real program!"

According to Terry Patten, supernormal stimuli affect not just our food consumption and health, they also affect our relationships. Terry believes that pornography and some advertising images, "hijack men's attention by inducing extreme, insatiable sexual craving. These images promote a sense of lack and need rather than sustainable enjoyment, connectedness to another, or happiness."

Terry argues that, "Women similarly are seduced by exposure to celebrity 'sexcapades,' soap operas, and romance novels. They are swept up in a passive feedback loop, wherein there is no risk of rejection and a momentary sense of excitement and connection is established. They are left with a painful longing for the fantasy figure of a Prince Charming who'll rescue them from a drab and uninteresting existence, compromising their ability to value and work for the real-world possibilities of actual, albeit imperfect, human relationships and a real life partner."

CASE STUDY—FLYING HIGH ON WAX WINGS OF ALCOHOL AND PORN

Tony is 36, recently single, and works as a computer repair technician. He called me to address his 'drinking and sexual problems.'

His girlfriend had given him an ultimatum to stop drinking or she would leave him.

In our first session he told me that he tended to drink more heavily on weekends. He had tried to reduce his drinking to just having a few beers, but recently at his best friend's birthday he got 'pissed'—so drunk, in fact, that he ended up getting arrested for drinking and driving and lost his driver's license.

Not surprisingly, his girlfriend was furious and walked out on him. He told me he wanted her back but she wouldn't speak to him. There were also other problems in the relationship—for example, she complained about their lovemaking and accused him of ejaculating too quickly and then falling into a post-sex slumber.

We explored his relationship to alcohol, sexuality, work, parents and women. His father had been a heavy drinker and was domineering towards his mother and him. Sometimes when he got drunk he was in a 'good' mood, and would flirt with other women. His mother would be upset but wouldn't say anything. She seemed to be depressed at lot. And when his father got drunk and was in a 'bad' mood, he could be verbally abusive. Tony shared stories of his father's abusive putdowns, especially around his music and friends.

Over time Tony also revealed that he hated his job. His real passion was playing electronic keyboards and he dreamed of playing in a band someday, but he hadn't played for years. His drinking started in High School at dances. Fueled by fears of humiliation, rejection and being shamed publicly, he was too shy to ask girls to dance. So, he started getting drunk to mask these feelings. Ever since then he had used alcohol to loosen up around women.

Relationships with women, however, never lasted for more than a few months. He got into computers through his love of keyboards, and found he was pretty good at it, so getting a job was easy. However, it was not what he really wanted to do. He recently saw the movie *Shame* and it freaked him out—he wondered if he was developing a porn addiction.

We worked together for many months and explored his patterns with Voice Dialogue and a method called the 'Clear Your Beliefs' process.

In one Voice Dialogue session, I invited him to move over and step into the part of him that feels shy or lonely and wants to reach for a drink or for some porn. From this place he could feel the fear in his belly and the desperate longing to connect with a drink or with a woman. Then I invited him to move back to the centre position so we could work on loosening his identity to the addicted lover in him.

After there was more awareness, I invited him to move to another position and become the object of his desire. It was potent to witness him become that which he desired. The essence of alcohol was a spirit that was inviting him to be a lover of life! His desire was for his own passion and soul, which he projected onto women. He saw that he had picked up a kind of curse or spell from his father who modeled projecting his soul onto women. He gained the insight that his father had also used alcohol to self-soothe because he didn't like his work; his spirit was bottled up in the bottle of spirits.

One of Tony's core beliefs was that he was fundamentally bad. No matter what he did, he was never good enough for his father. As a result he used alcohol to feel high and boost his confidence, so he could avoid feeling inadequate. When I invited him into a process of feeling the core belief 'I'm bad', as if he believed it completely, then he felt a lot of fear in his 'gut'. In the process we transformed this false belief and he felt a whole lifetime of stress and conditioning begin to melt from his body.

After we uprooted the old belief he felt spacious, and then tremendous joy as he accessed his Inner Treasure. Out of this new way of being he realized the truth that he is fundamentally good, that he had in fact always been good in the core of his being. His dopamine naturally increased. Unfortunately, all his life he had constantly been trying to 'perform' to please others for approval so he could convince them he was good and not bad, but it always backfired.

On a core level Tony suffered from shame about who he was. He felt fundamentally flawed and inherently bad from the abusive treatment he received from his alcoholic father. As young children we need our parents for survival, and so we have a lot invested in seeing them as 'good'.

As a child it is hard to imagine taking your parent aside and saying, "You know, Dad, we all love you, but I think you have a drinking problem and you are scaring all of us with your temper. So would you please go get some help?"

Instead, as little children, we will make up a story that there must be something seriously wrong with us for our parent(s) to be treating us this way.

USING ADDICTIONS TO MANAGE EMOTIONS

Tony was caught in the spell of his father's alcoholism. He and his father were like Icarus in the Greek myth where he flew too close to the sun and his wax wings melted, sending him crashing into the ocean. Like his father, he also started doing work he hated just for the money, and was not following his passion for music.

Alcohol and porn became the way he self-medicated the pain of not going in the direction his soul wanted. They became his demon lovers for releasing stress. As a result he couldn't relate to women as equal partners without objectifying them for his sexual and emotional needs. Alcohol and porn were like the wax wings that he used to get 'high' and fly to the sun of spirit. His wings would eventually melt and he would end up crashing into the ocean of self-doubt and depression.

Fortunately, he got help in time because he was in great danger of developing greater bi-polar swings of using alcohol as spirit to bypass his feelings of inadequacy and artificially boost his dopamine.

Often people will use alcohol or sex to manage their emotions. In his TEDx talk on "Why We Suffer," Michael Dowd speaks passionately about how both of these supernormal allurements affect our brain physiology.

As mentioned earlier, he says, alcohol was not something our ancient ancestors had to contend with. With elevated status, men's testosterone rises and is a supernormal allurement for some women as it raises their testosterone too. Alcohol and sex are second chakra addictions and are often used to either soothe turbulent emotions or get access to emotional flow or raise dopamine. Dowd suggests that this is why some high profile ministers end up having affairs. If we compulsively keep busy all week, then on the weekend we can use alcohol to numb out our workaholic tendencies and relax. Unfortunately, our instinctual drives take over, and pretty soon we are caught in the labyrinth of addictions to compensate for low dopamine levels.

A USEFUL BRAIN MODEL

Dr. Daniel Siegel is a major contributor in the field of neuroscience. He is a psychiatrist and psychotherapist, and in his insightful book called *Mindsight*, he teaches a simple model of the brain, which he calls "a hand model of the brain".

In addition to the left and right hemispheres, there are also the four main parts of the brain—firstly the reptilian brainstem, represented in Siegel's model by your lower palm area. Then, if you hold your hand with your fingers straight up (as if you were taking an oath), and you curl your thumb in to the centre of your palm, this represents where the midbrain or amygdala, a part of our mammalian brain is.

Now, if you curl your fingers over the thumb, the top of your hand represents the location of the neocortex, and the two fingers that are curled over the thumb in the middle represents the location of the prefrontal cortex.

This model has been helpful to show that when we get traumatized—when we feel an insecure attachment with a significant other—the reptilian brain is activated. It is the most ancient part of the brain and reacts with a *fight, flee, freeze,* or *fold* response. Imagine a smoke detector that sounds an alarm that there is a dangerous fire. In the same way, a signal is sent from the amygdala, which is highly sensitive. It developed thousands of years ago when we had to know whether to fight, flight, freeze or play dead when a lion or saber-toothed tiger was chasing us.

The neocortex developed next and is responsible for 'meaning making'. The final part of the brain to develop was the prefrontal cortex, and this is where we can develop greater awareness. It gives us the ability to identify which supernormal stimuli are addictive for us and gives us the ability choose to respond more consciously. This ability can be impaired by addictions.

We need awareness and discernment especially in relationship situations when our partner appears to us as threatening. We are sensitive to something called prosody—if our partner speaks to us with a certain tone of voice, or with a certain look on their face, our amygdala instantly fires, our reptilian brain triggers, and we think we need to go on the defense because there is a 'lion' after us.

So, in Siegel's hand model of the brain, under a real or perceived threat all our fingers shoot up, and we 'flip our lid', as the common expression goes. Temporally, at that moment we go offline intellectually. We can't think clearly, and we are caught in a panic for survival, in a fight, flight, freeze or fold mode.

This explains why couples sometimes get into dangerous situations while driving a car. They are both instinctively 'fighting for their life,' but they usually don't see that they are replaying a scene from their past and re-traumatizing each other.

UNDERSTANDING OUR BRAIN-HEART-GUT-MIND CONNECTION

We need to have some strategies for calming our amygdala. If we can calm our reptilian brain, we can see that it's not a lion that is going to devour us—it's just our partner who is doing something we are reacting to. Once we've realized that, we can ask questions like, "What are the basic needs that aren't being met in each of us?"

We're learning that the heart and the gut are both centres of neuron activity. The heart, it turns out, is an electrical organ and may have as much as five times the magnetic field of our brain. According to Sara Gottfried M.D. and her friends at the Heart Math Institute, the latest science suggests that our adrenal glands listen to what the heart tells the brain around what stress or repair hormones to release. They both teach that for vital health it is essential to do practices to increase our heart intelligence or coherence.

The heart-brain is a centre of love. How do we know whether we love something or not? That's going to come from our heart. It's from our deep heart that our Inner Treasure like Essential Qualities of love, wisdom, forgiveness, peace and compassion arise.

Then there's the centre of neuronal activity in the gut. For example, if you're walking into a dark alley and you get a hunch that you're not meant to go there, your gut senses, "It's not safe to go down this alley," and if you listen to your body's advice, that actually saves your life. It takes discernment to know what is true.

One of the problems, Dan Siegel says, is that for years we haven't had a coherent definition of the brain. Science thought of the brain as just an organ in the head, but now a new definition is emerging that suggests the entire nervous system is part of the brain.

And then there's the mind. Dr. Siegel realized that there wasn't a coherent definition of the mind. At a conference he was attending he addressed forty scientists from various disciplines—anthropology, biology, psychology, and so on—all professionals who were supposed to be experts of the mind.

Daniel Siegel asked them: "Do we have a definition of the mind?" They looked at each other and were suddenly perplexed. It was like finding out that the emperor had no clothes on. What became apparent is that nobody in his or her training had been given a clear definition of the mind. A few people made attempts at defining the mind, but nobody could agree on a coherent definition.

Siegel was at quite a loss and so, over lunchtime, he went for a walk and pondered this, and came up with a definition. When he came back, he shared this with the room full of professionals, and every one of them bought into it.

The definition that Siegel came up with is: "The mind can be defined as an embodied and relational process that regulates the flow of energy and information."

The idea is that the mind is not just local, in the head or in the body; the mind is also relational—it is part of a field that encompasses both 'me' and the 'we'. So, if two people agree, then there are two 'I's, but there's also the 'we' of "Do we understand each other?" This is a third multidimensional perspective that starts to evolve as we cultivate it through conscious practice.

Of course, if you have many people, then the challenge is to go from honouring all the little me's, to including the great We.

THE RIVER OF INTEGRATION

Daniel Siegel has made some major contributions to the field of neuroscience and psychotherapy. One of the images that I find useful to hold and share with some clients is what he calls "the river of integration".

As he puts it, "You can put all the different categories of the DSMV—the Diagnostic Manual of Psychiatric Disorders— into this simple image: if you imagine a river flowing between two banks, you need the banks for structure, and you need the river for flow."

From the bank's perspective, the river looks too chaotic, it's always moving. From the river's perspective, the banks are too rigid. People who are too rigid usually have some childhood trauma that has influenced them to be rigid, and they try to manage their anxiety and protect themselves by being rigid.

People who are too chaotic were usually also traumatized and feel very anxious, so their life is like an emotionally turbulent river. To have a healthy balance, both structure and flow are needed. Too much rigidity, then there's no flow, there's no river possible for flowing. Too much chaotic flow, and then we flood the banks.

When a person is flooded emotionally, then they can flip their lid and go offline. They can't think clearly, and they don't know what direction to take.

The river is a simple but profound image, and very useful in therapeutic applications. In Voice Dialogue, for example, we can work with the opposites in someone to achieve a better balance of form and flow, thinking and feeling, and so on.

Another contribution from Dan Siegel that I find very practical to use in my work is the idea of the healing power of presence between therapist and client that I mentioned before, as well as working with the nine domains of integration to promote well-being. These include the domains of consciousness, horizontal, vertical, memory, narrative, state, impersonal, temporal and transpiration integration.

For example, I'm using narrative integration in writing this book so that I can harvest the Inner Treasure of deeper meaning and purpose from some of my life so far to benefit myself, and others.

Siegel also noted that, "Emotion is not just some primitive remnant of an earlier reptilian evolutionary past. Emotion directs the flow of activation (energy) and establishes the meaning of representations (information processing) for the individual. It is not a single, isolated group of processes; it has a direct impact on the entire mind."

He goes on to say that there is a difference between implicit memories and explicit memories. Explicit memories are ones you can remember. Implicit ones (like the ones I've mentioned in the introduction that came up when I was writing the essay about losing my dog and father) are buried in the unconscious and in our body.

Without help, it would have been too overwhelming for me to experience them in early life, so to protect myself, I would have had to either repress them or blow a circuit breaker. It took much healing later on to allow these feelings to arise.

Siegel teaches that there is a seahorse shaped organ in the brain called the hippocampus that integrates information from our implicit memories to become explicit memories. The hippocampus can be blocked by alcohol and extreme stress. This explains why some people act out violently during drunken or stressful episodes and then can't remember doing so later.

Many of my clients are suffering from the trauma of implicit memories. This was the case with Beth.

CASE STUDY—FEAR OF FEAR

Beth is 42 and runs a daycare from her home. She called me about anxiety around sexual problems she was experiencing with the man she was seeing. Every time she made love she started to feel like her emotions would 'go crazy'. She couldn't understand what was happening. He seemed like a nice man, but she was having a strong emotional reaction to him and was worried that she would never be able to have a relationship with any man.

We explored this feeling of her emotions 'going crazy' through her subconscious using the 'Clear Your Beliefs' process and Voice Dialogue. In the process I guided Beth into her imaginal realm, her subconscious to explore this feeling.

At one point, a buffalo came to her. When I dialogued with the buffalo, it said that it was a 'protector spirit' for her. When I asked the buffalo if it was safe to work on this issue, the buffalo said that it was fine, but wanted to supervise and would block me if the process became too overwhelming. I agreed, saying that I respected Beth's resistance and that I have no intention for her to get rid of her protection. I honoured the buffalo for protecting her thus far, and assured it that I only wanted to help her explore this feeling and belief. The buffalo then gave me permission to proceed.

When we went into the process of feeling this belief, Beth suddenly began to sob uncontrollably. After empathizing, I asked her what was happening. She shared that a buried memory came up of her being abused by an older man when she was a young girl. When he forced himself upon her, she felt so overwhelmed that her emotions felt crazy! As she shared her grief she realized that a lifetime of self-doubt and difficult relationships with men stemmed from this incident. It was so overwhelming for her as a girl that she had completely disassociated from the memory.

As she released the trauma and transformed the old belief, her body filled with a powerful life force. At one point she imagined this man standing before her once again, but now she was much more powerful than he was. She realized that she had the power to crush him. After feeling so powerless it was important to feel her power.

All of a sudden he seemed puny, and she started to feel empathy for him. She realized that he must have been seriously wounded to treat a young girl this way. Instead of despising him and crushing him, she now felt compassion for her inner little girl and for him. Now she was the empowered woman who could stand up for her little girl, and set the appropriate boundaries that her alcoholic father could never set for her back then.

She began to dance with joy, as the spell from her childhood, was broken. She realized that she was attracted to wounded men like her father who weren't really available to her. She was unconsciously trying to heal her father through her relationship with them. It was true that the men she met feared commitment, but she also wasn't available to commit to them for fear of getting too close. Now that the spell was broken she was free to cultivate healthy relationships that weren't haunted by the ghosts of her past.

ADDICTED TO LOVE OR STRESS?

For most of us, our first food came from the breast of our mother. On a biological level we also received the chemicals that were in her bloodstream. If she was healthy, our bodies benefited accordingly. If she had addictive tendencies like alcohol, then we may have developed a condition like fetal-alcohol syndrome.

If she was overly stressed, she may have had elevated levels of cortisol, which could have put her and our Reptilian Brain and limbic system on high alert.

During the miracle of birth, Nature ensures that we attach to our mothers through co-regulation of our nervous system to manage the stress of birth by a powerful hormone called oxytocin. According to Dr.

Mia Kalef in her book *The Secret Life of Babies—How our Prebirth and Birth Experiences Shape our World*, oxytocin plays an important role in the neuroanatomy of intimacy, specifically in sexual reproduction of both sexes, in particular during and after childbirth.

She writes: "It (oxytocin) is released in large amounts after distension of the cervix and uterus during labour, facilitating birth, maternal bonding, and, after stimulation of the nipples, lactation. Both childbirth and milk ejection result from positive feedback mechanisms."

Oxytocin also elevates endorphins, which help the mother and baby experience a natural high.

Dr. Kalef goes on to say, "Attachment is the first addiction... Alongside oxytocin lingers a powerful group of chemicals called endorphins. Endorphins act as strong 'addictors' in that any other chemical present alongside them will become addictive... Depending on whether a baby has been marinating in a cortisol or oxytocin axis, she will be addicted to the qualities of that axis:

"Oxytocin—the 'love' hormone + Endorphins—the 'addictors' = Addicted to Love.

"Cortisol—the 'stress' hormone + Endorphins—the 'addictors' = Addicted to Stress."

It seems that if our birth was overly stressful, we may be more wired for stress than wired for love.

EARLY CHILDHOOD STAGES

If all goes well in early childhood, a child evolves through predictable developmental stages. Eric Erikson suggests that there are eight stages of our psychosocial development. Margaret Mahler identified five stages of development in early childhood.

Anodea Judith in *Eastern Body Western Mind* links Erikson's eight stages with the development of our seven major chakras. She teaches that "Chakra One relates to the formation of the physical body and spans from mid-pregnancy to twelve months after birth, peaking at four to five months. It is the foundation of security and being grounded that enables self-preservation and forms the physical identity.

"Chakra Two develops from six months to two years, peaking at twelve to eighteen months. It is typified by duality, sensation, feeling, and mobility and is characterized by the conflict of separation vs. attachment. This stage focuses on the formation of an emotional identity, which is mainly interested in self-gratification.

"Chakra Three development spans a period from eighteen months to approximately four years. There is an attempt at autonomy. This is the formation of a personal ego identity, mainly focused on self-definition.

"Chakra Four development spans a period from four to seven years where loving becomes more conscious. This stage heralds the formation of our relational programs and our social identity.

"Chakra Five develops between seven to twelve years and is the stage for creative expression and the formation of a creative identity.

"Chakra Six develops through adolescence and requires an ability to recognize patterns and apply them to life decisions. There may be a dawning interest in spiritual matters, mythology, or symbolism, whether through music, lyrics, popular movie icons, or the latest fashion. When allowed to mature, this leads to the formation of an archetypal identity, whose interest is self-reflection.

"Chakra Seven is the stage of early adulthood and beyond and is related to the pursuit of knowledge, the formation of a worldview, and the awakening of spiritual pursuits. There is a search for meaning inquiring into the nature of life, the universe, and the Self within. This leads to the formation of a personal identity."

Judith argues that chakra development during childhood happens in a relatively unconscious way. Adult development, by contrast, is largely conscious. We have to want to develop, or it may not happen at all. If any of the developmental stages are incomplete, that particular chakra isn't functioning optimally and we can get stuck in an immature stage of development. Through conscious practice we can heal, transform and evolve in all of our chakras.

ATTACHMENT THEORY

Looking at childhood, we also see that from a Developmental Psychology viewpoint, a lot of gains have been made with a theory of development called *Attachment Theory,* begun by John Bowlby and then Mary Ainsworth. In the 1970's, Bowlby and Ainsworth devised a procedure called 'the Strange Situation' to observe attachment relationships between a caregiver and their child. Later, Mary Main and Eric Hesse, took the theory much further.

They set up a room with a researcher and some toys. A mother would come into the room with her child—between nine and eighteen months of age. What they wanted to see was how securely attached the child was to the mother. They would invite the mother and child in, and then the child would be introduced to some toys. The mother would then leave the room, and concealed observers would watch to study how the child would react, and especially how the child would react when the mother came back into the room a little while later.

The securely-attached child who had a healthy bond with his mother was initially upset, but when his mother came back in, was easily soothed and comforted. They co-regulated together, producing oxytocin and reducing the cortisol produced by the stress.

Another category is called *insecurely attached.* In that case they found three different styles of insecurely attached children.

One style of attachment researchers called 'anxious-ambivalent attachment.' In this experiment, when the mother left, the child got anxious and the researcher couldn't calm the child down. Even when the mother came back in, the child remained anxious for some time, and needed quite a bit of soothing and would cling to his parent.

Another insecure attachment style is described as 'anxious-avoidant attachment'. In this case, when the mother leaves, the child starts playing with the toys; and when the mother comes back in, the child doesn't seem to get upset, and doesn't seem to mind that the mother was gone.

At first they thought this was the 'independent' child, but what they later learned is that if the mother or caregiver isn't available, then the child learns to self-regulate by attaching to an object like a toy or a teddy bear or perhaps watching TV. They are very intelligent already, so they will self-soothe in some other way, with an object. They found that often the child had a history of suffering significant periods of separation from his or her parent.

The other insecure style is called 'disorganized/disoriented attachment.' Again, the mother leaves the room. This time the infant exhibits intense movements, such as hunching the shoulders, putting her hands behind her neck and so on, as if stressed and trying not to cry. When the mother comes back, the child is very confused and the mother/caregiver in some instances is perceived as somewhat dangerous. In this case, there may have been too much chaos in their home environment. Nothing is certain at home, so the child is in a disorganized, confused state.

Co-regulation happens when the child can go to her mother to be soothed for her anxiety, but in this case, she doesn't know which way to go. And so she feels highly confused.

Research suggests that these attachment styles will play out later in life in adult relationships. The adult who was a securely attached child often becomes a securely attached adult and is attracted to another securely attached partner. These relationships usually exhibit harmony through co-regulation.

The insecurely attached child that has the anxious-ambivalent style of attachment becomes an anxious partner later in relationships, and he will often feel abandoned if his partner isn't there for him. He could be ambivalent or aggressive, and dramatic in the expression of his anxiety. It's like he is in danger of losing his needed connection with his mother or caregiver. His response to uncertain situations is like an overactive fight response.

The 'anxious-avoidant' style will use an avoidance strategy in relationships if they're not getting their needs met. They will get busy doing something, like focusing on the computer or watching endless TV. They try to avoid conflict because they don't want any disruption that reminds them of their past trauma. In conflict, they normally want things to be quickly smoothed over, or they want to leave. They also can be prone to being overloaded quite easily. In relationships, two insecure people will often find each other.

The other style mentioned is the 'disorganized/disoriented attachment' style. These people usually have a hard time with relationships because it feels so confusing, disorienting and perhaps even dangerous. Relationships feel overwhelming to them, and this also depends on the partner that they end up with.

If an insecurely attached person ends up with somebody who is a securely attached person, this can help him to regulate, and calm his nervous system. The secure partner can help him evolve towards what's called 'earned security' or 'healing attachment'. This is one reason why a secure relationship with a trusted therapist can be so healing.

Usually, however, we find that two insecurely attached partners find each other and, depending on their styles, react accordingly. If we look at two professionals, like two accountants or lawyers who are married and both have anxious-avoidant styles, they might seem calm on the exterior. Often there doesn't seem to be too much going on—they're both intellectual, so perhaps there doesn't seem to be a lot of passion in their relationship. They may be fine with that, but may also feel like something's missing.

Two anxious-ambivalent people can be very explosive. Where there is one person who is 'anxious-ambivalent' and one that's 'anxious-avoidant'—which is quite a common combination—then one is pursuing, and the other is usually distancing.

You can also have a combination of styles because we have two parents—father and mother. You might have had a secure attachment with your mother and an insecure attachment with your father. Developmental Psychology and Attachment Theory have been helpful in looking at some of these early family patterns and how they play out later in life. These patterns shape our habitual addictive responses as we attempt to self-regulate and self-soothe.

Daniel Siegel teaches that there is a part of the brain called the hippocampus that integrates implicit memory and explicit memory. Excessive alcohol or stress can impair our hippocampus. This is one of the reasons we can't remember how we behaved when we were drunk or abusive so stay in denial.

Whatever is normal in somebody's family system, the children will internalize. Children are innately intelligent when it comes to getting their needs met, so they will adapt to or rebel against the rules of their family system.

In the section on Voice Dialogue—Theory and Process in the next chapter, we'll be looking at how the first 'selves' that make up our personality are formed based on the explicit or implicit rules of our family.

For example, if in our family system our parents are anxious avoidant styles, we may also have an anxious avoidant personality style that follows from that. Alternatively, we can be just the opposite—we could be a rebel to that family pattern and try to fight to get our needs met in our family system. Our fighting disrupts everybody in the family because they're all anxious avoidant styles and want to avoid conflicts.

If we are more wired for stress, it fuels our insecure attachment style. If a couple can learn to use their bodies to co-regulate each other's nervous system, they can develop earned security or what some call 'healing attachment'. Recent studies have begun to investigate the role of oxytocin in various behaviours including orgasm, social recognition, pair bonding, and maternal behaviours. For this reason it is sometimes referred to as the 'bonding hormone'.

Knowing this, we can consciously use practices like conscious hugging to elicit oxytocin and foster healing through co-regulation. I like to call it 'hugging to heal.' We can also do practices like conscious movement to stimulate the natural flow of oxytocin and dopamine.

By now, you might be aware of a developmental stage you need some work on. You also might see some of the destructive or habitual patterns in your own life and family. Or, you may be in need of some help on your journey. In the next chapter, we will meet allies, mentors and elders for the path.

CHAPTER 3:

ALLIES, MENTORS, AND ELDERS ON THE PATH

"We do not believe in ourselves until someone reveals that something deep inside of us is valuable, worth listening to, worthy of our trust, sacred to our touch. Once we believe in ourselves, we can risk curiosity, wonder, spontaneous delight or any experience that reveals the human spirit."

— E. E. Cummings

Three: How can we clear barriers to accomplishing our goals in life?

In a world that is increasingly obsessed with social media and online 'friends', it is ironic that so many people go through life feeling so lonely, preferring (and sometimes refusing) to share their problems or seek guidance from mentors and elders and therapists.

This chapter explores some of the allies, mentors and elders we can find on our path. We will explore how even some of the famous names in history have experienced their own struggles and crises.

In this chapter we will also look at addictive tendencies in the third chakra. These include amphetamines, cocaine, caffeine, work, anger and power, according to Anodea Judith.

JUNG'S MIDLIFE CRISIS

Dr. Carl Jung said that when clients came for therapy, they were symbolically twenty-one or fifty years of age. Typically from twenty-one until thirty-four we try to get established in life. If this doesn't go well, we likely have a quarter-life crisis.

From about thirty-five to fifty-five we are established in life, but often a lack of meaning and purpose can lead us to a midlife crisis.

Jung experienced a midlife crisis himself when he experienced a conflict and fallout with his mentor, Sigmund Freud, due to Jung's views on spirituality.

When Jung was a boy, he came from a long line of pastors, like his father and many uncles. Naturally, he was also expected to become a theologian. During confirmation, he expected a big experience… instead, it was a let down, leaving him very disappointed. He must have been seven or eight years old at the time, and confused about not having the spiritual confirmation that he had hoped for.

Things shifted when he became aware of his powerful dreams. In his autobiography, *Memories, Dreams, Reflections*, he talks about having a number one personality and a number two personality by age ten.

He writes that his number one personality was a typical ten-year-old boy. His number two personality was an old man who was about two hundred years old, and came from a different time period. He engaged in dialogue with this inner figure, but it seemed strange to him as a boy, so he kept it to himself.

This was his discovery that—we have different dimensions of the psyche, different aspects to our inner world. And so for Jung, awareness of the inner world of the psyche started at a very young age.

Later in life he decided to not be a pastor like his father, but to become a medical doctor instead. His father approved because he thought the field of medicine to be a respected one.

This was the time when Sigmund Freud was getting popular. Freud was a respected leader in the psychology movement at the time, and had students such as Alfred Adler, Wilhelm Reich and Heinz Kohut. Many of his students went on to form their own schools of psychology.

Freud and Jung started sharing ideas, and Freud was quite impressed by Jung's ideas and vice versa. They met regularly for many hours. Freud was an older Austrian man, a well-known Neurologist and seen as the father of Psychoanalysis. He was a father figure and a mentor to Jung.

Jung was Freud's favourite colleague and seen by others in the Psychoanalytic community as destined to take over the lead from Freud. At a certain point though, they had a major disagreement about Freud's perspective on sexuality and spirituality. Freud thought spirituality was nonsense and an attempt to return to the womb. Jung, on the other hand was convinced there was something that he called a 'religious instinct'. I once went to a Jungian lecture where the presenter summed up Jung's essential ideas as contained in the 'transcendent function'—this could be accessed by holding the tension of a pair of opposites while tuning into a third order of consciousness that emerged.

Freud contributed much to the field of psychology and his theories are the basis for many of the psychological ideas of the theorists in the conventional medical field (see Rowan's chart, Column One, for ego repair). Jung ventured further into the spiritual and instinctual dimensions of the psyche (see Rowan's column three for psyche or soul).

When the differences between them became untenable, Jung felt disappointed, but decided to leave the Psychoanalytical Society. Later, as he healed, transformed and evolved soulfully, it became his path of individuation as he developed his own theories. His wife Emma Jung also became a writer and Jungian psychotherapist. They had five children together and lived in a stone house on the shore of a lake near Zurich.

After leaving the Psychoanalytic Society, Jung focused on offering private practice serving his clients. The status-seeking part of him went through quite a drop in popularity and status. This contributed to his midlife crisis as he lost his upward mobility. He saw his self-improvement persona was a mask that kept him from descending into the depths.

Now, with more time on his hands, he began journeying deep into the underworld of his own dreams, trying to find coherence for some of his theories. A big breakthrough came when he allowed himself to play.

Through a process Jung created called *Active Imagination*, he learned to dialogue with the eight-year-old boy in his psyche. He loved to build sandcastles. He would go down by the water and create sandcastles with moats and waterways.

This really affected his dreams. He discovered the archetypes of his 'personal unconscious' through this play. Children playing in nature access the Inner Treasure by doing profound inner work in their psyche, witnessing the process of tadpole transforming into frog, and caterpillar into becoming a beautiful butterfly.

Children's play is a form of intelligent work that they're developing. Play develops the child's whole brain. Lack of play in nature can emphasize their left hemisphere brain development over the right. If we stop them playing in nature, we can end up socializing them into objectifying nature. A kind of autistic behaviour can develop where they're not reading other people's signals and cues in the 'collective we' of culture and nature. They can become anxious avoidant and use phones or computers or TV screens to self-regulate and increase dopamine. Jung soulfully healed and integrated his inner child through play in nature. His *Red Book* is an amazing collection of his dream work and art.

As mentioned in the last chapter, Jung also studied religious traditions and indigenous people all over the world. He travelled widely, even going to remote places like Africa. On his journeys he learned that the local shaman could see when somebody was experiencing soul-loss, their eyes looked cloudy as if they weren't really present and vital.

The shamans knew they had to do a ritual to help the person recover their soul again.

If we are experiencing soul loss like this we need to recover our essence from within as Jung did. The word psyche or soul points to our essence. The Jewish Tradition calls this essence our 'Divine Spark' that gives us aliveness and soulful vitality.

Jung then looked at rituals of initiation and the collective traditions to formulate his ideas about the 'collective unconscious' that all of humanity shares. In his book *Man and His Symbols*, Jung explores these cultural symbols extensively. He was also a major influence on the ideas of mythologist Joseph Campbell.

Jung's midlife crisis included spiritual crisis, and through his dreams he connected with an inner figure that he called 'a wise old man' or 'Philemon'. Once he learned to dialogue with him, his wise inner figure started guiding him. Eventually, he was led to a wise feminine figure called 'Salome'. In Jungian Psychology, the term anima means soul, and Jungians see the anima or soul as feminine.

He dialogued with this inner feminine contra-sexual figure as a symbol of his soul. He said women have a contra-sexual animus figure within—the masculine spirit for the feminine. Many post-modern Jungians believe that we all have both anima and animus—a masculine spirit and feminine soul within each of us.

By interacting with his inner world of psyche, he explored his own unconscious through dream work and Active Imagination. When visiting the United States he was interviewed and asked whether he believed in God. His answer was something like, "I don't believe, I know!" Unlike his father, he didn't have to rely on blind belief.

At one point Jung witnessed his father become deathly ill, and in the process reject his belief in God. Instead, he leaned toward a blind faith in medical science. Science, however, was not able to save him.

It seemed his father's spirituality was based on blind belief, not on direct experience of Gnosis or 'True Knowledge.' This led Jung to investigate the path of Gnosis: to the wisdom of direct experience beyond blind belief.

With his map of the inner world of the psyche, Jung influenced many therapists to integrate the soul back into psychology, and thus to heal the split of soul and science.

A FICTIONAL DOCTOR'S MIDLIFE CRISIS

One of my favourite films highlighting the polarization of objective impersonal science and subjective personal care in the health profession is called *The Doctor*. It was released in 1991 at a time when I was swirling in my own mid-life crisis. This film was a good mirror for what I was going through back then.

The main character in the film is Jack, played by William Hurt. He is a successful surgeon, married to a caring wife and co-parenting a young son. They live in a luxurious house in the San Francisco Hills.

As a surgeon he holds the responsibility of people's lives in his hands and uses a lot of humour in order to deal with their pain. Some of it quite funny, but there is also a caustic quality to his humour. He is insensitive to his patients and starts to belittle some of his colleagues. This applies especially to one of his fellow surgeons—Eli, a compassionate doctor—but Jack still takes sarcastic shots at him.

Jack also has a business partner, another surgeon, who he jokes with. Their relationship is playful but has an immature quality to it that is particularly evident in the way his partner shirks from his ethical responsibility around a patient he injured. He wants Jack to cover his back by lying to the authorities. Like adolescents, they also tend to leer at women as sex objects.

Jack starts to have problems with his throat, and it turns out that he has to go in for a biopsy. It's ironic because he has to go to see a female surgeon, and he usually acts patriarchal and sexist toward women. He starts trying to use his charm to chat her up, but she's not buying any of it, in fact, she's quite impersonal towards him. So he gets a bitter taste of his own impersonal treatment towards others.

He's been very impersonal with his clients but now he's expecting care from her just because she is a woman. He makes an assumption that because she is female she 'should' be caring. His sexist attitude bugs her. As a result he ends up getting some cold impersonal energy right back from her that he is not too happy about. This is a reflection of his usual behaviour toward others.

Then it turns out that he has advanced throat cancer and he has to go down to the basement of the hospital for radiation treatment. He was on the top floor symbolically and literally as a surgeon. He thinks he is special but is forced to go through the whole intake procedure like other ordinary patients.

Meanwhile, he's expecting preferential treatment from the nurses, and they're getting a little ticked off at his arrogance. He tries to use his rank and his position to try to get to the front of the queue and this causes resentment in the staff.

One day he meets a young woman named June. Her head is shaved as a result of her treatment, and she wears a kerchief over her head because of her advanced stage of cancer. In fact, she hasn't been given very long to live. Eventually Jack starts to feel humiliated, powerless and eventually humbled.

Even though she looks like she's only in her early twenties, she seems like a wise elder compared to Jack.

Jack is attracted to her as a fellow companion on the cancer journey and looks to her for support. He hasn't been very attentive to his wife or his son, and we can see his avoidant tendencies in these relationships. His son is becoming avoidant too, just like his father. Jack's wife is keeping busy with all kinds of activities. They are drifting apart and their marriage is suffering.

Jack gets closer to this young woman, June. It seems like he has a crush on her, but he is actually attracted to her authenticity and the realness of her immediacy in facing death. That kind of intimacy is something that he lacks and is longing for.

There's one scene where it looks like she hasn't got long to live, so he talks her into a spontaneous plane trip. They rent a car and go for a wild ride to watch the sunset. Jack feels passionate and alive. He has projected his passion and soul onto this young woman but is still unconscious of it. In Jungian Psychology, the anima is Latin for soul. He becomes animated in her presence and becomes animated in nature, witnessing the beauty of the Soul of the World. Painfully, the young woman suddenly seems aware of the projection and his attempt to escape reality.

Later, he calls home on a payphone, insensitively waking his wife, Anne, and makes a confession as to where he is and whom he is with. Anne feels betrayed by Jack's closeness to June since it was missing in their relationship.

Eventually, June dies and Jack is devastated. He is forced to wake up and see the gravity of his situation. When it's time for his operation, he fires the impersonal female surgeon and asks Eli to do the operation, the surgeon he has consistently ridiculed. There's a powerful scene when Jack says to Eli, "I'm sorry for treating you so poorly." Eli snaps back with a playful response: "Well, Jack," he teases, "I've always wanted to slit your throat, and now I've finally got the chance!"

In another scene we see Jack maturing as he confronts his business partner for his unethical behaviour and announces that he won't lie for him by covering up the facts of his negligence. Jack takes responsibility for speaking the truth and matures. Eli demonstrates his caring compassion and excellent skill as a surgeon as Jack's operation turns out to be successful.

At the end of the film, Jack acts like a more caring doctor or healer. He also repairs the relationship with his wife and son. We see him maturing into being a mentor as he teaches his new students to be more compassionate. We witness the transformation from the beginning when he used to be very impersonal, to finding balance by integrating his personal side.

This film reflects the essence of some of my journey of rebalancing impersonal objectivity for clarity and personal subjectivity for caring. It also reflects some of the rebalancing currently needed in our medical system.

MANAGING OUR STRESS

In a talk at Naropa University in 2013, Doctor Sarah Gottfried, Harvard-trained MD, yoga teacher, mother and author of *The Hormone Cure*, shares that as a Doctor in the U.S., she was only given seven minutes to treat each of her patients. Her caseload increased to thirty to forty patients per day and her cortisol levels became dangerously high. She became stressed, overweight, had a low sex drive and went to couples counselling for help, blaming her husband for how she was feeling. She was fond of drinking wine to relax, but it was spiking her cortisol levels.

When she went to her Doctor, he recommended she go on Prozac, birth control pills, eat less and exercise more. His advice didn't feel right to her as it implied that if she only had more will power, she could surely succeed. She decided to take her health into her own hands and explored an integrative, Functional approach to wellness. She has now healed the causes of her imbalances, lost the extra twenty-five pounds, recovered her sex drive and completed couples therapy. She now finds meaning and purpose teaching women how to manage their stress and hormonal health. She is at *www.sarahgottfriedmd.com*.

BRAIN SCIENCE MENTORS

A few years ago I went to see Daniel Siegel at a talk at the Dalai Lama Centre for Peace and Education in Vancouver, and he said that he went through a very similar impersonal training when he was a hospital intern. His mentors focused on teaching him to be impersonal with his patients. When he tried to enquire into how their health was and how they were feeling, his supervisors reprimanded him saying, "We don't ask how they are feeling, that's not our job. Do you want to be a psychiatrist or something?"

Dan got quite discouraged about his choice of profession. He decided to take a break and travel to British Columbia and went salmon fishing on the West Coast. He had somewhat of a midlife crisis of his own.

He did a lot of research and realized the imbalance in his life. In one example, he told a story about being in the lunchroom with a number of other doctors, some of whom talked about resenting their patients. Siegel had to admit that he felt the same way towards some of his patients.

I was amazed to hear a well-known doctor admit this candidly on stage with hundreds of people witnessing. My sense is that he realized that, as an impersonal doctor, he was expected to always be the expert, the 'fixer.' The patient would come in with a problem that he was supposed to 'fix.' And if he couldn't 'fix' them, he would feel like a failure. He realized he had been taught to see a patient as a problem to be fixed.

A polarization of an impersonal doctor who always needs to play the role of the powerful fixer, and a patient who needs 'fixing,' results in what Voice Dialogue calls a *polarization of the opposites*. It forces the patient to always play the role of the personal, vulnerable, sick one.

Siegel started to investigate the polarization. My guess is he realized that if he could embrace his personal vulnerability and be an ordinary human being, instead of an impersonal expert, maybe his patients could get in touch with their own inner doctor, their own inner healer. He then started to investigate a more compassionate approach to healthcare.

Encouraged by his candid sharing, a number of people in the audience started asking him about the soul… about whether he believed in the soul. He said something like, "Well, in medical science we don't talk about the soul because we can't measure it in a double blind study, but I believe there is a soul or some essential part of the human being." Siegel said that he had been invited to many conferences that have had prominent spiritual teachers as the presenters. He was also one of the founders of a new integrative movement called Interpersonal Neurobiology or IPNB.

Siegel said his approach to wellness now is, "It's all about meaning and connection." He said these spiritual teachers were teaching the same thing in essence—it's all about meaning and connection. Siegel said, "You know, we just use different language." He is helping to bring what I would say is some soul back into the medical community. Siegel integrates the personal and impersonal energies with awareness and presence.

He has also brought in mindfulness practices to his work with patients. He discovered this organically through his work with his patients, especially children. Later on someone told him, "It looks like you're practicing Buddhist meditation!"

He was then introduced to Jack Kornfield, who is a psychologist and a senior Buddhist meditation teacher, and also Daniel Goldman, who conducts a lot of research in mindfulness. Eventually Siegel went to a ten-day Insight Meditation Retreat, and he saw a real parallel to the work he was doing and the work that some of the modern Buddhist teachers were doing. Soon he started to integrate meditation and mindfulness into his approach of working with patients and found it to be very powerful.

Another doctor that Siegel connected with is Jon Kabot-Zinn, who has a series on PBS called *Healing and the Mind*. One episode highlights Jon Kabat-Zinn's clinic in a U.S. hospital where patients are sent after they have not seen any progress elsewhere. He demonstrates that yoga, meditation and mindfulness have extraordinary results with these patients.

Jon Kabat-Zinn also had meetings with the Dalai Lama and shared his research on the effects of the integration of science and spirituality.

Great strides have been made in brain science in the past two decades. In his book *The Brain That Changes Itself*, Norman Doidge says that the brain is malleable. He uses the term neuroplasticity to infer that the brain can change itself. Medical science used to think that patients with severe brain problems had to live with their condition or go on powerful medications indefinitely.

They would see a psychiatrist who believed the medical model of prescribing medication was the only method to control serious cases. But now, with the breakthroughs of recent neuroscience, we see that the brain indeed has a neuroplasticity and can heal itself.

According to Doige, "Neurons that fire together, wire together." The brain can indeed grow new neural networks through meditation and mindfulness. Research also shows powerful healing and transformation are possible through methods like Voice Dialogue because it works with different states of consciousness and enhances awareness. One medical research study showed that Voice Dialogue helped those with Awareness Deficit Disorder (ADD), an early precursor to Alzheimer's Disease (AD). Voice Dialogue practice cultivates more awareness so develops our prefrontal lobes.

Modern brain research is also shedding light on whether we are left-hemisphere or right-hemisphere dominant in our orientation to life. Psychotherapist Ian McGilchrist has some insightful TED talks about the difference between the left hemisphere and the right hemisphere of the brain. He uses informative animation to demonstrate the difference. Looking at a bird, he shows that its brain is like a wedge; the left hemisphere is the point of the wedge and the right hemisphere is the wide-open part of the wedge. The bird needs the right hemisphere to be ever alert for danger, and it needs the left hemisphere to focus in on pecking at seeds. The right hemisphere sees the big picture and the left focuses on the details. The same is true for human brains.

What has happened according to him is that for many generations there has been an emphasis on left hemisphere development, whose functions are more 'masculine' or 'yang.' A lot of our educational institutions and industries are focused on logic, linguistics, linear thinking—all 'L' words of the left hemisphere.

McGilchrist makes a compelling argument that you can see this left hemisphere dominance through the change in art over the ages. A society that primarily values people with left hemisphere dominance rewards the people with these gifts more by giving them high salaries and status. This kind of power then dominates in a patriarchal society.

Even in the medical system you end up with left hemisphere dominant specialists that are impersonal technicians, that don't exhibit much care for others or themselves. They are often getting exhausted from overwork. The right hemisphere, on the other hand, is more intuitive, and open to the big picture. It takes in more of the gestalt and works with imagery.

Right and left hemispheres can be thought of as a pair of opposites. We don't want to polarize and choose one side or the other. For wholeness, we want both hemispheres online and more. So the overarching principle is that there's a bridge that connects the two opposites.

THE MAGIC THEATRE

The first time I encountered the idea that we contain opposites within ourselves and have many 'selves' was when reading about the Magic Theatre in Hermann Hesse's book *Steppenwolf* in my early twenties:

"Harry consists of a hundred or a thousand selves, not of two. His life oscillates, as everyone's does, not merely between two poles, such as the body and the spirit, the saint and the sinner, but between thousands and thousands. Every ego, so far from being a unity is in the highest degree a manifold world, a constellated heaven, a chaos of forms, of states and stages, of inheritances and potentialities. As a body everyone is single, as a soul, never."

I came across this idea of our soul's multidimensionality again many years later through Hal and Sidra Stone and the psychospiritual theory and process they co-created called Voice Dialogue.

VOICE DIALOGUE THEORY AND PROCESS

Hal and Sidra Stone founded *Voice Dialogue—The Psychology of the Selves* and the *Aware Ego Process* over forty years ago. Hal Stone originally trained as a Jungian analyst and drew upon some of the essence of Jungian Psychology, such as working with dreams, active imagination, archetypes and the essential idea of holding a pair of inner opposites with the transcendent function of awareness.

Sidra trained as a psychologist in New York and she too was impressed with Hermann Hesse's *Magic Theatre*. When Hal and Sidra came together in the 1970's they began to facilitate each other's process and discovered they could dialogue with their vulnerable inner children. This was a revelation for them both, and they began to explore each other's inner 'Magic Theatre' of many selves.

In Voice Dialogue, our essence is called our psychic fingerprint, a kind of blueprint of our uniqueness at birth. It is like the essential blueprint of a particular seed. Our personality could be compared to the shell that contains and protects our essential vulnerable blueprint. It's important to have a healthy body or shell to protect this vulnerable essential blueprint inside.

The different selves of our personality form to protect our vulnerability and develop based on our unique family system. Our inner rule-maker formed to assess, "What are the rules of this family system, so I can get my essential needs met here?"

In Voice Dialogue, we work with our inner opposites with an aware centre. So, for example, thinking would be one side, and feeling is on the other side. Some people identify with being thinkers, some people identify with being feelers.

Some doctors and professionals identify as impersonal, some as personal. If, in the prefrontal lobes we access awareness, then we can hold both perspectives and say, "It would be healthy for me to access thinking and feeling, and personal and impersonal energies." This forms a triangle of opposites held in awareness.

In the ancient philosophical triangle on the opposite page, the bottom corner is the thesis, the opposite corner is antithesis, and the top is synthesis.

THE PHILOSOPHICAL TRIANGLE

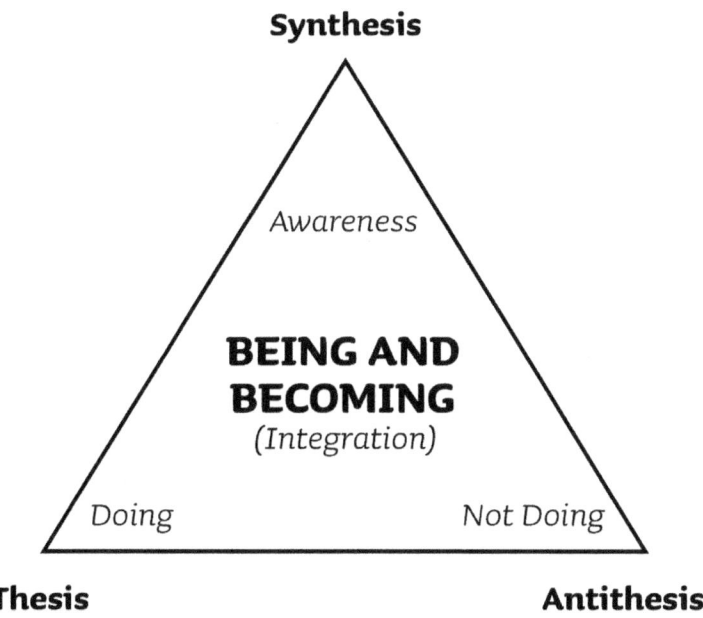

In the example of a doctor who is identified with impersonal thinking, we can see that as his thesis. Feeling and personal energy are his antithesis side. With awareness at the top point, he can be aware of both impersonal thinking and personal feeling. Awareness simply witnesses without judgment or action.

Meditation helps foster increased awareness and so does Voice Dialogue practice. In the centre of the triangle is integration. This is what is referred to as the 'aware ego process' in Voice Dialogue theory. It's where we have the freedom and choice to act with awareness. With our healthy ego we draw on awareness to choose consciously the balance of thinking and feeling, personal and impersonal energies we want.

We are working with three levels of consciousness here: the

horizontal plane of the opposites, the sub-personalities or selves, the vertical plane of awareness, and a middle place that integrates all three levels. The middle place is the aware ego process and is best described by metaphor— its role is like a juggler who can juggle these two different balls, or an orchestra conductor that has two different musicians to choose from and can coordinate their playing.

If you're the impersonal thinker, you have only one instrument to play. If you're always the personal feeler, you still only have one instrument to play. But from the center you have a blend of thinking and feeling, or two different instruments, so you have much greater choice conducting your symphony in life.

SPEEDING OUT OF CONTROL

The best part about finding allies, mentors and elders is that we can incorporate what we learn from them and pass it along to others. In my case, I found excellent use of Voice Dialogue, personally and in my practice as a therapist.

One of my clients—Ed—was a busy salesman for a large engineering firm in the US. At age forty-three he was doing well financially and had recently been promoted to team leader of his division. He called me because he had nightmares and suffered from panic attacks when he had to give a talk to his staff.

The nightmares usually consisted of him speeding down the freeway in a powerful sports car. At first he felt excited, but then the car sped up and he worried he was going too fast. He panicked when he tried to stop because there were no brakes! As he prepared to crash, he would awaken from the dream sweating with terror.

Realizing that it was 'only a dream,' he started to breathe again. Then he would hop out of bed and make some strong coffee to shake off his tiredness.

Soon he was back behind the wheel of his sporty SUV and speeding down the freeway to work. Once he arrived at work, he noticed that he was snapping at his colleagues more than before.

This is a very common dream for busy professionals. Hal Stone teaches that dreams can be literal or symbolic. It's best to consider the literal interpretation of the dream first. Ed's dream may be guiding him to get his brakes checked before going on that trip!

In Ed's case the dream was symbolic. Engines are measured in horsepower. He had become so revved up with the mastery and proactivity stage of accomplishing his goals that he was out of balance.

His main map for life was acquiring more money and power. Power and status can become such powerful addictions because they are socially sanctioned and celebrated. We are rewarded with a promotion even if our company is engaged in unethical behaviour. His lack of sleep, workaholic tendencies and excessive use of coffee were taxing his adrenal glands and driving up his cortisol levels so he was heading for burnout.

Ed was 'successful' but his psyche was telling him he was out of balance. With more responsibility, he was afraid of not performing. His confidence was slipping and he used coffee…driving him all day and night. We discovered a mythic dimension to his panic attacks. Pan was the Lord of Nature in ancient history. When he feels separate from Nature he is more likely to suffer from panic attacks when he is afraid. He imagined his panic as a knock on his door from Pan, inviting him to connect with his body and nature again.

Using Voice Dialogue I helped Ed find a better balance of power and vulnerability so he could separate from his negative triangle of perfectionist, pusher and critic while embracing his vulnerability. He was driven by fear of failure and to compensate he tried to achieve perfection through status or higher income.

His perfectionist would set the bar high, but his critic always told him, "It's never good enough," so the pusher would push him harder! This pattern of internal sabotage was steering him toward a literal accident or an emotional crash as he burned out from being a workaholic.

After some mentoring and psychotherapy he found a better balance between productive activity and much needed down time.

I created a simple rebalancing process for him. He imagined that he was driving his car by pushing on the gas with his right food while noticing the increased tension in his gut and solar plexus. Then I got him to ease off on the gas and move his right foot to the brakes to slow down. He could feel his body relax. I invited him to imagine pulling over to a beautiful beach, stopping the car, turning off the ignition, letting go of the steering wheel, and releasing control. Finally, I instructed him to feel his left foot, relax, and release into balance..

I suggested he jot down any negative beliefs, such as fear of failure, and to embrace these feelings and thoughts as if he were embracing his vulnerable inner boy. I asked him to relax and look at the vast clear blue sky for a sense of spaciousness and peace, and when ready, to start the car again and see if he could retain his relaxed state while pretending to drive. My suggestion was to focus on his senses and the present moment instead of racing into the future driven by his fear of failure.

Over time, he joined a men's support group and learned to balance his thrust for power with his need to relax and play with friends. Then we looked at his career to see if he was experiencing meaning and purpose. It turned out he was only in it for the money, and now that he was established financially he reflected on what career would be meaningful for him.

With the Inner Treasure of his new clarity, he let go of the position of supervisor and went back to sales where he had more freedom of choice. He saw it as a promotion for his health, relationships and soul. It turned out that he loved dogs and always had a dream of moving to the country to raise seeing-eye dogs for the blind. As he remembered what he loved, his heart opened and he explored that as an avocation.

WHAT DO WE VALUE MOST?

In just about any major city we can see the story of our shift in values expressed in the architecture. At one time the church, temple, or mosque was always the tallest building in the town, pointing to our greatest values as a society. Jungian psychotherapist James Hollis points out the tallest buildings are now the Banks, Insurance and Pharmaceutical Companies. Symbolically we can see this as a shift from valuing the power of the divine or our greatest values to the egotistical pursuit of money and power.

Maslow's *Hierarchy of Needs* is often presented as a hierarchal pyramid with self-actualization at the top. Some business professionals find this to be a useful map for accentuating personal growth as self-actualization. Used this way, this could be the crowning symbol of Column Two of Rowan's chart. If you remember, Column Two is about ego growth or improvement. It's useful to acquire the mastery and power of cultivating a healthy ego in our youth, but there are limits to ego growth as we mature.

Remember that Columns One and Two are symbolic of becoming a healthy caterpillar—the caterpillar is constantly consuming any leaves in its path; in other words, it's like an egocentric consumer addicted to over consuming.

Modern industrialized nations are often called consumer societies because of this. There is a point where over-consumption is not a good thing, especially now that we collectively recognize that there are in fact limits to industrial growth. Multinational companies now have more power than many countries and use their money to promote their agendas.

There comes a time when each one of us is called to enter the cocoon of transformation, in order to evolve soulfully. This applies to individuals, couples, organizations, companies, religions, countries and indeed humanity itself. Maslow taught that self-actualization includes manifesting what he called 'B values'—love, compassion, courage, and so on. Later he included the need for aesthetics like beauty and spirituality.

Author Duane Elgin conducted a survey asking people all over the world: "How grown up do you think humanity is? When you look at human behaviour around the world and then imagine our species as one individual, how old would that person be?" The overwhelming majority of people thought of humanity as a teenager. We could say that the caterpillar is a like teenager that needs to enter the cocoon of transformation in its journey to becoming a butterfly if it is to evolve soulfully.

Duane Elgin, in his book *Promise Ahead: A Vision of Hope and Action for Humanity's Future*, suggests that we can see evidence of the human family having the maturity of a teenager. We can see this in actions like living recklessly in how we consume resources, placing a high value on external appearances and possessions, and clustering ourselves into 'in versus out' and 'us versus them' groupings based on ethnicity, race, gender, and so on.

If humanity is like a teenager, I would argue that humanity is an addicted teenager. The way we mindlessly consume our natural resources without considering whether our consumption is sustainable smacks of major addiction to me.

If we are to shift from getting too egocentric at the pinnacle of Rowan's column two, then we need to enter the humbling cocoon of transformation of column three to become soulfully 'ecocentric'. In the experience of my journey and with many clients in midlife, ego thinning is needed. It happens through losing the dominance of the little me, thinning my identities, my status, and my stuff. We need to address our addiction of rigidly identifying with the little me.

We can get caught thinking that something in the future will save us, instead of rolling up our sleeves and realizing Ghandi's wisdom, "We must be the change we are seeking!" When we awaken to our Inner Treasure, we are empowered to co-create in partnership with Divine Reality.

My mentor, Atum, once said there is a real pusher in the consumer culture. When you link the protestant work ethic with original sin, you get a culture that feels guilty about the past and is constantly pushing for a better future, while avoiding the present moment.

MYTHIC AWARENESS PATH

Atum has been a soulful mentor, helping me explore my personal mythology to discover the Inner Treasure buried in my wounds. I like to call this the mythic awareness path. It is important for narrative integration to understand your myth. The story I tell myself may be keeping me trapped in a very limited experience of life. Uncovering your personal myth can liberate your story into a greater narrative. In the alchemy of transformation, we need to do the soul work of investigating the patterns in our leaden consciousness. Hidden in our past there is gold in the shadows.

The shadow is what we don't know about ourselves. It can be light or dark. Robert Bly called it the "long bag we drag behind us" filled with unacceptable parts of ourselves. Often we get a sense of our shadow through projection. Like a projector we project aspects of ourselves onto the screen of another. When we see someone we really don't like and could never see ourselves like him or her, it's likely a reflection of our shadow. If we see someone who we greatly admire and think, 'I could never be like him or her,' it's likely the disowned gold in our shadow.

CYCLES OF SEVEN YEARS

Some traditions say there is a major change that happens every seven years or so. In indigenous cultures, wise mentors and elders initiate youth into the next phase of their soulful life at a seven-year cycle. In our culture, without the guidance of mentors and elders, adults around the age of twenty-eight often experience quarter-life crisis because of this. As a result of missing this important initiation into mature adulthood, many of us suffer from a midlife crisis at thirty-five or later.

Twenty-eight years of age is often described as the time of Saturn return. Anodea Judith says that in approximately the first twenty-eight years of our life we are evolving through the seven major chakras unconsciously. At approximately twenty-eight we are faced with an initiatory challenge. There is the pull backwards toward regression into childhood through addictive tendencies because the prospects of stepping into a meaningful and purposeful adulthood look so daunting.

Alternatively, there is an opportunity to transform and evolve into the next stage of consciousness through the conscious integration of resources in each of our chakras.

If we can catch the necessary initiation at twenty-eight, then we can shift from the mastery and proactivity stage of life to the meaning and purpose stage through mystery and presence. If we don't catch the transformation here, then we usually get another crisis and opportunity later on in midlife crisis.

Reflecting on my own crisis, my family system was negatively impacted by immigration, war, too much moving, and addiction, cancer and loss. Your family system may have different wounds so will constellate a different pattern. I will share some of my story because it serves to illustrate how important it is for us to have allies, mentors and elders to help us at crucial times on our journey—and how lost we can become without them. They can help us recover the Gift in our wounds.

In the next chapter I'll share some of the seven-year cycles that happened in my life leading to my quarter-life and midlife crisis. Eventually my midlife crisis became a midlife awakening process by remembering the Home of the Soul.

CHAPTER 4:

HOME OF THE SOUL AND SOULFUL RELATIONSHIP

"Your task is not to seek for love, but merely to seek and find all the barriers within yourself that you have built against it."

—Rumi; *Translation by Coleman Barks*

Four: How can we clear our barriers to deeper intimacy for greater relational vitality?

In this chapter, we will begin to explore healing our barriers to deeper intimacy in relationships. At this stage we see in nature that the caterpillar enters the cocoon. In the story of Isaac's Treasure, Isaac starts to dig under his hearth and actively seeks for the Inner Treasure. In another story, Mullah has lost his wedding ring and thus is disconnected from the feminine and symbolically from his wholeness.

Rumi tells a version of the story of Isaac's Dream in which the Dreamer had squandered the wealth he had inherited. Rumi points out that when we inherit wealth we don't know what work it took to get it. In the same way he says, "we don't know the value of our souls, which are given to us for nothing."

In the movie about the doctor, Jack looks about thirty-five, the same age I was in 1989 when my midlife crisis was most painful. Like Jack, I was married with a young son and was a workaholic. I too was identified primarily with my left hemisphere of reason and order and avoided my vulnerability. I used alcohol and other substances to unconsciously get release and reflexively try to manage my stress. But, unlike Jack, my marriage ended in a painful divorce.

Jack gets throat cancer and it becomes a catalyst for him to heal, transform and evolve in his career and his relationships with his wife and young son. My father got lung cancer and died during his midlife crisis. I was fortunate to come out of denial and get help from mentors to heal my addictive tendencies.

Author and eco-theologian Michael Dowd also got cancer. According to Dowd, a cancer cell is one that thinks it is separate from the rest of the body. It begins to multiply and create other cells that also think they are separate. His condition became meaningful to him when he realized that when humans think they are separate from the Earth community, humanity becomes like a kind of cancer to the Earth.

His healing path led him from managing his pain of separation by using supernormal stimuli like drinking alcohol, to cultivating a deeper connection to Spirit or Reality.

In the fourth chakra the addictions are tobacco (smoking), sugar, love and marijuana, according to Anodea Judith. The recent film, "*Fed Up*" looks at how our runaway addiction to sugar is creating a culture of obesity. See fedupmovie.com.

In this chapter we begin the descent into soul. This is the cocoon stage of digging within to reflect on the patterns of our life and our path so far. Within our deepest wounds we can glimpse the Inner Treasure. I'll share some of my wounds to show how they eventually became a womb to birth new life.

MAGIC AND PLAY OF CHILDHOOD

My favourite place to live in rural Nova Scotia was a place called Sandy Point. As I shared earlier, in this part of childhood I enjoyed playing with my friends and dog in the forest. I was also fortunate to have a healthy magic and play stage of childhood.

Like many seven-year-old Canadian boys, I enjoyed playing hockey with friends and was enrolled in Cub Scouts. Then, at age eight, I was confirmed as a Catholic.

For my eighth birthday my father chaperoned me and my friends since my mother had to work. During the party he got quite drunk and disappeared into his bedroom. He lay down, passed out and set the bed on fire by dropping his cigarette on the mattress.

My friends and I smelt the smoke and rushed in to see him lie back down on the smoldering bed. He yelled that it was under control! He had thrown water on it and it was OK now.

I felt humiliated; it was not OK. Later I found out my Cub Scout Master also had a drinking problem and squandered our dues on alcohol. Then we moved from one part of Nova Scotia to another and tragically my parents gave my beloved dog away.

The loss of my dog broke my heart.

MASTERY AND PROACTIVITY

By the time I was fourteen we had moved many times and were living in Northern Ontario, on a military base called Camp Borden. My father taught accounting there. At school my teachers said that academics came easily to me, but I could use some help. I had many friends and enjoyed building forts in the woods, playing hockey and going to the movies.

The next year my father retired from the military and the only place he could find work was in Hamilton, Ontario, so we were forced to move there against our will. He hated his new job working as an expeditor at a steel mill. Then his health and relationships deteriorated. To cope with his pain, he ramped up his drinking. Conflict became our way of being together.

My father got drunk at a party one night, was arrested for resisting arrest and put in jail. Subsequently, they committed him to a psychiatric ward for severe alcoholism.

By the time I was sixteen I was smoking pot. I got busted for two joints and served thirty days in jail. I also got kicked out of high school and rebelled against my military father by becoming a sixties-style hippie. That year, I nearly died twice, once in a near-drowning and another time in a high-speed car chase. A friend raced his Mustang car across a one-way bridge while forcing another driver to back down!

In his insightful book, *David and Goliath – Underdogs, Misfits, And The Art Of Battling Giants*, Malcolm Gladwell quotes criminologist Todd Clear who says, "For a child, losing a father to prison is an undesirable difficulty. Having a parent incarcerated increases a child's chances of juvenile delinquency between 300 and 400 percent; it increases the odds of a serious psychiatric disorder by 250 percent." Like David, I was going to need a trusty slingshot to battle this giant issue.

My parents divorced later that year and my father moved to Vancouver. When he left our family, we finally found some peace, but by then my addictive tendencies were firmly entrenched. The next year I left school, got a job in a factory, moved out of my mother's house and got my own place. My teen years were very turbulent. At age twenty, a friend wanted to go on an adventure to Vancouver, so I left Hamilton behind to go with him. It seemed like an irrelevant coincidence that my father lived where we were headed, but retrospectively, it feels more like a meaningful synchronicity.

My father seemed much happier living in Vancouver. At twenty-one, while living in Vancouver, I started reconciling with my father. With his support and guidance I found work and started an apprenticeship as an alarm systems technician. I bought a car and rented my own apartment. On the weekends I enjoyed camping with friends, going to a concert or to the pub. My diet consisted of eating lots of highly processed fast foods. I drank coffee and alcohol, smoked cigarettes and the occasional joint.

When I was twenty-five, shockingly, my father died of lung cancer, after using a lot of alcohol, caffeine and nicotine to ease his pain. My emotional life was thrown into a sea of turmoil and it threw me into a quarter life crisis.

Fortunately I had a mentor at work that helped me to complete the mastery and proactivity stage I was in. Unfortunately, he too was caught in the same addictive tendencies as my father and I. There didn't seem to be any psychospiritual mentors in sight at that time, so I used work and my other addictive tendencies to self-medicate while managing the pain of my loss. I had to wait for another decade before another tsunami of crisis and opportunity hit!

By twenty-eight, I was a journeyman alarm systems technician and started my own alarm systems company with a partner. We had a couple of employees. My workaholic tendencies were in full swing. My diet was composed of highly processed foods, supplemented with coffee and cigarettes to keep me going, with alcohol and marijuana to settle me down and keep my emotions at bay. It's no surprise that I was single.

In 1986, at age thirty-two, I got married, and was blessed to inherit a wonderful five-year-old step-son. We bought our first house. My business was finally taking off. Finally, I was becoming 'successful.' Everything seemed to be improving. I felt at the height of mastery and proactivity and I even gave up drinking and smoking. My new responsibilities led to working long hours.

Then in 1989, at thirty-five, under way too much stress, my flimsy house of cards came crashing down. I got divorced and lost my wife and stepson. Eventually my work felt meaningless, so I sold my business. My diet remained mostly unchanged, as it was one of my reliable coping mechanisms. That was until the autumn of 1989, when everything began to change.

For most of my adult life up to age thirty-five, I was caught in the ordinary life of separation. The call to a more meaningful and purposeful life came many times over my first thirty-five years, but I had avoided it consciously or unconsciously. At 35, I was given yet another opportunity to answer the call, or stay caught in separation and suffering.

After my marriage broke apart and I sold my business, I felt confused because I had lost my identities of husband, father, business owner and technician. At first it was extremely painful because I was brokenhearted over my loss of my stepson. I started to suffer physically and existentially. I had no idea what to do with my life. Life seemed meaningless.

I fell into a painful midlife crisis. The call to the inner world of the psyche came in the form of symptoms caused by unbearable losses and a deep yearning for a meaningful and purposeful life.

At this stage of my journey, some key allies, mentors and elders started arriving to assist me: first in the inner world, in the form of the wise old man in the dream, then in the outer world.

I had become seriously out of balance from doing so much in the mastery and proactivity phase of my life. Fortunately, my psyche guided me toward relaxing into mystery and presence as a new way of being.

MEANING AND PURPOSE

Within the next few years I was blessed to meet many mentors who assisted me to awaken into a deeper sense of mystery and presence in order to cultivate a soulful life of meaning and purpose. But first I had to descend farther into the depths of suffering. To manage my pain I started drinking again.

In Alcoholics Anonymous there is an expression that "De-nial isn't just a river in Egypt." There is also an old Japanese saying: "First the man (or woman) takes a drink, then the drink takes a drink, and then the drink takes the man (or woman)."

I started getting worried about my drinking habit and in the fall of 1989 I came out of denial, went to see an addictions counsellor and finally admitted I had a drinking problem. After sharing some of my history with her, she said because both my father and grandfather were alcoholics, I was in danger of becoming one too. Luckily, I wasn't there yet.

The counselor asked me if I had heard of the Men's Movement, and I told her I hadn't. She told me about Robert Bly and a retreat centre called *The Haven* where they teach counselling and hold men's retreats. She also directed me to Banyen Books in Vancouver and the owner, Kolin Lymworth, who was involved in the men's movement. I only had one session with this counsellor but I'll always be grateful for her wise guidance, as it profoundly changed the direction of my life.

At Banyen Books I bought an audio program by Robert Bly called *Iron John* and a book called *The Flying Boy: Healing the Wounded Man* by John Lee. I also bought tickets for the upcoming one-day men's retreat with James Hillman and Michael Meade and a catalogue of events happening at the Haven Retreat Centre.

Robert Bly introduced me to the deeply subjective soul of masculinity. By using mythology, like the Grimm's stories, in his workshops, he led me into the heart of narrative integration. Ancient stories are like maps of the psyche. When J.R.R. Tolkien created *The Lord of the Rings*, he was using the art of storytelling to create a social commentary on the culture of that time. Before there was psychology, mythology was used by wise teachers to help students heal, transform and evolve soulfully. People like Joseph Campbell saw the great myths as subjective stories and maps of the Hero or Heroine's journey.

The Flying Boy: Healing the Wounded Man by John Lee resonated profoundly with me. He used the story of Icarus from Greek mythology to look at the dynamics of fathers, sons and addiction. Icarus's father Daedalus was a brilliant inventor who created a complex labyrinth to contain a dangerous bull, by order of King Minos. Daedalus soon fell into disfavour with the King, however, and was imprisoned on an island in a tower with his son Icarus. The King controlled the sea so Daedalus devised a plan to escape by air.

He collected feathers with his son and used wax to create wings for him and his son. He warned Icarus to fly close to him at moderate height, for if he flew too low the damp would clog his wings and if he flew too high the heat from the sun would melt them.

When the time came to escape, they flapped their wings and flew over the island. The shepherds were amazed and wondered if they saw gods. Eventually Daedalus and his son were over the sea, and Icarus was thrilled to be flying. Despite his father's warnings, however, he was attracted to the great warmth of the sun and flew toward it as if he could fly to heaven. The heat of the sun soon melted the wax holding his wings together, and they fell apart. Tragically, Icarus plunged into the sea and drowned.

His father cried out for his son but it was too late, he had perished. He then saw the feathers floating on the surface of the sea and realized his son was dead. Eventually he found his son's body and buried it. He called the land Icaria in memory of his son, and the sea became known as the Icarus Sea.

That almost literally happened to me as a teen. I nearly drowned in a lake after getting high on alcohol and pot.

Author John Lee also struggled with addiction, and courageously shares his story of addiction and recovery as a mentor to the rest of us. He is a good example of someone who was wounded but became a wounded healer by transforming the wound into a womb that births new life. Now he is a healer and psychotherapist by finds meaning and purpose helping others to heal, transform and evolve soulfully from their addictive tendencies.

This myth helped me realize that I too was a 'flying boy' like Icarus, as was my father and my grandfather. We were caught trying to fly too high on alcohol. Could the wings of alcohol carry us to spirit? No, they were made of wax and melted. We went crashing into the sea of addictions.

My father guided me to be a skilled worker, but his addictions to work, alcohol, sex, caffeine, tobacco and the occasional joint were causing him to fly too close to the sun and setting a poor example for me. He literally fell into the sea and came down with pneumonia. When the doctors investigated further they found out that he had advanced lung cancer. Then he died tragically at forty-seven years of age. His midlife crisis became fatal. His father—my paternal grandfather—also got caught in addictive tendencies. They both crashed into the ocean of the unconscious, resulting in poor health, turbulent relationships and meaningless and purposeless work.

Immature fathers or mothers who are caught in addictive tendencies like Icarus, are flying too high and aren't giving the guidance their sons and daughters need. With so many single-parent families and absent fathers, many young people today lack healthy guidance. So it's no surprise that when they attempt to fly high on addictive substances, they crash into the ocean of depression.

If they are sent to a conventional doctor they are likely given a prescription for potent medication to clip those wings. For many of them, the medication may help keep them on the ground—but it also clips their imagination, creativity and emotions.

There is a helpful resource online where young people are trying to imagine this differently at www.theicarusproject.net.

FIREWATER

If a youth receives a prognosis it can become a rigid identity. Perhaps we can bring some imagination to diagnostic terms like 'bi-polar disorder'. Like a magnet, there are two poles or directions. The element in the first chakra is earth. The element in the second chakra is water. The sea is often used as a metaphor of the unconscious. The third chakra element is fire.

The fourth chakra is the home of the air element. Alcohol is often called 'firewater' by indigenous people. If alcohol or 'firewater' is an addiction of the second chakra, then we can see that these two poles or directions are in a dynamic tension. One direction is downward toward water and the earth. The other direction is up toward fire and air.

Let's look at the addictive tendencies in the third chakras again—amphetamines, cocaine, caffeine, work, anger and power. We can see the pull upwards in these 'uppers' towards the power of fire.

Many people are trying to self-initiate by spreading their wings in the attempt to fly into the fourth chakra, but end up crashing into the second chakra sea of emotions and depression.

High-speed car chases, for example, are unconscious attempts to use horsepower as the thrust under the wings to take off and burst into a more meaningful and purposeful life. Even Gandalf the Grey from *The Lord of the Rings* had to transform and evolve into an even wiser wizard. Shadowfax, his winged horse of power, helped him transform and evolve.

Anodea Judith says that the first three chakras are about developing a healthy ego, and the third chakra is about developing the will of our personal power. She teaches that humanity needs to transform from the love of power (third chakra) to the power of love (fourth chakra), while keeping grounded and integrating the healthy functioning of all the lower chakras. The fourth chakra is the centre of our seven major chakras, the multidimensional place where we can embrace heaven and earth, the vertical and the horizontal.

DEMONS AND DAEMONS

In the First Nations Medicine Wheel there are seven directions; upper, lower, inside and the four cardinal directions. When we attempt to use a substance like alcohol or 'firewater' to fly to the Upper World of Spirit, we can get high but can become ungrounded. As previously mentioned, the attempted flight to spirit ends with a crash into the ocean of despair. We need to reach upward for spirit and unfold downward into a soulful life. We need all the elements and all the directions so we can firmly root in the earth and reach our branches up high and out wide to offer the fruit of our Natural Gifts.

My own transformational understanding of this concept emerged when I went to see Robert Bly. He spoke passionately about how the First Nations Elders were shaking their heads in disapproval, back in the 1960's when hippies experimented with drugs. In the First Nations tradition certain psychotropic plants are seen as plant spirit medicine. The shaman needs to have an intimate relationship with the plant and the person to help with healing and transformation. When we take these substances recreationally, we call our demons to ourselves. Then it takes more of the same substance to get high, and more demons are summoned.

In conscious ritual, the sacred substance is used as part of an initiation. You don't decide the amount to take—the shaman does. If you decide how much to take, your ego is in charge of your initiation and it goes poorly. The shaman knows how much to give you. A person with little ego may only require a small dose; someone with a big whopping ego may need much more of the spiritual medicine to face his or her demons and make the necessary transformation.

In one example of indigenous initiation, the initiates journey up the sacred mountain and is given the sacred medicine by the healer. Then they sit in a circle of stones and are instructed not to leave, sometimes for days. In the dark their demons come to haunt them and their fears show up. If they can face their fears, the demon turns into their *daemon*, a Greek term pointing to their unique genius and inner gifts.

When they leave the mountain and return to the healer, they share their story. The healer and the elders hear the genius in their stories and reflect it back to the initiates. In some traditions, initiates are given a new name to demark the transformation, and mentors are assigned to help them build a relationship with the Inner Treasure of their particular medicine or Inner Gifts.

The healthy side of the mastery and proactivity stage of life is the ability to know what you want and know how to get it. If we don't know what our Inner Gifts are, it is easy to aim the arrow of our proactivity in the wrong direction.

If you do have a sense of what your Inner Gifts are, you can set tangible, measurable goals for manifesting them. There is a lot to do in getting established in life: getting an education, a place to live, a way to get around, a job, perhaps even start a family. This is a time of much doing. Some people don't do enough and some do too much. We need discernment to choose wisely.

There is a shadow side too. If we feel inadequate or don't know our gifts, then busyness, success and status are used as a compensation to avoid how we feel. We can easily polarize, identifying with limited personal power rather than feeling and embracing our vulnerability. A common disappointment for men and women occurs when they climb the ladder of worldly success only to find it leaning against a wall far from their soulful calling.

To briefly summarize my own journey: At thirty-two it looked like I had it made—I was happily married and co-parenting a stepson I loved, CEO of my own successful business, a journeyman alarm technician, owner of my own home and a newer vehicle. I even had a ski cabin on a local mountain. I had become masterful at setting goals and accomplishing them despite the trauma of my upbringing. But, I used busyness and success to climb the status pyramid and avoided my vulnerability. And then my upward mobility took a nosedive.

Like many children I was forced to be overly responsible and grew up too quickly. In the mastery and proactivity stage of life I became too identified with doing and became a workaholic. I used supernormal substances like highly processed food, alcohol, cigarettes, sex and pot to numb the pain of disconnection and as a pseudo reward. By the time midlife rolled around I was burned out. My work was more of a job than a calling even though I looked successful by conventional standards.

When my strained marriage ended and I sold my electrical business, I felt 'lost in a dark wood'. All my identities were suddenly gone. I was no longer a husband, father, business owner, technician. The existential questions started to haunt me as I slid into meaninglessness and midlife crisis: What is love? What and who do I love? Who am I really? What is meaningful? What is my purpose?

THE TURNING POINT

My midlife crisis happened because I was caught in separation, using supernormal stimuli to ease my suffering from this existential pain. After seeing the addictions counsellor, I decided to attend the Men's workshop, but on the day of the workshop with Michael Meade and James Hillman came along, I felt very nervous.

Children raised in chaotic alcoholic family systems often have a lot of residual fear running through their bodies and suffer from a kind of PTSD. This certainly was the case for me. The venue for the workshop I attended was located on a University campus. Having been kicked out of high school in my teens, anything linked to post-secondary education felt like forbidden territory. Having spent time in jail with a lot of intense men, I was terrified to be caged up again with potentially violent men.

Upon entering the University building, I saw a line-up of over a hundred men. It looked very intimidating. Doubts crossed my mind about whether this was a good idea or not.

As the door to the auditorium opened up ahead, I heard loud drumming coming from the main room and the sound of men's voices chanting. As the line edged closer I could see some men open the door, grab a couple of guys and pull them across the threshold, all the while paradoxically chanting, "Go back, go back, go back!" It was unnerving, but now I became caught in the stream of men heading toward the turbulent sea.

Robert Bly wrote that there are "four things that are no good at sea—an anchor, a rudder, oars, and the fear of going down." The fear of going down was coursing through me and trauma from my childhood and chaotic family began flashing before my eyes. What was I thinking paying good money to willingly sail right into this Bermuda Triangle! I could be hanging out at the beach! I considered leaving but I was more afraid of looking like a coward. As I got closer to the door, I started to panic. My inner alarm was sounding.

And yet, somehow, I managed to stay.

My turn finally came, and I braced myself for the worst. It was an intense first experience. These men had transformed the auditorium into an ancient cave with African drums and masks. It was simple but effective. The threshold was like a portal to another world; inside it was like an ancient cave of masculinity that took us right back to our roots as Paleolithic hunters. Outside the door that I just came through was a different world, the busy world of modernity and domestication. The men sitting on the floor looked like a wild tribe of monkey chanters from Bali, all unified with their one-pointed chant.

I was stunned when I heard my name being called out from the middle of the pack—I was sure that no one I knew would ever come to anything like this! And yet, a fellow alarm technician who also owned his own security company called out to me. Here was some safe protection for my inner alarm. We always had a friendly word for each other when we met at the alarm suppliers. He welcomed me by making a space beside him, and we soon became allies and soul friends.

Meade and Hillman worked their magic with deep mythic stories, drumming and poetry, while 'hunting in the forest of the soul' and I was transfixed. I hated poetry in school, but this poetry was coming from the blood and guts of men who knew the agony of deep wounds and the heights of ecstasy, like the great African American poet, Etheridge Knight, writing from his prison cell. The rusty gates of my heart were being pried open through the art of ritual, personification and metaphor. I began to understand that relationship is all about subjectivity—how can we know what we love unless our heart is torn open?

Michael Meade teaches that a mentor is someone who can curse or bless you. In many myths, the hero or heroine is put under a spell or a curse. Often a spell comes from the maternal line and the curse comes from the paternal line, but they can come from either. The mentor is the one who can see your spell and help you turn it into a blessing. This is an example of where the wound becomes a womb and births new life. Meade teaches that the blessing-curse of the individual wound, is very precise.

My wounds are particular to me and can keep me in the spell or curse, or they can lead me from an unhappy fate to a meaningful and purposeful destiny. Meade has found that many of our best young leaders are the leaders of gangs or have suffered in prisons. At this workshop, both of these mature elders, Hillman and Meade, were mentoring youth to become powerful leaders.

Upon reflection later, this early unconscious choice of careers in protection and alarms made sense as my attempt to protect others from being hurt by violation or fire. I found meaning and purpose in protecting them with alarms when they felt unsafe as a way to work with my own sense of violation and lack of safety in early childhood. My new vocation as a mentor and psychotherapist is symbolically about freeing myself, and others from the prisons of our conditioning and addictive tendencies to uncover our Inner Treasure for soulful living.

This was the first time I had heard the Sufi mystic Rumi quoted, and his words set my heart on fire with longing for this mystical kiss that we want: "the touch of spirit on the body".

I realized that deep down my drinking alcohol/spirits was reaching for this spirit, but instead I was settling for the cheap wine, the fool's gold.

Rumi teaches that there is fool's gold or false gold to remind us that there is real gold. My dream of meeting the wise old man gave me a taste of this ecstatic mystical kiss! In my contracted protected state I was blocked. Once I relaxed deeply, the ecstatic energy of being truly alive could begin to flow.

One of the men in the group spoke about the recent death of his young daughter, and I'm sure every man there felt an immense wave of grief. What was incredible to me was the way Meade and Hillman honoured his sorrow with an Irish ritual and then invited all our grief to emerge. It felt like an authentic Irish Wake without the need for alcohol. This man, Michael Talbot-Kelly, later became a close friend, colleague and business partner. We both subsequently trained to become mentors and psychotherapists and formed the Meaningful Life Design Centre and Natural Gifts Society together to help others.

The men's group that helped organize and sponsor the event included the owner of Banyen Books, Kolin Lymworth, and his friend and store manager, Michael Bertrand. At the end of the workshop with Meade and Hillman, they invited anyone who wanted to form a men's group around this soulful way of connecting through ritual and myth, to stay afterwards.

It seemed like everyone stayed, and we formed into about ten men's groups. My group included my buddy from the alarm industry and eight other men who also lived in my part of town.

One of the organizers generously volunteered to meet with us for six weeks to help get us started. At first, I felt intimidated in the group because about five of the men were psychologists or psychotherapists. At the time, I wasn't into psychology in the least.

By the end of the day-long workshop, much healing had occurred and it felt like my life had profoundly changed. I felt reluctant to leave and go back to the life I had been living. The organizers for this event were part of an organization called Vancouver M.E.N. (Men's Evolvement Network). As part of my counselling practicum years later, I acted as a steward and leader for the Vancouver M.E.N. for a year: helping support individual men and help men's groups form. This was a meaningful way for me to give back and complete the circle.

After a while, my alarm industry friend dropped out of this original men's group, and I felt on my own. We stayed connected though, and he stayed with me during a relationship break-up. I was glad to support him. It also didn't take long for me to see that the men in my men's group were all very human. Their challenges in life were just as real and painful as mine. Over time, a deep sense of camaraderie emerged as we healed and soulfully explored the shared landscape of wounds and giftedness together.

Just after I began attending my first men's group, I was called to go to a men's retreat at the Haven Retreat Centre on Gabriola Island, entitled *Men, the Body and Energy*, led by two male therapists who were close friends and colleagues. Both of their wives were also therapists and were co-leading a retreat next door called *Women, the Body and Energy*.

We met for five days, and it was incredibly powerful. The dynamics between the younger male therapist and his father were especially potent. The younger therapist was about my age then, and his father was about the same age, as my father would have been had he lived. His father was there for the first time and was a recovering alcoholic.

This stirred up the complexities of my relationship with my father, especially all of the painful issues that remained. The older therapist was very skilled at giving his younger colleague support.

The two therapists guided the group into some powerful practices and rituals. At one point, I discovered my own estrangement from my deceased father and grandfather, and the sense of loss I was experiencing between my stepson and I.

My paternal grandfather had ten children, and my father was the eldest. My grandfather enlisted in the Infantry during the Second World War, and left my father in charge as the new 'man of the house' at the age of twelve, recruited to help his mother with his then four siblings. He ended up becoming his mother's surrogate little man. When my grandfather left for war he wasn't a drinker, but he saw a lot of death on the front lines and came home a raging alcoholic.

My father and his father began to battle with each other, often violently, especially when my grandfather would go to the Legion to drink with his war buddies, and then come home drunk with a woman that he had picked up. My grandmother was horrified, and my father tried to stand up to his father but was badly beaten.

Apparently the violence was so bad that everyone feared for my father's life. So at sixteen, a Catholic priest forged my father's birth certificate so he could run away from Ottawa and join the Navy on the West Coast of Vancouver Island.

It didn't take long for my father to become an alcoholic himself. One night, in my early twenties, when he and I were getting drunk together, he told me that when his ship was away for many months the men would get unruly and resist orders. Five hundred men without any women to temper them can become an explosive force.

My father said that there were rum rations given to the men, and they would gamble to see how many they could win. Sometimes they would anchor the ship close to a deserted Island, and the Officers would pull out the over-proof rum. Filling the lifeboats with sailors and heading for shore, they would get smashed and let off steam before skulking back to the ship, hung-over.

Even when my father was commissioned to work at a Canadian Armed Forces Base the men were permitted to run up a tab at the Mess (Bar). My father was very disciplined and controlled in areas concerning work, but when off work his knees buckled under the influence of alcohol and he became a mess. Sometimes most of his pay was gone before it ever made it home.

I suffered a similar fate as my father, in also being made the 'little man of the house.' I have a letter from my father, written in 1966 from his ship at sea when I was about twelve years old. It was a real treasure when I found it stuffed in the family Bible in my thirties. I could finally hear the love my father felt for me, while also seeing the set-up: "While I'm away, you're the man of the house. Make sure you look after the girls for me! Love, Dad."

When he would come back home from sea I would look forward to welcoming him as my returning hero and handing him back my role as the responsible 'man' of the house. Unfortunately, his drinking had gotten worse and just like he did with his father, he and I also began to combat for who was the 'responsible man' of the house. We both lost!

BODYWORK

One of the most significant experiences I had at that first men's retreat at the Haven was an intense release of energy. Both therapists were skilled body workers, and they had all sixteen of us men lie on our backs with our knees up and legs bent wide while we were instructed to do pelvic thrusts. Then the two therapists roamed around and did bodywork with us individually. There was powerful music playing in the background, and I was shocked to start hearing men scream and sob.

Finally, it was my turn, and the therapist pressed on certain pressure points on my body. Then *wham*, energy like a coiled serpent at the base of my spine shot up my spine and burst through the top of my head. It was more intense than in my dream of the wise old man! Unlike the other men, I didn't scream or sob, I felt incredible rapture, joy and bliss. All of a sudden I could really hear how beautiful the music was, and I started to laugh ecstatically.

It felt like I was experiencing a full body orgasm, but there was no need to ejaculate. My laughter was so infectious, some of the other men started cracking up too. It felt wild. Men were screaming, sobbing and howling in laughter all at the same time. It was a safe way to release what we had bottled up.

Wow, who needs drugs? Dionysus, the god of wine must have broken out in song. I'm sure that Pan, the Lord of Nature, started playing his flute!

Later I read an insightful book by the Psychotherapist Guy Corneau called *Absent Fathers, Lost Sons* that got to the crux of the problem between fathers and sons. Soon after this, I went to a weekend workshop with him, and at the end of the first day he asked us to come back the next morning with an item that represented our relationship with our father.

I felt stumped and wasn't sure what to bring. Finally I checked in the family Catholic Bible that I had never opened. While leafing through looking for pictures, I was surprised to find the wonderful letters I mentioned earlier, written from my father to me. I had concocted a negative enemy image of him due to the many hard times in my teens, and now I was breaking through the protective wall to an earlier period of my life.

These early memories were part of the magic and play of my childhood, where my father and I could still express our love for each other. The next day I shared the letters with the men, many of whom were deeply touched.

ENTERING THE COCOON

Soon afterward I went to another men's workshop and felt a deep connection with one of the presenters, Ian MacNaughton Ph.D., author of *The Body, Breath and Consciousness*, and the President of the BC Association of Clinical Counsellors. At the break I told him that I was really moved by his willingness to be so vulnerable with us, sharing his stories of nearly drowning and getting sick by releasing energy up his spine too forcibly. I said that I could relate to both pieces. I asked if he was taking on new clients, and he said he was, so I got his number and booked an appointment.

My journey with Ian as a mentor and psychotherapist lasted many years. Through his soulful care and skillful guidance I answered the call into deep healing and transformation and eventually thought of myself as his apprentice. He became like a loving father to my soul.

Like many therapists, Ian has trained in many disciplines and modeled lifelong learning, constantly learning new healing modalities as they come online.

The journey with Ian could fill the whole book, but I'll highlight some meaningful pieces relevant to this chapter. Ian invited me to start researching my Family System more earnestly and do research for a genogram or family tree.

The first genogram I did was very healing. It told a much bigger story than the one I was telling myself. I couldn't really understand my own life and symptoms until I could see what had come down the pike to me, and my immediate family. I saw the effect that World War Two had on my paternal grandfather, and how it drove him to using alcohol, cigarettes and womanizing to ease his pain.

His trauma carried through to many of the members of our family. My father's addictive tendencies then seemed to be a normal consequence of his traumatic upbringing. As previously mentioned, my father ended up dying tragically of lung cancer and alcoholism. What I discovered was that many of his siblings also died tragic deaths related to this early family trauma.

Suddenly, I could see my own addictive tendencies in a new light. I thought I was a rebel, but I realized that I was a conformist to my family system and the culture's habitual pattern of managing stress. Other members of our family were traumatized in other ways.

MEANING IN THE PAST

Ian's invitation to create a family tree helped me see the bigger story or myth that I was a part of. I discovered that there are three rivers coming together in my bloodstream. English and French from Europe, and Algonquin First Nations from Trois Rivieres, Quebec. This had a profound impact on my identity. I realized that I am a 'Metis Acadian Canadian' or 'mixed blood' person.

Alcoholism, which at its roots is a spiritual problem, affected the First Nations people particularly strongly because when they were first exposed to it, they felt a strong high and thought it must be a sacred substance. They were so susceptible to alcohol addiction because they were under a lot of stress as the life they knew was being completely altered from hunting and gathering to farming. They also originally valued spiritual experience more than material possessions.

Alcoholism is one of the oldest illnesses known to humanity, and the Bible has many warnings about the excesses of alcohol:

Drinking leads to poverty.

—Proverbs 21:17, 23:21

Strong drink produces sorrow, woe, contentions, babbling, wounds without cause and redness of eyes.

—Proverbs 23-29-30

TOBACCO AND ALCOHOL AS DEMONS OR MEDICINE

I realized that some of the conflict and addiction of the English, French and First Nations People was in my bloodline. No wonder there has been so much stress and wounding in my family system!

My mother had said that my paternal Grandmother 'smoked herself to death'. She was in great pain due to her husband returning from the war as an alcoholic. He had also betrayed her by sleeping with other women. She began to smoke heavily to numb out. Tobacco is a fourth chakra addiction and concerns matters of a broken or blocked heart. Her Algonquin ancestors would have used tobacco to pray with, so she must have felt very disconnected from her Ancestors and from her Catholic upbringing too. There is a deep existential suffering when there is no sense of Spirit to turn to.

Tobacco for the First Nations people was always used as a sacred medicine before the Europeans came. In the Algonquin medicine wheel, tobacco is placed in the East and is seen as a gift from Great Spirit or Great Mystery. It is used to show gratitude for the gift of life and all of the Creator's Creation.

The movie *Elizabeth: The Golden Age*, set in the 16th century shows the first contact between the English, First Nations and tobacco. It depicts Sir Walter Raleigh journeying to the New World and bringing First Nations Braves back to England. The First Nations men give a gift of tobacco to the Queen as a sacred gesture.

The Queen is shown receiving this tobacco flippantly and smokes it recreationally with her ladies in waiting. To the First Nations Tradition at the time, this was sacrilege. The ritual is sacred; the bowl represents the feminine and the stem the masculine part of the peace pipe. The two brought together the masculine and the feminine in union. The tobacco is seen as sacred; the smoke takes your prayers up to the Creator, the Great Spirit, the Great Mystery or the Great Web.

I have often wondered how this disrespect for tobacco and alcohol influenced my father's death by lung cancer. It's hard to tell what caused his death, but he smoked a lot of cigarettes, and he chronically abused alcohol. That's how he managed his pain and emotions. He probably had cirrhosis of the liver. My shell-shocked grandfather used caffeine, nicotine and alcohol to manage his stress, so it isn't surprising that my father learned to manage his stress the same way.

These two substances, tobacco and alcohol, were originally used as sacred substances; these days, they have become secularized in popular culture. The First Nations population suffered so much alcoholism because they didn't have a long-term relationship with it as the Europeans did. Culturally, there was no acquired alcohol tolerance, nor accepted thresholds of consumption. Similarly, Europeans, lacking cultural filters to tobacco, ended up with lung cancer and smoke related addictions. Whether it was addiction in both cultures or disease in the First Nations, these both spread like wildfire in the population that lacked immunity and historical exposure.

Exploring my family tree and myth has helped me to understand how addictive tendencies flourish under stress in our traumatized culture. I now feel forgiveness and compassion for myself, and my family for using supernormal stimuli to manage our trauma and stress. My family wound is becoming a womb that is birthing the gifts of meaning and purpose.

OUT OF BALANCE

Ian and I did a lot of healing work around my early losses. Before I met Ian I picked up a parasite on a trip to Mexico. I'm still not sure if this foreign organism was the cause, but when I got home, my balance was severely affected. My doctor sent me to specialists for two years to no avail.

This is when I experienced first hand how impersonal some people who work in hospitals can be. I'm sure that it was learned behaviour, but receiving such lack of care left me feeling like an object or a broken machine in need of fixing.

FALLING INTO THE EARTH

To explore my balance issue, Ian invited me to try an experiment. He spread out a thick mat on the floor and asked me to let myself fall onto the mat face down. He encouraged me to try not to stop myself from falling. He said he would assist me to stay safe in the fall.

I stood and then fell forward. When I hit the mat with his support, he suggested I keep my eyes closed and keep feeling the falling sensation.

I noticed some anxiety but then let go. All of a sudden, it was like I was dreaming, and I saw a high-rise apartment building. I was falling beside it, and if I looked down I would speed up and feel anxious. If I became curious and looked in the rooms as I fell past them, I slowed down. It was like seeing scenes from my life and each floor was another layer of my psyche. It was fascinating. When I looked down again, my fall sped up. I prepared myself for the crash.

Instead of hitting the earth, I merged into the earth and then became the earth. It was like I was the earth looking into space. There was absolute stillness. After a while I heard a sound, and cracked up laughing. After some time Ian asked me what was happening and what I was laughing about. I told him I was laughing at my experience, and the sound I heard was *home*, not *ohm*. There is no place like home! Home is where the heart is! It felt like I had merged with the Soul of the World.

Merging energetically into the earth was profound. I felt such a deep peace. Later I heard the mystical terms, the 'Ground of Being' and 'True Nature,' which seemed to describe my experience. My sense was that each human body is as a cell in the great Body of Gaia. Again I use this term *Gaia* as a subjective personification, not as an entity separate from us.

If we are aligned with being the Body of Gaia and serving this Great Body, we are in harmony and feel purposeful and at home as part of the soul of the world. If we feel separate, we lack purpose and aren't at home in our body or the world.

Later I found a quote that came at a synchronistic moment by Albert Einstein that points toward this deep experience:

"A human being is a part of the whole called by us universe; a part limited in time and space. He experiences himself, his thoughts and feeling as something separated from the rest, a kind of optical delusion of his consciousness. This delusion is a kind of prison for us, restricting us to our personal desires and to affection for a few persons nearest to us. Our task must be to free ourselves from this prison by widening our circle of compassion to embrace all living creatures and the whole of nature in its beauty."

He is using the pronoun 'he' to describe a human, not his experience, as was the convention of the day, but my experience felt deeply feminine.

REUNION AND INITIATION

Eventually, I reconnected with my stepson when he turned about fourteen years of age. It was meaningful to invite him fishing and to create a coming-of-age ritual with him. To prepare, I bought him a First Nations necklace of an eagle feather, as a protective symbol to watch over him during the next seven-year period of his life. The gift of the eagle's keen sight seemed to have worked, because he was the only one of us to catch a fish.

He was very proud of this and whenever trouble came knocking on his door he would ask me if we could go fishing. I knew this was his code for, 'Can we have a deep talk?' When he was nineteen I brought him to his first men's retreat with Michael Meade and Malidoma Some. When I witnessed the men loving him in the way he needed most, through mentoring, I realized the truth in the ancient saying, "It takes a whole village to raise a child."

THE CALL

After a couple of years of deep therapy with Ian, I explored what I felt called to do with my life. Under his recommendation, I went to a psychological testing firm called Young's Ferris and they conducted forty hours of career testing with me. In the end, they presented me with an extensive assessment and recommended that my top three careers possibilities were Teaching, Ministry or Psychotherapy. I decided that psychotherapy held my greatest interests, and that as a psychotherapist I could incorporate a teaching approach and soulful aspect like Ian had modeled, integrating all three disciplines in my chosen vocation.

In the next chapter we explore the soulful relationship between masculine and feminine.

Being deeply loved by someone gives you strength, while loving someone deeply gives you courage.

—Lao-tzu

CHAPTER 5:
TRANSFORMATION: OUR UNFOLDING SOUL

"Someday, after we have mastered the wind, the waves, the tides and gravity, we shall harness for God the energies of love. Then for the second time in the history of the world, we will have discovered fire."

—Pierre Teilhard de Chardin

Five: How can we clear barriers to our inner resources?

In the second and third chapters we looked at some of the territory of the Inner World of the Psyche. In Chapter Four we explored the Home of the Soul and Soulful Relationships. In this chapter we will continue with the theme of Soulful Relationships and explore the Unfolding Soul, in which Essential Qualities (EQ) arise as inner gifts from the Home of the Soul, our True Nature (TN). This begins our path of individuation. The acorn cracks open and unfolds toward its destiny as the magnificent Oak Tree.

The Sufis and many other mystics say our True Nature is the Source of Love. Sufis also speak poetically about the '99 Names of Love.' When we tap into our True Nature, the Home of our Soul, it is like digging deep in the Ground of Being, or tapping into an underground stream. If we dig a well with the shovel of our daily practices, we can tap into this underground stream and receive the healing waters of Love's Presence.

The mystics say that the form Love takes is based on our deepest need and sometimes gets objectified in the outside world. If we are stressed and pray for Peace, then Deep Peace is likely the form that Love takes. If we pray for Forgiveness, then it's Forgiveness or tolerance.

Sufi master Hazrat Inayat Khan teaches that 'Spirituality is attained through the heart'. When we enter the Deep Heart, we enter Mystery And Presence. By facing our fear with presence, compassion and courage arise as Inner Gifts, and so on.

If we reflect on the journey of our mythical characters, Isaac uncovered his Inner Treasure when he dug under the hearth in his own home. The hearth is a symbol for his heart. He had to go on a journey, then return to know his home, his heart, as if for the first time. 'Home is where the Heart is.'

Right behind our human heart is the Great Heart, the Greatest Mystery! The First Nations elders say the longest journey is the distance from our head to our deep Heart. As Isaac digs into the Ground of the Great Heart, the Essential Qualities of Generosity and Gratitude emerge, and he is so moved that he sends the captain of the guards a precious ruby in gratitude for pointing the way to his Inner Treasure.

A ruby is often a symbol of the heart, and the heart is the seat of the soul. When the sun fills the ruby with light, it radiates its illumination. The sun is often a symbol of the Source; the Home of the Soul, and our Soul is a ray of that Sun. This Sun shines freely on all beings.

We each have an inner captain of the guard that protects our Inner Treasure. When he or she becomes autonomous he forgets whom he is working for and scoffs at his dreams and the dreams of others. He has been protecting us for so long that he forgets what he is protecting. When we become identified with the part of us that protects us, we can also become so defended that we forget about the Inner Treasure that we are protecting.

The captain serves the king and queen of the palace. If we aren't aware of our inner palace and the inner king and queen that reside there, then our selves become egotistical and self-centred. The inner king or queen can become tyrants too. They can easily be seduced by the fool's gold that is dangled in front of their noses by those who want to sell us something. We can also get caught in protecting what little fool's gold we have. Then the pursuit of happiness becomes a constant seeking for more outer gratification.

The addictions in the fifth chakra are opiates and marijuana, according to Anodea Judith. This is our centre for clear communication. In Voice Dialogue we ask ourselves which voice is speaking. Is it the self that is addicted to supernormal allurements? Indulging in opiates and marijuana can keep us locked in fantasy and block our clear vision.

By resting into the Ground of Being I was beginning to enjoy a deeper sense of stillness, calm and inner peace. These are EQ (Essential Qualities) that arise as a gift from the Source, the Home of our Soul. This is the Inner Treasure of true gold Rumi speaks of. I felt profoundly connected in the wild natural places of the BC wilderness and found easy access to the peace of my inner nature.

Eventually, through Ian's support, I healed some of my addictive tendencies and started exploring the world of meditation. He was exploring Buddhist meditation, so suggested I try Vipassana or Insight Meditation. I joined an Insight Meditation group. Buddhist Teacher and Psychotherapist Jack Kornfield was a major influence in that tradition.

Most of the teachers I have been drawn to have psychological and spiritual dimensions to their work. That was so with Ian and my next mentor, Atum, who introduced me to the four worlds of the soul.

I first heard about Atum in 1992, as described earlier in the introduction, through an article I read entitled *The Midlife Passage*. That same summer I went to a retreat with him at Hollyhock on Cortez

Island. Every summer I trained with him until 1999 when I enrolled in his spiritual guidance training program, then later in other trainings.

In 1999, Atum began teaching his two-year program *The Art of Spiritual Guidance* in Vancouver and Hollyhock. In the program, we trainees met five times per year for a total of twenty-six days over two years.

I enjoyed the two-year program with Atum immensely. We dove deeply into our personal mythology, shadow, dreams, typology, and God-ideal. Then we learned to soulfully guide others.

Atum also does spiritual pilgrimages to the birthplaces of the mystics. Right after the training, he embarked on a pilgrimage to Assisi, the birthplace of Saint Francis and St. Claire. I had been thinking about doing a pilgrimage to Halifax, where I was conceived, and then to my birthplace in London, England, because I hadn't been there since age two. Forty-five years had elapsed since then, and I was turning the same age as my father was when he died.

On the last day of the training, Atum gifted me with a card of an image of Saint Peter's Basilica, which was unknown to me at the time. On the inside it had a meaningful phrase penned by Atum. I wasn't planning on the Assisi pilgrimage, but Atum's message spoke to me so deeply that I signed up. It was time to follow synchronicity again.

I wanted to track what had meaning for me. I realized that I could stopover in London, perhaps find a way to do a ritual at my birthplace, go to Rome with Atum, participate in the pilgrimage, and visit the birthplace of Saint Francis, all on the same trip. Halifax would have to wait until another time.

Just prior to leaving for Assisi in 2001, the bombing of New York's Twin Towers shocked everyone. In response to the possibility that the bombers may have crossed the border from Canada, the Vancouver Airport was turned into an armed camp.

With all the uncertainty, we didn't know if our plane was going to get off the ground, but eventually it did. However, the stopover in London at Heathrow Airport was absolute chaos.

We missed our connecting flight, but got through the pandemonium to Italian Airlines on the lower level. I couldn't believe the difference. The Italian Airline Agents were so relaxed, "Don't worry, we'll get you on the next plane, no problem, your bags will be in Rome when you get there!"

When we arrived in Assisi, Atum led us on a pilgrimage through the holy sites of St. Francis and St. Claire's birthplace. We meditated in the cave where St. Francis is said to have had his first illumination. It wasn't in a church but in a dark cave in the belly of a mountain, which birthed the greatest light for him.

Atum, grounded in so many mystical traditions, along with Jungian and Transpersonal Psychology, inspired me to do a ritual based on the story of St. Francis and his parents. St. Francis was also a wild partier in his youth, then he went to the crusades, was captured and put in prison. When he was released, he came back home and worked for his merchant father. Later he confronted his father on his greedy oppression of his workers. He was locked up for a time in his father's prison. He also named the hypocrisy of the Catholic indulgences of the time and was shunned. He found solace in nature, the poor, and friends.

His story resonated with mine. I wanted to separate from the negative impressions I received from both of my parents while honouring the positive ones. By studying this period of history I also got to reconcile with my Christian roots. I could see how St. Francis stewarded a spirituality that was deeply connected to nature and how Christianity has wandered from that connection.

When I came home from Assisi, I felt like I had received a great gift and a deep healing. As soon as I arrived, Atum called me and asked me to assist him in his next two-year training. I explained that I was also taking a three-year training in Process Counselling at Langara College with Jungian Psychotherapist and Process Work Diplomat, David Roomy, and might have to miss a weekend occasionally. Atum was fine with that.

So I did the two-year *Art of Spiritual Guidance* Program again with Atum—this time as his assistant. My journey with Atum continues to this day as I continue to do post-graduate training with him.

At the same time, I was enrolled in the three-year training in Process Counselling at Langara College. In that training I enjoyed diving into deep Process principles, Dream work, Body work, and Group work, and I met a wonderful group of friends and colleagues who lived locally—so I had a supportive local therapeutic community developing.

During the training, I underwent forty deep Process Work Counselling sessions with David Roomy as part of my course requirement and then twenty-five supervision sessions with him to graduate as a Process Counsellor.

When David Roomy retired, he asked me and some of the other senior students to take over the Process Counselling training. In this way, I became an instructor at the Community College, teaching Process Counselling.

MEANING AND PURPOSE

At forty-two, in 1996, I was single, in therapy and answering the call to become a psychotherapist. I was a member of a soulful men's group and a dedicated practitioner on a psycho-spiritual path. My diet had improved somewhat. I no longer used coffee, alcohol, cigarettes or pot to numb out. My workaholic tendencies disappeared as I learned how to balance activity and rest.

Vancouver winters can be quite dreary at times with all the rain. Many single people suffer from feeling blue, living on their own. I came down with a nasty flu one winter and had a wicked fever. The fever was so high that I started worrying about my health. I stubbornly didn't want to call anyone and 'bother' him or her when I was feeling so vulnerable. After a couple days, the fever still wasn't subsiding, and I thought, 'I'm going to die on my own and nobody will know. I don't want my life to end this way!'

I realized that I didn't want to be single anymore, but I was just afraid to commit to a relationship again because I was hurt when my first marriage broke apart. I decided to go to the store and buy a thermometer and take care of myself. I vowed to live more fully and find a partner to share my life with, someone who was willing to dance together in the ecstasy and the agony.

"Give me burning! I want burning!"

—Rumi

In the middle of the first training program with Atum, I came down with another fever, but it didn't seem like the flu. That night I had a dream of one of Atum's mentors, a woman named Helen Luke, a Jungian Analyst who was 91 when she died. She was a very wise woman. In the dream, I was shaking all over with a fever. Helen came to me and kindly said, "Don't resist the fever, don't resist the fire, just surrender to it!" and so I did. The next day I felt a lot better, well enough to complete the retreat. The wise old man had come in a dream many years before, and now the wise old woman visited me.

The next night I watched a PBS program celebrating Helen Luke's life. The program was very meaningful. I watched it with a close friend named Joani, from Seattle. We had become soul brother and soul sister to each other over the many years of studying with Atum. In the book *Anam Cara*, John O'Donahue uses the term 'Anam Cara' to express the concept of soul friends.

Since I had sisters and I enjoyed hanging out with my younger sister a lot, it felt great to foster connection with a soul sister. In the PBS program, James Hillman, Robert Johnson, and the famous film director Peter Brooke all celebrate Helen Luke's life. They all say she was one of the world's great wise women.

Before Helen died at 90 years of age, she said she was going on a walk with the three wise men. Robert Johnson said that when Christianity acknowledged Mary as ascending to Heaven, there was hope for Christianity to move from a trinity to a 'quaternity'. My dream of Helen Luke seemed like a symbol of that emerging quaternity where masculine and feminine god images are honoured equally.

To cultivate more meaning and personification, we can also see

Sophia as "wisdom" or the feminine face of God. In Gnostic tradition, Sophia created the material world, therefore Sophia could be seen as the subjective feminine face of the Creator, and God the Father or *Abba* could be seen as the subjective masculine face of God.

My relationships with women were healing but in the romantic area I was still stuck in the old paradigm. One of the retreats I did with Atum was called *the Alchemy of Relationships*, and in it I began to glimpse a new possibility for how couples could journey together on a soulful path. I realized that I needed to become whole inside first.

Michael Meade tells an insightful folk myth about becoming whole in an ancient story from Borneo called *The Half Boy*:

In a small village in Borneo, a woman gives birth to a son but he is only a half boy. He has one left eye and only his left arm and leg. As a half boy he keeps thinking half thoughts, later he only gets half of his homework done in school. As he grows, he causes trouble in the village because he's so hard for people to look at. People turn away, and this disturbs his parents. Everything they try to do to make him whole doesn't work.

The teachers try to teach him to act whole, but it doesn't work and he becomes very disruptive.

Discouraged, the half boy leaves the village and heads down a path. He walks for a long time. Eventually he comes to a river, and on the other side of the river he sees another half boy who is the opposite half of himself. He has only a right eye, a right arm and a right leg.

At this moment, we probably think to ourselves, *'The two half boys have found their other half and will come together and live happily ever after.'*

No, it didn't work that way. They waded towards each other and when they met in the middle of the river, they fought, wrestled and went under the water. In the heat of the conflict the water boiled and pretty soon the river took them downstream. Every once in a while a foot would come up, an arm would come up, a head would come up, and they'd go under again. They wrestled and wrestled like this for a long time.

Eventually, there was a turn in the river. The boy crawled out of the river onto the bank. One whole boy emerged from the river, and he started to walk, but he was wobbly. He wasn't certain of the direction but he walked, and he walked, and he walked some more, and then he saw a fire in the distance.

Beside the fire, there was an elder. He said to the elder, "I'm lost and don't know where to go." The elder said to him, "Welcome, back. You've come back to where you started. This is your village, and we have been waiting for you to come home. The people have not been able to dance since you left. If we enter together everyone will dance. It's time to celebrate!"

The whole boy was welcomed into the village, and a great celebration and dance began. The boy danced his wholeness and everyone was reminded to dance theirs.

Meade suggests that in a village that is whole everyone dances together, but in this particular village they had stopped dancing. Perhaps they had become fundamentalists? When this happens, the youth become half boys or girls. The elders and youth need to dance together for wholeness to occur. The inner elder and inner youth within each of us need to dance together as well. When Meade asks youth what the river of conflict is for them, they often say alcohol, drugs, prison, and so on.

Inspired by this story, I decided to create a ritual to energetically separate from all my past unsatisfying romantic relationships with female partners. Inspired also by the Jungian way to work with Active Imagination and what I was learning from the African elders, I created a ritual of separation and honouring to transform the old paradigm.

Like Mullah, I had literally lost my wedding ring and it was quite a search to find it. The ring even had my former wife's name engraved on the inside. The ring is a symbol of wholeness and marriage, so I cut it in two and buried one half in the earth and dropped the other half in the ocean. It was a symbolic gesture to show that I was ready to let go of the past pattern.

I also found some photos of my former wife and me and cut the photos, separating us. Then I found saplings to represent every woman I had ever gone out with. Then I cut them in half and planted them separately. Symbolically, I let the negative patterns of the past go and wished each woman well. I was ready to heal and move on, and I wanted the same for them.

It was a powerful ritual, and within weeks, three good-hearted women seemed interested in me. I had never been this popular before, so it increased my faith in the power of working with symbolic ritual. I had the challenge of deciding which potential partner was the right one to commit to! I got clear on being ready to commit, and made a list of qualities that I wanted in a partner. Soon afterwards, I met my present wife Sue.

In *Love and Awakening*, John Wellwood suggests that for relationship to be a conscious path we need a heart connection and a soul connection. We can have a heart connection with many people, and even our beloved pet. "A soul connection is a resonance between two people who respond to the essential beauty of each other's individual natures, behind their facades, and who connect on this level. This kind of mutual recognition provides the catalyst for a potent alchemy. While a heart connection lets us appreciate those we love just as they are, a soul connection opens up a further dimension—seeing and loving them for who they could be, and for who we could become under their influence."

A soul connection is often about challenge. Someone with whom we have a deep soul connection won't let us get away with being too small or let us shrink from our destiny. I also like Wellwood's poetic, subjective definition of spirit and soul. He says, "Spirit is love of the universal, and soul is love of the particular!"

As far as I could tell, most couples seemed to be living in polarized egocentric relationships. I was tired of this and kept myself out of intimate partnership for quite a while. I concentrated on deepening intimacy with my friends, with my men's group, my spiritual group and, with my psychological training group, while trying to imagine and understand what a soulful relationship between lovers could be like.

If I back up a couple of years to 1999 again, some friends of mine put together a sacred music festival in Vancouver, and I volunteered to help with the organization. During the event, I met a wonderful woman named Shasta. I already knew her husband Brian for many years from the soulful men's retreats I attended. Brian and I had become friends, but I hadn't met his wife Shasta yet. I was delightfully surprised to find out they were life partners, and they have since become very close soul friends of mine.

Fast forward to 2001 and another Sacred Music Festival where I meet my soulful life partner Sue. We met within the container of our mutual love of sacred music. It turns out we also love all kinds of other music. We're particularly fond of folk festivals, dance, singing, camping, kayaking and are both lifelong learners.

Process Psychology has a term called the *high dream*. It refers to this great Mystery that brings two lovers together. It's important to remember the high dream so that you don't descend into a low dream while attending to the everyday activities of journeying together.

Sue says that when we first met at the festival she felt a great stillness between us. This Essential Quality of stillness and the mutual love of music and meditation give depth and life to our high dream.

I was yearning for more than just a sexual partner. I wanted a good friend too, someone who did meaningful and purposeful work in the world and someone who walked a psychospiritual and interspiritual path. I didn't know if that was possible, but that's what I put on my list.

All of a sudden, there was Sue! It took me a while to realize it, but she had all the qualities I was yearning for. She was a passionate schoolteacher making a difference with children; a loving mother with grown children, and she was part of a Mindfulness Practice Community inspired by Thich Nhat Hahn. She lived just a few blocks from me.

I attended a Sufi group regularly and Sue wanted to come because she loved to sing. Devotional singing is a big part of this universal Sufi Tradition. I was interested in the Buddhist group because I wanted more focus and discipline to sit properly in meditation. It took a few more meetings to discover all this about each other.

After Sue and I met at the Sacred Music Festival, synchronicity played its trump card when a mutual friend phoned Sue one day and invited her to his birthday party. He told her he was inviting a storyteller named Dave to tell stories to the children and lead a Sufi dance. Sue's ears perked up, and with bated breath she said, "Dave! Is this the same soulful Dave from the Sacred Music Festival?" You know the answer!

When our friend's birthday came rolling around, I was excited to see he had invited Sue, and we ended up sitting at the same table. He asked me to share the children's story and then to lead the twenty plus people in a Sufi dance. I agreed and taught them the dance and the chant that went with it. The chant was, 'All I ask of you is forever to remember me as loving you. Ishq Allah, Ma'bud Allah.' This last phrase means, 'God is Love, God is the Beloved or God is Love, Lover and Beloved.'

I instructed the dancers to gaze deeply into each other's eyes, looking past the personality into the eyes of the Beloved Source. As the old expression goes, 'The eyes are the windows of the soul.' We whirled around and attempted to see the Beloved in all of Creation. Finally, we sent any love we felt to whoever in the world needed it most.

There's a trinity of Love in the Sufi ideal—Love, Lover, and Beloved. This is one reason it is called the 'Way of the Heart'. So there we were, falling in love through this dance of the heart. We were sharing this very experiential dance and, of course, it's very easy to fall in love through that! In the end, we sat in our chairs and shared what we were passionate about. We discovered many interests in common. Later, she invited me to hike the next day with her son. I thanked her for the invitation but regretfully I had to work. I wasn't too swift on the uptake and forgot to ask for her phone number!

That night I pinched myself for not asking for her number. Fortunately, the next day I called my friend and he kindly gave her phone number to me.

Sue and I had both had been married once before and were now divorced. When I met her she had two grown sons, and by then my stepson was grown up. It felt good to meet someone who was in a similar stage of life in that way.

The third time we connected was a week later when I asked her out to lunch and an afternoon movie. I couldn't help but check my list and saw we had a lot in common.

I had an epiphany later in the movie theatre watching the romantic film *Amelie*. There's a scene in the film where the lovers are trying to connect with each other and hoping synchronicity will somehow draw them together. All of a sudden I realized that the couple in the film was like us. Finding each other was our destiny. Sue was the answer to my prayers.

I wasn't going to snooze again, so I turned and boldly said, "This is for Amelie!" and kissed her deeply on the lips as she met mine fully. Instantly, we fell head over heels in love.

After the film, we tried to find my car in the underground parking but felt so drunk on love that we couldn't remember where we left it. We started following the arrows painted on the ground and then burst out laughing, remembering that it was just like one of the scenes in the movie.

We finally found the car and made it to the meditation group in time. Being head over heels in love while doing sitting and walking meditation is challenging to say the least, but our responsible selves kicked in and we saw it through. My heart really just wanted to burst into song.

At the end of the class, I asked Sue if she would be interested in seeing my apartment just a few blocks from where she lived in a group co-op. She sounded enthusiastic.

When we walked up the stairs to my house, I felt smitten and drunk on the spiritual wine of love. I couldn't resist and picked her up and carried her across the threshold and said, "Welcome home!" I've never been so sure of any other relationship in my life. Sue seemed to just melt into my arms, and we made passionate love that night.

The next morning she woke to the sound of music, and when she entered the living room, she saw me dancing joyfully to Leonard Cohen's

Dance me to the end of love! She joined the dance, and we have been dancing this dance of love and awareness through soulful partnership ever since.

When we met, we embraced relationship as a soulful path, which is easy to do when things go well. At other times, it is very challenging because our limited selves dominate, and we act in selfish self-interest. It's painful at times to make the descent from the high dream to the low dream, but we are learning to walk the middle path.

When our limited selves take over we are asked to bow to a deeper love. There is an essential teaching from Hal and Sidra Stone Ph.D., authors of *Partnering—How to Love Each Other Without Losing Your Selves* that is a guiding light for us when we fall into forgetfulness:

"Relationship is the Teacher, Healer and Guide."

INTERSPIRITUAL RETREAT

We moved in together soon afterwards and shared many passionate adventures. One of our most meaningful memories was a wonderful interspiritual retreat in Vancouver that was life changing for both of us. Some of the teachers included the Dalai Lama, Rabbi Zalman Schachter-Shalomi, and Brother Wayne Teasdale.

Brother Wayne was a Christian monk and a Hindu Sannyasin. At the time of the retreat, he was one of the leading figures in the interspiritual movement. He dressed in orange robes and had trained with Bede Griffith in India. Bede was born as Alan Richard Griffiths and also known by the end of his life as Swami Dayananda. Bede was a British-born Benedictine monk who lived in ashrams in South India and became a noted yogi. He went to India originally to convert the Hindus, but he became converted when he experienced the richness of Hinduism, which made his Christianity blossom. Bede founded his own Monastic Ashram in India, and Brother Wayne ended up studying with him there.

I was especially touched by the diversity of people and doctrines represented at this gathering: First Nations elders, the Dalai Lama, and many other Traditions. About two hundred of us meditated together, people from Buddhist groups, Sufi groups, Jewish groups, even Whirling Dervishes! It was so rich for us to share together. One of the highlights for me was that they chose different locations each day to represent the different Traditions.

On one of the days we met in a large Christian church. The First Nations elders came in, walked all around, circled everyone, played their drums, and then called in the sacred seven directions. They called in the upper world, the lower world, the four cardinal directions, and the inner direction. They respectfully honoured all our relations, including all of Creation, the Soul of the World.

Sue and I were so moved we cried with joy. We realized that while this little church was only a hundred years old, the First Nations people had been living here for thousands of years, which felt primordial. Often settlers built their churches on land that is sacred to First Nations people, as a way to harness sacred energy there. We were moved that the organizers showed respect to the Musqueam people, the traditional keepers of the land on whose unceded territory we had been granted permission to meet.

It was so beautiful to witness each Tradition respectfully honouring each Tradition's diversity and celebrating what they each had in common, instead of fighting over whose Name for Ultimate Reality was right. St. Francis would have approved.

Essential Qualities like love, peace, compassion, courage, forgiveness, and patience are the true gold of our Inner Treasure. When our leaders instruct us to chase after material objects to give us happiness in the form of pleasure, we may miss the deep joy that arises simply as a gift from the Ground of our Being. This can happen for an individual and for a collective.

To awaken, a society can also reflect on its Inner Treasure. An awakened society then becomes a collective symbolic soulful butterfly. Anodea Judith PH.D, in her book, *Waking the Global Heart—Humanity's Rite of Passage From The Love Of Power To The Power Of Love* articulates the transformation that is desperately needed on a global level in times like these.

RECOGNIZING OUR INNER SELVES AND EVOLVING OUR EGO

In the film *The Doctor*, Jack comes to terms with June's death and feels deep grief and compassion for losing a trusted friend. Then he humbly makes amends with Eli, the surgeon he formerly mocked. He trusts him to give him the care and skill needed for his operation. He finds his integrity and says 'no' to lying on behalf of his partner.

Jack and Anne are undergoing major life transformations. They aren't making a transition but are going through a metamorphosis. They are symbolically dying to their old stage of life and relationship that they were locked in and being reborn into their next stage of life and relationship. By resting deeply in the Home of the Soul, our True Nature, we surrender the attachment of our small selves to their dominant egocentric perspective. Then we are initiated into the Self, Soul and Spirit.

To foster soulful relationships with others, so our partnerships heal, transform and evolve soulfully too, we need a healthy inner garden as an individual and as a couple. We need to weed out what is overgrown and plant new seeds of possibility. This means each partner takes full responsibility for healing, transforming and evolving from their past hurts. To take responsibility for yourself means to be able to respond compassionately to your inner selves.

In Voice Dialogue, The Psychology of the Selves and The Aware Ego Process, the goal is also to heal, transform and evolve so we can live with greater freedom and choice in our lives. If we can determine what kind of unique psychic fingerprint we have, we can guide our unfolding soul in the particular direction of our destiny, otherwise we end up suffering from living an unhappy fate. The constant question we are asking in Voice Dialogue is, 'Who is speaking now; speaking out loud or internally?'

When Freud used the term ego, he described it as the executive function of the psyche. Hal Stone thinks this is still a useful term. In Voice Dialogue we don't try to get rid of our ego but we embrace it, honour it and encourage it to heal, transform and evolve. If we completely identify with our ego, then we think that is all of who we are.

First we need some perspective on our ego. There is an old saying that the ego makes a lousy master and a wonderful servant. We can learn to be aware of our ego, help it transform and evolve, and then enlist its skills in the service of manifesting our soul's gifts. Being facilitated by Hal and Sidra Stone helped me to heal some of the remaining hurts with my parents and to integrate their wonderful gifts to me.

OUR INNER SELVES IN CONFLICT

Shakespeare said that, "All of life's a stage..."—and indeed this can be used as a metaphor for transforming ourselves. The term personality comes from the Greek work persona. In Greek Theater there are two masks, one with a smile for comedy and one with a frown for a tragedy. When the actor dons the mask he or she is clear they are not the mask but the being peering through the mask.

Our personality is like a collection of masks we wear. Depending on the occasion we will wear and present different masks or faces. This is what the saying 'two-faced' points to.

If we completely identify with a particular mask, then we disown our other masks for the moment. If we identify with our mask too strongly, we forget who we really are. For that moment we have forgotten our True Nature. When we get lost in identifying too strongly with our masks, we start to feel inauthentic and trapped in a story that is too small for us.

The word *authentic* has the root word author in it. If we can take a larger perspective on the stage of our life, we can see larger perspectives from the view of the stage light, the audience, the director and the producer. We can become an authentic leader with authority in our life.

The mask we identify with most is called our primary identity in

Voice Dialogue. Actually, our primary identity can be a collection of primary sub-personalities. For example, Jack in the film *The Doctor* has some primary selves or identities of Surgeon, Husband, Father, Impersonal Logical Thinker, Judge, Joker, and so on. One moment he can be wearing the mask of 'Impersonal Surgeon' and the next, the 'Joker'. His disowned selves start to be revealed throughout the film: Vulnerable Cancer Patient, Personal Caregiver, and Compassionate Mentor. As his character transforms, he starts to integrate the opposites and he becomes the caring and skillful Surgeon—and finally the compassionate and wise mentor.

His wife Anne also has some primary identities or selves as Wife, Mother, Pleaser, and so on. Her disowned identities are of Impersonal Thinker and Vulnerable Child for example. As the film unfolds, she too starts integrating her opposites of personal and impersonal selves.

Let's take a closer look at some of these selves and how they operate in our inner world of psyche and in our interaction with others. For example, I'll often hear someone say, "That was so stupid of me!" We hear this judgment all the time and think it's normal. But is it natural? Did we speak to our self like this when we were very young? What's actually happening here? The person is hurting himself or herself with self-criticism, and you might be the one that gets judged next!

The person might not realize that there are actually at least two selves inside. There is the inner critic that is calling another part of them stupid, and then we could say that the other self is a victim to the critic. There is a violent battle going on inside, but the person is usually unaware of it.

The practice of Voice Dialogue is one solution. If individuals, mediators, therapists and facilitators were trained in the art of facilitating inner selves they could bring more consciousness to communication.

If the original person who said, "That was so stupid of me!" asked themselves, "Who just spoke in me?" they could use their awareness to illuminate their inner stage and see the two characters playing out their parts in their inner tragedy. They could catch the performers in their act. With awareness they can clearly see the inner polarization of power and vulnerability and not get overly identified with either side. With loving compassion, they could embrace the two opposite selves within.

The one inside that is criticizing their behaviour is usually trying to protect them from making a mistake and looking foolish. It is protecting the self in them that made a perceived error. Unfortunately they have learned a caustic way to reprimand their self. Our inner critic's style of communicating is often learned from someone in our past who judged us, and now we have internalized that attitude and use it against our self.

With wisdom, we can decide whether to consciously externalize this inner battle or take it to a process for healing. The inner critic can be transformed into the voice of discernment and serve our soul's unfolding. Or, the person who is witnessing the first person criticizing him or herself can be alert to their inner polarization and use compassionate communication in conveying this to the other person.

BONDING PATTERNS

According to Voice Dialogue theory, when a couple first meets there is a lot of inner dialogue going on between their inner selves. There is a primary bonding pattern that happens between their 'inner child' and their partner's 'inner parent'.

In Attachment Theory, once the bond is established this person becomes our primary attachment figure. Once this attachment is present, patterns from childhood, both positive and negative, begin to resurface. If we learn to expect this, as a natural phenomenon, then we are not going to be so surprised when it starts happening and we can employ conscious relationship practices to heal our old wounds.

Hal and Sidra Stone in *Partnering—How to Love Each Other without Losing Yourselves* give a comprehensive map for couples to begin exploring their bonding patterns. In their experience working with hundreds of couples, they say that love is not enough—we need awareness too! Like a garden, if we want a conscious relationship, we need to dedicate time to tending it.

A committed relationship has many facets to it and we will need a way to integrate the opposites if we want to operate as two conscious, whole people. We need to have both warm personal energy for deep love and care, yet we also need cool impersonal energy for clear thinking and planning. There are many complex decisions to be made in running a household and we need care and clarity.

Often couples are originally attracted to each other because they are opposites and need to integrate his or her opposite, represented by the other person. For example, in the film *the Doctor*, perhaps Jack was attracted to Anne's warm, caring side and she was attracted to Jack's cool rational side. Later however, he started to feel smothered by her personal energy and tried to distance from it. She felt abandoned by his cool controlling and withholding.

They are two half people trying to become whole by coming together. This isn't wholeness; it's fusion and just the first stage in the journey of conscious partnering.

In Voice Dialogue, each person is often a reflection of what is disowned in his or her partner. What comes naturally to each of them is what is challenging for their partner. They are like the irritating grain of sand in the oyster for each other. Hal and Sidra say that the Intelligence of the Universe has brought them together to heal, transform and evolve.

To transform, they need to shift their consciousness to awareness. Then, they need to hold the tension of the opposites within themselves and welcome this irritating grain of sand within them, and embrace it. Over time and with practice, it becomes the priceless pearl of integrating a disowned self.

When a man and woman, 'fall in love', and commit to each other, they become primary attachment figures for each other. One of the psychological dynamics that happens in this phase of pair bonding is that his inner boy seeks to connect with her inner mother, and her inner girl seeks to connect with his inner father. If this all goes well, a positive bonding pattern established.

When a mother gives birth to a child there is an umbilical cord attaching them to each other. Even when the cord is cut, there is an energetic connection between them that creates a needed bond between parent and child. This energetic connection needs to be nurtured for the health of the child.

Similarly there is an energetic link between father and child. Research shows that if in early infancy the father holds the newborn to his bare chest, this energetic connection can be strengthened. This energetic connection happens between a couple's inner children and inner parents as well. Voice Dialogue calls this our energetic linkage. Each couple will have a unique blend of this energetic linkage depending on many factors.

If we take two figure-eight symbols, one for the woman and one for the man, we can construct a visual for this. The parent in the woman bonds on one side with the boy in the man on the same side. The girl in the woman bonds with the parent in the man on the other side.

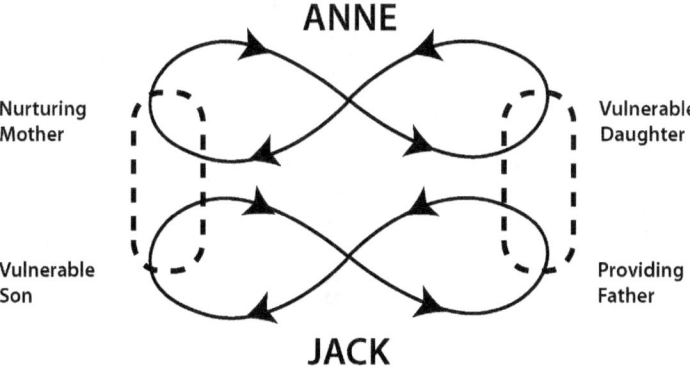

A positive bonding pattern feels good because both people have agreed on some level to take care of some their partner's basic needs. The relationship is still in an immature phase to the degree of the unconscious dependence between inner parents and inner children.

For example, she may always need to be the one to be nurturing. He may always need to be in the role of provider. This was the ideal relationship for many couples in the 1950's; everyone knew their role and stuck to it! Those were the unconscious rules of engagement and still are in many parts of the world.

In this case, his inner boy bonds with her inner mother for nurturing; and her inner girl bonds with his inner father for providing.

If either person tries to change the dynamics—for example, she starts earning more than he does or he starts to exclusively look after the children—their positive bonding pattern can flip into a negative pattern if there isn't a high degree of consciousness regarding the change.

Depending on many factors, like their attachment styles, which relationship stage their parents were in when they were born and the modeling from their own family systems, this can throw them in chaos. It can feel like hell to be in the boxing ring with no rules or referee!

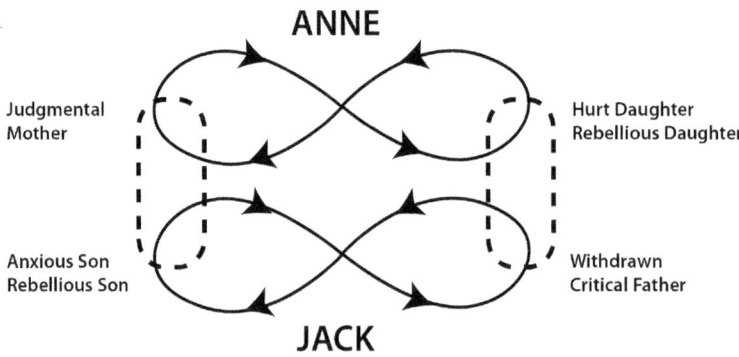

In the traditional model, the man probably feels powerful as the provider and might feel vulnerable if his wife now takes on that role. It might remind him of being vulnerable with his mother as a boy. Perhaps he rebelled against his mother and now will rebel against his wife—she becomes the stand-in for his past conflict with his mother. He might be more identified with staying in the powerful control position like his traditional father did. In fact, his parents or buddies may give him a hard time because they judge his new role as a form of weakness.

The female partner, too, may feel powerful in the mother role and feel vulnerable if she has to get her husband's approval for spending. This can remind her of being with her controlling father as a girl, when he used her allowance to control her behaviour—getting her allowance depended on whether she was 'good' or 'bad' in her father's eyes. She may have rebelled against her father and now rebels against her husband, as he becomes a stand-in for the past conflict with her father.

There are endless variations on this theme. The fundamental pair of opposites is power on one side of our teeter-totter, and vulnerability on the other side. If the power side has all the weight, the vulnerability is hanging up in the air—having no fun, so to speak.

There isn't much movement or play. There is mostly conflict and power struggle. If we look at the teeter-totter again, the middle point is the fulcrum; this represents awareness. To balance a teeter-totter, the flat board is placed on top of a stable triangle.

Did you ever stand in the middle of a teeter-totter as a child and use your two legs to gently rock from one side to the other? This is an image of what the couple needs to practice internally if they are to evolve toward a conscious partnership. Instead of polarizing to either side of their inner opposites, child or parent, they need to straddle both sides of themselves and embrace both their inner power and inner vulnerability, then relate to their partner with presence and awareness from the centre.

This centre position is called the *aware ego* process in Voice Dialogue. From a centre we can access awareness and hold the tension of the opposites, then decide what balance we need to implement. The aware ego process is not a fixed place; it's a process that evolves the more we practice it.

The centre is like a juggler that can now juggle more balls than before. A juggler needs awareness to be fully present. If they take their eyes off the balls, then they drop them.

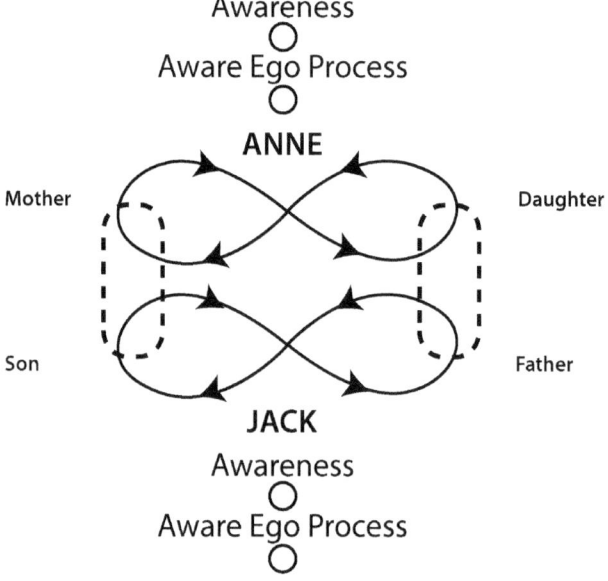

Bonding Pattern with Awareness & Aware Ego Process

Each time we relate to our partner from the centre, we begin to evolve more. This isn't a linear process, however—if we are sick with a cold or tired from lack of sleep, we can fall back into our old patterns. It's important to have patience and compassion for our self at those times and not expect our self to be perfect, or else the inner perfectionist takes over, followed by an inner critic who keeps raising the bar saying, "It's never good enough!"

MUTUALITY AND PARTNERING

Trying to stay in love's first stage can become addictive if we limit each other's evolution. This is like attempting to stay in childhood.

Drawing on the work of Dr. Margaret Mahler and her discovery of the stages of early childhood development, Dr. Ellyn Bader and Dr. Peter Pearson of The Couples Institute, have posited similar developmental stages couples have to navigate through for deepening maturation. The first stage lasts about six months to two years and is an emphasis on bonding to form connection and a secure attachment with each other. Couples often get arrested here trying unsuccessfully to maintain this symbiotic bond. They are in danger of breaking up and some are called to therapy for help in evolving to the next stage.

The second stage begins when they are called into a healthy differentiation where they define themselves, express their needs, thoughts, feelings and desires, establishing that "We are different."

The third stage is about individuation. It is called "practicing" where they assert, "I like my independence." In this stage, partners go out and explore the world. They often focus on their work, their hobbies, and there is not so much intense focus on the relationship. Partners will slip into independent periods of looking for greater connection.

The fourth stage is called the "mutually interdependent" or "Rapprochement" stage of "Moving close, moving away."

Finally, the fifth stage is the "synergistic stage" of being together—"One plus one is greater than two." This is where a couple is "integrating intimacy into ongoing life and sexuality, committing to joint projects/work and leaving a legacy."

When we learn to take responsibility for our selves, then our judgment of others decreases. We evolve beyond positive or negative bonding patterns toward a conscious partnering process that I call mutuality and partnering. This requires a healthy inner triangle where we can hold the tension of the opposites.

If we use Jack, Anne and their son Nicky from the film *The Doctor*, we can flush out their positive and negative bonding patterns. Jack carries the primary selves of husband and father as 'cool impersonal provider', and his disowned self is his 'vulnerable dependent inner boy'. Inside Anne there are primary selves of wife and mother as 'warm personal caregiver', and her disowned self is her 'vulnerable dependent inner girl'.

Lets assume that when they met, they were in the early romantic stage of their relationship and all these selves were lighting up in a positive bonding pattern. The two lovers had enough novelty to keep interested in each other; clearly there was enough of a connection that they decided to move in together and birth a child. This was a move toward greater security and predictability. They felt safe with each other, and secure routines are established.

What they might not have been fully aware of, however, was that as soon as they had a child together, she became a mother and he became a father. The complexity of their bonding pattern was drastically changing. Their attachment styles and psychological sophistication would determine how well they navigated this evolutionary stage.

Hal and Sidra say this is often the beginning of the end for a couple if they are in an early symbiotic bonding pattern. Unless they understand the psychological dynamics of what is happening to them, both people can be under tremendous stress, and this creates cortisol spikes in their brain and nervous system while taxing their adrenal glands.

As Anne became a mother, her son needed her, so the bond between them increased. However, the inner boy inside her husband could start to feel abandoned at this point. This is a dangerous point for many men. Nicky as an infant had his mother's full attention and breast, but Anne was also the inner mother for Jack's inner boy—and she was also the inner wife to his inner husband. If Jack's inner boy felt abandoned, he may have unconsciously looked for the nourishing breast elsewhere.

In the film Jack flirts with other women and fantasizes about smoking cigarettes again when he is stressed. Tobacco is a fourth chakra addiction used to soothe a broken or blocked heart, and sex can be a second chakra addiction when it is used to pacify our emotions (or we can use ejaculatory release to let off pressure). There are many symbolic oral breast substitutes as supernormal stimuli to soothe our inner wounded children—sugar, ice cream, sucking back bottles of beer and sucking on cigarettes or a joint, to name just a few of them.

When Jack became a father he may have suddenly felt tremendous responsibility to provide for his child for the next twenty-plus years. He may have felt compelled to work more because being a provider is the primary way he had seen love modeled by his father and his father-in-law.

His increase in status makes him feel more powerful, while his vulnerability is buried. He keeps Anne at arm's length. When he tries to hide his vulnerability, Anne ends up carrying it. By not attending to his inner child he projects the need for a mother onto her. Then he judges her for being too 'smothering' and pushes her away even more. We see them becoming estranged and then independent as they journey through the differentiation and individuation stages of their relationship.

It's interesting that Jack develops throat cancer. The throat is the centre of the fifth chakra, the centre for communication, prayer and praise. He hinted that he had a history of smoking cigarettes to deal with his stress and anxiety. We can also see that his communication style was being witty at other people's expense. He was also arrogant and cold at times, signifying a block in his fifth energy centre. It's not surprising that he would develop throat problems. He was caught in separation.

When considering the cause of serious conditions like cancer, it's important to watch out for getting too dogmatic about making a diagnosis. It is helpful to wonder at possible underlying causes for each individual's history.

The more Jack used work to avoid intimacy with Anne, the more she felt abandoned. Neither lover was getting their needs met if they identified exclusively with being parents or workers. Many exhausted parents end up putting time for love making with their spouse at the bottom of their list. If lovemaking happens at all, it is often used as a stress reliever at the end of a busy day.

When we are exhausted, we can overcome our tiredness by getting aroused enough to ejaculate: then collapse in exhaustion. This results in an addictive high, usually followed by a low within minutes, days or weeks.

This kind of lovemaking can become unfulfilling, incestuous sex between an inner child and an inner parent. Her inner daughter may get into pleasing his inner father if she wants an increase in 'allowance'. His inner boy can get into pleasing her inner mother if he wants her approval or soothing. The lovemaking starts to get routine and boring, or perhaps the opposite happens—there are fantasies or affairs to unconsciously get the novelty back in the relationship.

If the couple can learn to hold the opposites within themselves like novelty and security, power and vulnerability, subjective and objective perspectives, love and awareness, provider and caregiver, parent and spouse, they can learn to live more consciously and soulfully.

CHILDREN GETTING CAUGHT IN THE PATTERN

We see Jack and Anne's young son Nicky getting caught in their negative bonding pattern. As Jack is less available to Nicky, he likewise distances from his father. He is learning to repress his vulnerability just like his father does. A negative bonding pattern develops between father and son. He is undergoing his own process of differentiation and individuation.

Nicky has more of a positive bonding pattern with his mother. This usually will become more challenging once he enters his teens. If he tries to individuate from his mother and she is totally identified in the role of mother, he may experience her as smothering like Jack does. Nicky can turn cold toward his mother and reject her just like he has watched his father do.

If he doesn't witness his parents' relationship evolve beyond differentiation and individuation, then this immature pattern will likely continue in later life with his future romantic partners.

STOPPING THE CYCLE

Jack and Anne are caught in a painful midlife crisis as the film unfolds. Fortunately, by the end of the film a midlife awakening process transforms them both. They evolve into the mutually interdependent stage, and as they both begin to integrate their opposites, their relationship as lovers gets back on track, and they start collaborating on parenting and decision-making.

When couples get stuck, it is best to approach healing together, because couple's mentoring and psychotherapy is different than individual psychotherapy. Traditionally, couples counselling has treated the two people as if they were two individual clients. This has had a very poor success rate because the accent was too much on the individual. If each individual individuates, then it might feel like the best solution is to go his or her separate ways.

Hal and Sidra Stone present a radically different model for couples by saying that the relationship itself is the 'Third' perspective. They imagine the relationship as the Teacher, Healer and Guide. This helps each person to orient to this Third, this other perspective. We can learn from this Third perspective what is needed for each partner to heal, transform and evolve to the next stage.

Initially, the facilitator is a temporary stand-in for the Third; however, the couple can be empowered to learn how to access this perspective on their own. They are both needed to tend the mutual garden of their soulful relationship.

Often one partner is self-possessed and might not be receptive to therapy. The other partner often feels lonely and may suggest getting help. The self-possessed partner may be resistant or defensive at the suggestion of therapy.

Sometimes only one partner in a couple is willing to come to therapy and the other person isn't. What I've learned over the years is that there are many ways to work with healing, transformation and soulful evolution—therapy is just one of them. I've met men and women who will do something physical to effect transformation, for example plan, and execute a renovation. In the process of taking a section of their house apart and rebuilding it, they are transforming their home and their psyche at the same time.

If the person coming to therapy is presently in a relationship, the therapist needs to watch out that he or she doesn't take sides too strongly. This can create positive and negative bonding patterns between therapist and client. If the therapist stays in the power seat of good-then-bad parent, the client is forced into good child or rebellious teen, either against their partner, or the therapist.

The deepest resources come from within the client's own heart and soul. The soulful therapist or facilitator hopes to teach their client to fish rather than just give them a momentary break from starvation. If the client learns how to facilitate their own process, then they contact the inner healer within himself or herself and eventually become free of therapy. As they heal and evolve, they can become a healing catalyst for others.

When we learn to see the relationship as the 'Third Presence,' as Teacher, Healer and Guide, we begin a path of soulful relationship. With practice, we foster mutuality and partnering. In the next chapter we turn to the quest for deeper meaning and purpose.

Human beings are not born once and for all on the day their mother's give birth to them, but life obligates them over and over again to give birth to themselves.

—*Gabriel Garcia Marquez*

CHAPTER 6:
THE GIFTS OF SOULFUL MEANING AND PURPOSE

"Every being is intended to be on earth for a certain purpose, and the light of that purpose has been kindled in his or her heart."

—Sadi – 13th Century Sufi Mystic

Six: How can we clear barriers to our inner gifts so we can live with deeper meaning and purpose for vocational vitality?

Do you remember our map for meaning and purpose from the introduction? Here's a reminder:

MAP = TN (True Nature) + EQ (Essential Qualities) + NG (Natural Gifts) – PR (Personality Resistance) + MN (Meaningful Need).

In this chapter we'll look at our Inner Gifts (or Natural Gifts), and continue to explore some of the barriers we need to clear to uncover them for cultivating a soulful life of natural vitality, deep presence, intimacy, meaning and purpose.

The Sufi teacher Sadi taught in the 13th Century that "every being has a certain purpose in life." He suggested that "our purpose has been kindled in our heart." Sufi teacher Hazrat Inayat Khan agrees with Sadi, and adds that our ultimate purpose is to make God a Reality and to "be the truth." What is the heart? By the word *heart*, he isn't speaking of our physical heart, but the "Great Heart."

Hazrat Inayat Khan is referring to "Great Heart" as our True Nature, the Home of our Soul. "Clear Mind," he says, is "the surface of Great Heart, and Great Heart is the depth of Clear Mind." To refer to our Unfolding Soul, he often he often used the term, "God Seed". As we rest in mystery and presence, this divine seed within each of us unfolds and leads us toward our unique destiny of living with deeper meaning and purpose.

In the Christian tradition, an aspect of finding your purpose is to discover what your "Spiritual Gifts" are. Some people are born with the gift of music, or teaching, or craftsmanship, and so forth. Part of our purpose is to give these gifts to others.

In the Jewish Tradition this is referred to as your "Divine Sparks." Michael Meade teaches that each of us has a unique spark. If we project our spark onto the movie or sports star, they burn more brightly. If we only see their brilliance and not our own, we start to feel diminished. This gives our inner gold away.

The First Nations elders also say that each person and creature has a unique purpose. For example, the dog has the gift of loyalty; the cedar tree has the gift of healing; the owl has the gift of wisdom; the butterfly has the gift of transformation. If we dream of a dog, it can mean we are carrying the gift of dog medicine. Perhaps this gift from the dog leads us to find meaning and purpose in being a loyal service provider.

For example, one of my maternal ancestors was called 'Medicine

Fish Woman'. She must have carried this spiritual gift or medicine to be given this spiritual name. Her original Algonquin Midewiwin Tradition (the right path) was also referred to as 'the way of the heart'. In the Midewiwin Tradition, they honour the 'Great Mystery' and the Gifts of the Creator with tobacco, in a sacred ritual. When she was nineteen she embraced the Catholic Tradition as part of her wedding vows to a man from France. In the initiation, she was given the name Marie. Interestingly, the fish is often used as a symbol for Christ.

SOULFUL DIALOGUE

Addictive tendencies in the sixth chakra include hallucinogens and marijuana, according to Anodea Judith. Addictive tendencies can be seen operating in numerous chakras at once. A twenty-eight year old First Nations single mother and nurse that I'll call Sarah, came to see me because she was overweight, feeling exhausted and suffering from Adrenal Fatigue, addictions and relationship challenges. She was exhausted from her imbalanced way of living.

After her shift at the Hospital, Sarah would stop off at a grocery store to pick up groceries along with a reward of sweets like ice cream, chips or cookies. Sometimes she would rip open the bag of chips or cookies and start devouring them right in the car. If she were particularly stressed, she would 'wolf' down the whole bag. To relax, she said she likes to drink wine and smoke marijuana occasionally.

As a nurse she was concerned about health in others, but her own health was getting out of control. Recently she had a scary dream of a bear chasing her. Working with Voice Dialogue again, I interviewed the 'single mother self' and found out that she took her five-year-old son to daycare when she was at work. Her son was getting overweight and she felt guilty about not being able to be a stay-at-home mom to care for him. Even though her son was safely at daycare, she felt like she was on call twenty-four hours a day as a mother and a nurse.

When I asked this self when she first came into Sarah's body as the 'mother self' she said, "When Sarah was only seven years of age, she had to look after her mother and her younger sister. She needed a mother so I came into her life." As the new mother to her mother and sister she became the super responsible caregiver. When I asked where she lived in Sarah's body, she indicated her chest. I asked her, "If you were a major household appliance what appliance would you be?" She laughed and said, "That's easy, a fridge. Everyone can come to me anytime day or night and drink my milk." We came back to the centre to reflect on this self.

Next I facilitated her 'nurse self'. She told me she loved her job in the beginning, but it became more stressful once she had a child to look after as well.

When we came back to the centre position after facilitating each of these selves she felt much lighter and less stressed. We explored how each of these selves requires energy to run, like the fridge working twenty-four hours a day, they are taxing her adrenal glands. We worked energetically to give her some space.

Then I invited her to explore her dream about the bear chasing her. First I interviewed the part of her that was fearful of the bear, and learned that this fear was held in her stomach area. When she starts worrying she eats sweets to soothe herself. As the fearful one, she started sharing her fears of not having enough resources to look after herself and her son. Whenever she tried to confront her former husband around missed alimony payments, he would get angry and sometimes fly into a rage, and so she ended up avoiding dealing with the issue. He seemed resentful that she got custody of their son, and was critical around how she was raising him.

After empathizing with her about how scary this must feel, I invited her to come back to the centre position again. From the centre we worked energetically with the part of her that was afraid so she could relate compassionately with this part of her without becoming it. She began to feel even calmer.

Then I invited her to move over and become the bear in her dream. She was a short woman, but when she stepped into becoming the bear she seemed to become tall and very powerful. As the 'mother' bear she stood right behind Sarah's seat and extended her powerful arms out wide as if to embrace Sarah.

I asked the bear why she had come into Sarah's dream. 'Mama Bear' told me that its role was to protect Sarah, but Sarah was afraid of her power. She was getting exhausted and needed the deep rest associated with hibernation. She was eating junk food as a reward for working so much but it was not healthy. She could benefit from eating a more natural diet of wild salmon and local berries like her ancestors have done for thousands of years.

'Mama Bear' also said that she was trying to be a vegetarian for the wrong reasons. I asked, "What do you mean?" The bear said that she became a vegetarian for intellectual reasons after watching a disturbing documentary, which was noble, but the reasons were not valid. Again I asked, "What do you mean?" and the bear explained that the documentary showed animals living in squalid conditions.

Of course she shouldn't eat those kinds of animals for two reasons. The first is a protest against this kind of treatment of animals, and the second is because the animal isn't healthy. She could however eat animals that were healthy, well treated and came from a natural setting.

'Mama Bear' continued, saying it also helps to show gratitude and to honour the animal that gives its life as a gift so Sarah can have natural vitality.

I asked the bear if there were specific practices Sarah could follow to help her physical health become more vital. The bear suggested she should learn more about her grandmother and her First Nations traditional ways. She could go hiking in the forest, picking berries with her son, or place him with her sister-in-law for support. She could then let go of the mother and nurse roles for a while, and hibernate for rest.

She could also regularly go for a walk or hike with her friend. The bear also said it lived in her shoulders and was really powerful. She needed to learn to growl at her ex to make sure he followed through with the financial support. If she learns to be more playful she won't need to get drunk or high to attract a lover.

After we came back to the centre and reflected on her process she realized how she and her son were using junk food to self soothe just like her mother had. With her new understanding she was breaking the spell.

WISE ADVICE FROM MAMA BEAR, BUTTERFLY & EAGLE

Clients are often amazed at the wisdom they hold within themselves, and the answers their 'disowned selves' can provide. In Sarah's case she was energetically getting burnt out by working twenty-four hours a day identifying with the role of mother and nurse. She learned to put herself last and focus all her care on others to her own detriment. Her adrenal glands were taxed to the limit, and if she didn't correct her course soon she would suffer a collapse to get the rest she needed.

The young vulnerable part of her was terrified, and her inner mother learned to give that part of her treats as rewards to avoid the pain, just like her mother had done when she was little. During our sessions she realized that the sweet junk food was a poor substitute for the loving arms of the mother bear who could set healthy boundaries for her health and relationships.

Sarah's primary identity was to be a responsible caretaker and pleaser. She had learned to please her mother and receive sweet rewards to get her basic needs met if she complied. It worked with her mother, but identifying with this strategy was no longer working for her as an adult.

Her mother was also disconnected from her First Nations Tradition. She wasn't able to be a nurturing presence for Sarah, so Sarah had to please her mother to get the love she needed and in doing so she psychologically became a 'mother to her mother'.

Because she had become good at pleasing others, it was normal that Sarah had gone into nursing. She spent long hours pleasing patients hoping to be appreciated and loved, but her patients were in no position to meet her needs. So she reached out to her substitute inner mother—the reward eater—who would reward her with sweet food.

In a follow-up session I asked her if she had a favourite animal? She said she was fond of eagles. I invited her to move into a position in the room to become the eagle. She moved close to the balcony and looked to the vast blue sky. I asked the eagle to scan the big picture of her life so far and then zoom into the detail that is most important for her now. The eagle said, "To cultivate meaning and purpose at work she needs to stop smoking marijuana. It is clouding her natural vision. It would help to learn a more natural approach for healing herself and her son than what the conventional medical system teaches."

As she transformed and learned to balance the opposites within her, she started dreaming of butterflies, and often noticed them on her hikes. She intuitively sensed they were leading her from survival to a more soulful way of being as she learned to walk the beauty way of her ancestors. She also felt more connected to nature.

By working with her 'disowned selves' she learned that she needed to integrate her 'Mama Bear,' 'Eagle' and 'Butterfly' as allies from the wisdom of her instinctual body. They connect her to the soul of the world, and give her perspective and wisdom around her process so she could learn to take care of herself and others in a healthy way. Over time she found more meaning and purpose by integrating the traditional wisdom of her ancestors. She also began to study Functional Medicine to learn a more integrative approach to healthcare that explores root causes of disease. In this way she learned to integrate the subjective truth of indigenous wisdom and objective truth of medical science.

Sarah learned that she needed to balance caring for herself with caring for others. As she stopped managing her stress unconsciously with addictive tendencies and cooked healthier meals for herself and her son, they both lost weight and their symptoms disappeared. She also began to understand that when she identified with her inner mother to look after her former partner's inner boy, this contributed to their disconnection and sexual problems. When she understood how relationships are meant to evolve through stages of maturation she could see how their relationship didn't survive the differentiation and individuation stages. Eventually she joined a shamanic journey circle and learned the art of meaningful healing and ritual. Integrating the message from her symptom and dream helped her to heal her barriers to transforming and evolving soulfully in her health, relationships and vocation.

In the film *The Doctor*, Jack had the gift of healing but needed to clear some barriers of personality resistance to become a true healer. The same was true for Sarah.

The Heart in alchemy is often symbolically referred to as the philosopher's stone—this is the place where we can reconcile and integrate the opposites. There is a difference between having a job or career as a doctor or nurse, and it becoming your calling or vocation. In order to be a true healer, one must be able to hold and embrace the opposites of care and clarity, subjective truth and objective truth, love and wisdom, personal energy and impersonal energy, power and vulnerability and so on.

Then your vocation becomes your sacred calling and you become a healing presence in whatever the calling is. You become a representative for Reality—the bridge for integrating subjective Mystery and objective Science.

Isaac found the Inner Treasure within his Heart, sent the ruby (his Heart) to the captain of the guards in gratitude (embraced his inner protector and his vulnerability) and was transforming his house (his body) into a temple to celebrate the spirit of guidance that comes through his psyche and dreams.

THE SOUL'S CODE

If you remember, one of my first mentors early on in midlife was James Hillman whom I met back in 1989. He wrote a transformational book called *The Soul's Code*, which essentially deals with the idea that each infant is born with unique gifts.

Certainly, we have the genetic influences of both parents, but there is also something unique, and that something unique he calls *the soul's code*.

Hillman also refers to it as "the acorn myth"—namely, within every acorn is a blueprint of a mighty oak tree. He says, "The acorn myth is a worldwide myth that says that the roots of the soul are in the heavens, and the human grows downward into life.

"A little child enters the world as a stranger, and brings a special gift into the world. The task of life is to grow down into this world."

"The perspective is that we came to earth as a stranger and slowly, as we mature, grow into the world, take part in its duties and pleasures, and become more involved and attached."

This essential concept is common in Africa and many other cultures around the world. Earlier I spoke of Malidoma Patrice Somé, the Dagara Shaman from Africa and how his culture interviews the fetus to discover what Natural Gifts the fetus is carrying. The Dagara then build a shrine to celebrate this incoming child and to remind them of the innate gifts he or she carries. These gifts determine the person's life purpose.

In the First Nations vision quest, there is a ritual of initiation for youth coming of age. The youth sometimes will make a pilgrimage to the sacred mountain and pray for a dream or vision. During the vision quest, if the initiate dreamed of an animal, this would be considered part of their sacred medicine. Working with this medicine would introduce them to their inner gifts and purpose.

Sarah was finding her spiritual medicine in her dreams, in the cocoon of my office, in her journey circle and on her hikes in the forest. She was becoming a modern and traditional 'medicine woman.'

If she hadn't reached out for support, then her son's health might have gotten worse and he may have become a youth at risk. His symptoms and her love for him called her into action to heal transform and evolve soulfully.

YOUTH AT RISK

Malidoma Some once said something that I'll never forget, about how his tribe works with youth. "It takes a whole village to raise a child." Using a modern metaphor, he said that when they have, what we would call a 'youth at risk,' they imagine that the youth is like a telephone that is ringing. He said, "In our culture, we don't silence the telephone; we pick it up to find out what the message from spirit is."

"The youth is dancing a rhythm not their own, so we bring in a rhythm specialist; a shaman. The shaman dances into the chaos with the youth until they have learned what the message is, and then they dance the youth back to their natural rhythm."

It turns out that the message from spirit is that the whole village is off track when youth are not being initiated into their gifts and life purpose. The village is not whole. The elders need to correct the situation in the village.

The message is coming through a particular youth because he or she is more sensitive than the older people and will pick up a disturbance in the energetic field of the village. This youth is like a receiver that picks up signals, but is not skilled enough to decipher the message. The youth then goes into apprenticeship with this shaman to learn the healing arts in order to interpret the messages from spirit as a healer.

There are different initiation rituals for various traditions and unique ones for boys and girls. Ancient stories often contain examples of initiatory ritual.

SPIRIT IN THE BOTTLE

One of my favourite stories from the Grimm's Brothers about discovering your unique gifts and genius for meaning and purpose is called The Spirit in the Bottle. I often tell it at soulful men's gatherings when we look at our addictive tendencies and wonder about the creative potential that we have bottled up.

It goes something like this:

Once upon a time, in a vast forest, there was a hut. In the hut there lived a woodcutter with his son.

Each day the woodcutter would go into the forest and chop down trees, and that's how they made their meager living. He dreamed of a better life for his son so he saved up what little money he could for his son's education.

Eventually, he sent his son off to university to get an education. The son was away for quite some time, and he was a good student, he did well in his studies and his teacher's praised him. But eventually the father's money ran out, and he was only half way through his education.

He journeyed back to the hut of his father, and his father asked, "Why have you come home? Did you finish your education?" The student said, "I'm sorry father, but your money ran out and school costs money, and when the money runs out, that's when the education stops!"

And his father said, "Well I don't know what I'm going to do with you. What can you do with only half of an education?" and the student said, "Not much, really. These days you really need a complete education to get a job. How about I help you in the forest, cutting wood?"

His father said, "You're not cut out for that—you've been sitting behind a desk all these years, you wouldn't be able to handle it. It's hard work. This is man's work!"

The son responded: "I could give it a try. It feels good to be back in the forest!"

His father said, "Well, I don't have much book learning, and I'm not very smart, but one thing I do know is we only have one axe." The student said, "Well, what about the neighbour, don't they have a spare axe? I could go check?" The father said, "Well, yeah, I think they might."

So the student went over and checked with their neighbour, and sure enough, he had a spare axe. He had just bought a new one and kept the old one as a spare, just in case. The student brought the axe back to the hut.

When he came back home, he saw that his father had cooked a meager dinner for them because there wasn't much money for food left. Then they both went to bed hungry that night. The next morning the father got up early because he was used to doing a long day's work.

The student had gotten used to sleeping in. After a while, his father felt impatient waiting for his son. He started banging around trying to make some noise that would awaken his son. It didn't look like his son was going to wake up, so he yelled out, "Hey you, Lazy-Bones, it's time to get up to go to work!"

His son finally crawled out of bed feeling groggy. They grabbed a quick bite to eat and then headed down the path into the forest. It was still dark and there were some stars out, even though the night was almost over. The student felt excited to be home, to be back in the forest and breathing the fresh, cool air of the early morning. They made their way deeper and deeper into the forest until finally they came to a clearing where the father had been previously working.

The father grabbed his axe, and he took a swing into the first tree. The student took his axe, and did the same, and they went on this way, chopping trees side by side all morning. The son was doing pretty well; he was young, pretty fit, and had energy. The father would look over occasionally and kind of nod his head approvingly.

They went on this way all morning until high noon. At noon the sun was at the highest point in the sky and it started to get hot. So the father said, "It's time for a break and lunch."

They sat down, and the father prepared a meager meal. He said, "It's time to get some rest." And the son said, "You rest father. For me, I want to go for a little walk and look for bird's nests." The father said, "Don't be a fool, you should rest, especially in the hot time of the day because we've got a long day ahead of us!"

The son said, "You rest, father, I want to go and explore the forest." The father started muttering under his breath, "What good does an education do you, if you don't even have any common sense!"

The son headed off into the forest, and he felt thrilled. He noticed the bird's chirping and looked up into the greenery for bird's nests. He was enjoying seeing the wild flowers and the mushrooms. He was so glad to be back in the forest again and recalled fond times as a boy. He headed deeper and deeper into the forest until eventually he saw a huge tree up ahead of him. It looked dark, like a big angry-looking oak tree. He felt drawn to the tree, and when he came near he suddenly heard a strange sound.

It seemed to be coming from the earth, below the tree. He heard it clearly this time: "Let me out, let me out!" He couldn't see anything but as he got closer to the ground, he heard it again—"Let me out, let me out!"— So he started digging at the roots of the tree.

"Who are you?" he cried out. The voice answered, "I'm in among the roots of the branches. Let me out. Let me out!"

The student dug among the roots until he found a dirty looking glass bottle. When he held it up to the light, he saw inside a misshapen being that looked like a frog, and sure enough, it jumped up and down, and cried, "Let me out. Let me out!" What would you do? Suspecting no harm, the student pulled the cork out of the bottle.

All of a sudden a spirit came out and began to grow into a big giant, half the size of the tree. Then the spirit growled in a thundering voice, "Do you know what your reward will be for letting me out?" The student said fearlessly, "No, how could I?" Then the spirit said, "I'll tell you! I'm going to snap your head off and separate your neck from your shoulders! That's your reward!"

The student was surprised and said, "You should have told me that before. I wouldn't have let you out of the bottle. But I'll be keeping my head on my shoulders. You'll have to consult with many others before I let you tamper with my neck." The spirit said, "More people indeed! You've earned your reward and you shall have it. Why do you think they shut me up in here in the first place, out of kindness? They did it as a punishment, for I am the mighty Mercurius. When someone sets me free I vowed to snap their neck."

"Not so fast," the student said, "I don't believe you are the same little being that was in that bottle. Prove to me that you are that same one and then I'll believe you and you can do what you want with me." And the spirit laughed haughtily and said, "Nothing could be simpler!" Then the spirit turned his body into wispy smoke and shrank to the size he began with and crawled back into the bottle.

Of course the son quickly grabbed the cork and plugged it back into the bottle and then threw it back under the roots of the oak tree.

Then he heard the spirit crying out again, "Please let me out, let me out. Please, let me out!" And the student said, "No, you can't fool me twice, why should I? You threatened my life! When someone threatens my life I don't let him go so easily."

And the spirit said, "Please, if you let me out, I promise, I'll give you a great reward; enough to last for the rest of your life."

And the son thought, "Well, I don't think I can trust this spirit, but he's not very smart and can't hurt me. I tricked him once, and I can probably trick him again."

So he reached down for the bottle, popped the cork, and the spirit came out again, and the student said, "Okay, where is my reward?" And the genie handed him a cloth.

The student said, "A cloth? What kind of reward is this?" and the genie said, "This isn't any ordinary cloth. If you touch one end of this cloth to any wound it will heal, and if you rub the other end on anything made of iron or steel it will turn instantly to silver!"

And the student said, "I don't know if I can trust you, just a minute." So he made a gash in the tree with his axe. Then he rubbed the cloth to the gash and the tree was healed instantly. He was amazed, he said, "Ok, now we can part!" He thanked the spirit for the gift, and the spirit thanked the student for setting him free. The spirit went on his way, and the student went back toward his father.

Once he got back to the clearing his father said, "Where have you been all this time? It's getting late and you've forgotten there's work to be done." His son said, "Don't worry father, I'll catch up. I'll have that tree felled in no time!"

He picked up his axe, and it was a bit dirty, so he cleaned it with the cloth. In the shadows, he couldn't see, but when he did that, it turned to silver. So when he hit the tree with the axe it twisted out of shape and the blade bent.

Then the father got angry and started criticizing his son, he said, "You idiot. We didn't have enough money to begin with! You take off in the forest; you only do half a day's work, and now you ruin the neighbour's axe! How are we going to pay for this axe? Sit down and keep quiet. I don't want to hear another word from you!"

The son hung his head in shame and sat there, and waited all afternoon watching his father work. The father muttered under his breath the whole time.

After a while the son started to get cold and hungry. His father worked later than usual trying to make up for lost time. Eventually, the son pleaded with his father to go back home and the father said sarcastically, "I at least finish something that I start! You can go home if you like but I have work to do!"

And his son went quiet again for a while and eventually his stomach started grumbling, and he got very hungry, so he pleaded with his father again and said, "Please father, I've never been in this part of the woods before and if I try to make my way back in the dark, I'll get lost." Eventually he convinced his father to make his way back home. All the way back home his father was still angry and didn't talk to his son.

When they got home the woodcutter told his son to go to town the next day to sell the ruined axe for whatever he could get for it. The next day the son took the axe into town to visit the goldsmith, who tested it and weighed it on his scales and said, "It's worth a lot of money but I don't have that much on hand." The son realized that when he rubbed the axe it turned to silver and he said, "Give me what you have and you can owe me the rest."

The goldsmith gave him a lot of money for those times. It was more money than the son had ever seen, or his father had ever seen. He thanked the goldsmith and made his way back home.

When he got home, his father muttered, "What took you so long?" So the student told his father the whole story about the axe, the goldsmith, the spirit, and his whole adventure.

His father was suspicious until his son reached into his pocket and took out half of his money to give it to his father and he said, "Father I want you to have a larger house and I want you to enjoy a life of ease now!" His father gratefully accepted. His new house was built, and his father was wealthy enough to retire in ease.

Then the student took the rest of his money and went back to university and completed his education, his second education. He eventually became a respected doctor.

Anywhere he went where someone had a wound, he would touch the poultice to the wound and it would heal. He also earned money; he earned the silver for his livelihood from being a healer.

WHAT DO STORIES AND MYTHS MEAN TO US TODAY?

That spirit in the bottle—that genie—in ancient times was called Mercurius. He is one of the Greek gods that was often called 'the god of the marketplace'. The exchange between our gifts and talents and earning a living is how our soulful vocation manifests in the world. Mercurius was often called 'the god of the pickpocket', too, because he was a trickster.

Mercury, the god, was the winged messenger in the Roman Pantheon, but before that, in the Greek Pantheon his name was also Hermes, guide of souls. Then there was Hermes Trismegistus, who was a master alchemist—and turning lead into gold was the ancient art of the alchemists.

In psychotherapy, this principle can be seen in working with the basic pattern or prima material of these heavy feelings as the leaden stage of consciousness. How do we transform these patterns into the gold of receiving our Inner Treasure? The symbol for Mercurius is depicted as two serpents with wings intertwining and meeting at the top of the staff. This staff belongs to Mercurius, and it's called the caduceus. Some say that where the serpents intertwine across the spine is where the seven energy centres of the body are located.

The student in the *Spirit in the Bottle* story has wandered deep into the forest and arrived at the world tree; he has listened to what is bottled up within him, and is learning the alchemy of transforming his 'leaden state' into the gold of healing. He receives the Inner Treasure in the form of a magical cloth or poultice from the genie and is discovering its healing abilities; he is awakening to the potential of his unique genius and inner gifts. Thus begins the second half of his education.

Michael Meade in *Fate And Destiny—The Two Agreements Of The Soul*, speaks about our first and second agreements. Our first agreement in life is to deliver our gifts, and the second agreements are all the other agreements life requires of us. The first agreement to give our gifts is primary if we are to live a soulful life of meaning and purpose. The first half of our education is needed to make a living and survive in the world. The second half of our education is about uncovering our unique genius and gifts, then giving them to the world. We might need to literally go back to school in later life in order to follow a calling rather than just have a job.

In the Half Boy story that I told earlier, the boy was only 'half' because he had not yet undergone the ritual of initiation to awaken his Inner Treasure as Gifts. When he wrestled with what was missing in himself, he discovered his gifts and purpose so could walk as a whole person. He wobbled for a while because he still needed recognition by the elder and by the whole village.

Our fictional characters have survived harrowing ordeals and have received the boon from their journey. However, they still might need to clear barriers to giving their inner gifts to a meaningful need in order to live a soulful life with deeper meaning and purpose.

The spirit in the bottle is an important story for me because the 'spirit in the bottle' at the base of my own family tree for many generations was alcohol. Once I got help to heal my addictive tendencies, the wound became a womb and started to birth some of my gifts. Then I followed the call to complete the second half of my education, becoming a 'wounded healer' and found meaning and purpose in helping others who are wounded or yearn for deeper meaning and purpose.

LEARNING FROM ANCIENT WISDOM

I remember being at a men's retreat once with Malidoma Somé where he shared about his being initiated as a young man into his African Tradition. He said that the Dagara people have an unbroken tradition that goes way back in time. Like I mentioned before, when a woman becomes pregnant in their tradition, the Shaman puts her under a kind of hypnosis and interviews the fetus to find out what gifts the child will be bringing into the village. This information is kept until the youth is ready to undergo initiation into adulthood.

In their cosmology, a person is also related to a particular element in the Dagara medicine wheel. Each element—earth, water, fire, mineral and nature—has particular gifts associated with it that determines your life purpose.

For example, Malidoma was born into the water element so he is a member of the water clan. Some of the gifts of the water clan are around healing, purification and mediation. Part of Malidoma's life purpose is therefore helping modern people to grieve their losses and to heal. The Dagara Tradition has a profound cosmology that intimately connects one with the sacred immanence within the natural world.

At this retreat, Malidoma did a divination for each of us and the divination placed me in the mineral clan. The people in the mineral clan are often storytellers and writers. They are passionate about helping others to remember their Natural Gifts for living a soulful life of meaning and purpose.

One Spring, Malidoma led another retreat at the First Nations Native Friendship Centre in Vancouver. We felt blessed to be allowed to use their beautiful cedar sanctuary for our mineral ritual to honour our ancestors. At a certain point Malidoma asked me, and my friend Michael, to be temporary priests of the mineral clan to organize building a mineral shrine.

I noticed that in the centre of the room was a First Nations Medicine Wheel painted on the floor. I instantly had an intuitive vision that I later shared with Malidoma. What I saw was that a Dagara Medicine Wheel could be temporarily overlaid on top of the First Nations Medicine Wheel as a shrine to honour the friendship of these two great indigenous traditions. He nodded his approval and we gathered the mineral clan members together to create a beautiful shrine.

It's an incredible experience working with others who are in your own clan. There is a deep sense of communication and united purpose. I had explored other clans in other retreats with Malidoma, but felt uneasy in all but the water and mineral clans. Brian was in the water clan too, and we are both engaged in healing. My birth sign is in water through Cancer. The mineral clan really resonates with me though because I'm drawn to stones, shells, stories and writing. Since the stories I'm attracted to are mostly healing stories, I could imagine my elemental typology as mineral water!

At one point Malidoma said he was encouraged to see men's groups and women's groups coming together to explore how to do ritual together. He said that we cannot go backwards and become tribal people again, but we each have an indigenous soul and we can remember how to do appropriate ritual for our time and place. He said the information is written in our bones.

That really rang true for me! I asked him if there were problems with alcohol in his village. He said, "At one time alcohol was only used for ritual but it is becoming a problem for some of his people too."

Modernity is creeping into his village and negatively impacting their youth and ancient way of life.

I can see how the supernormal allurement of all the trinkets that modern culture has to offer, could capture the indigenous imagination if they are not really grounded in their Tradition.

FIREWATER REVISITED

For another one of Malidoma's ancestor rituals we met at the Billy Bishop Legion in Kitsilano, Vancouver. The room we used was upstairs and the walls were plastered with pictures of military personnel from the Second World War. Downstairs we could hear the raucous sounds of the patrons drinking 'spirits' (firewater) in the bar below.

It seemed like a strange place to have our ritual, but then I realized it was perfect. I had brought pictures of some of my ancestors for the fire shrine and placed pictures of my military father and grandfather on the other side of the flames. Then as the drums sounded I poured out a lifetime of grief in their direction. It was an incredible purging.

Forty of us then made a procession to Kitsilano beach and began preparation for a water ritual. We built shrines to each of the four directions and one in the centre for earth. Those of us in the mineral clan created a beautiful mineral heart on the beach consisting of shells, stones and bones for our shrine. As nighttime fell, we placed candles all around the edges and in the centre to create a fiery mineral heart on the beach. At this shrine of remembrance, we invited each person to remember who he or she really is, and what their Inner Gifts are for living soulfully with deep meaning and purpose.

I had brought some tobacco and offered it to the fire shrine where the pictures of my ancestors were now resting. This gesture was to honour tobacco again as a sacred gift from the Creator, and to pray to heal my ancestors and myself from misusing this ritual substance. If you remember, my father died of lung cancer; he drank alcohol and smoked heavily until his last moments. His father had also become a smoker and alcoholic. His mother 'smoked herself to death'.

Then I took out a mickey of whiskey—my father's favourite spirit. For the first time since I was thirty-five, I filled my mouth with whiskey, but instead of swallowing it, I sprayed it out of my mouth onto the fire shrine and the fire flared up and crackled in appreciation of my offer. I again prayed for forgiveness for all the ways my family and I have misused this ritual substance. I poured the rest of the alcohol onto the ground and remembered that while Jesus was on the cross being crucified, his blood ran into the ground. This Earth is sacred ground! This wine, this blood, these spirits, now returns to the earth from which they came. The spirit in the bottle has been freed from my life and from my ancestors. I forgive us all!

Many of us felt called to disrobe and enter the cool waters of English Bay. The members of the water clan courageously assisted us to surrender to the watery deaths while praying for the water to heal and purify us. A curious seal poked its nose out of the water to see what was going on. After wrestling with the hungry ghost of the past, I staggered out of the water like the half boy, now feeling wobbly in my new-found wholeness.

I was naked and shivering, and the nurturing members of the earth clan assisted me to dress and prepare for the last leg of the journey home. Arriving at the entrance of the earth shrine, a beautiful African goddess greeted me with a warm hug and then I was buried in the womb of mother earth. Welcome Home to the place of belonging! People in the earth clan often have the nurturing gift of hospitality.

This transformational ritual was very potent for me. I have met many people in my work as a mentor and psychotherapist who are wrestling with their addictive tendencies. They try to quit drinking with their will power alone and then they end up smoking more, drinking more coffee and binge eating, or they quit smoking and start inhaling donuts. Knowing about the research in supernormal stimuli and how our instinctual brain is hardwired for craving reduces judgment.

Remember the Flying Boy story and the Icarus myth? Today we see many highly imaginative young people, but they're not very grounded. They tend to fly upward for a vision, but they're lacking mentors and elders for the return journey into soulful expression, so they pull up their roots. They need a healthy root system to their tree so they can spread their branches wide, and give the fruit of their Inner Treasure as Gifts.

Youth in isolation are extremely vulnerable if they have parents or caregivers with strong addictive tendencies. So youth need mentors to honour the vertical dimension for inspiration, and then to navigate the meaningful and purposeful descent into creativity.

The addictive tendencies in the sixth chakra are hallucinogens and marijuana. Instead of receiving a clear vision from our third eye of what our inner gifts and purpose is, we can get trapped in fantasy by these supernormal allurements, which are just pale imitations of the real thing.

In my experience Jung was right—there is a spiritual or soul dimension to addiction. Connecting with Self, Soul, Spirit, Mystery, and Nature is needed to heal a spiritual illness. My First Nations ancestors suffered terribly from the diseases brought by my European ancestors—Smallpox, Typhoid, alcoholism and aggressive domination. My European ancestors suffered terribly from their misuse of alcohol, tobacco, caffeine, sugar, drugs and other supernormal stimuli. It's time for deep healing, respect, reconciliation and peace. We need to bring the best practices of Spirituality and Science together for healing our mutual addictive tendencies.

MORE FORMS OF TYPOLOGY

Typology is an important place to continue exploring what your unique purpose is. The Sufis are thought to be the originators of the Enneagram, an archetypal symbol with nine points to it. Some spiritual directors, therapists and coaches use it to help their clients to discover which of the nine Enneagram types they are dominant in. Each of the nine types has particular strengths to integrate and barriers to overcome.

In their book *The Wisdom of the Enneagram*, authors Riso & Hudson bring more depth to each type by articulating nine levels to each type as well. For example, someone could test as an Enneagram type One, the Perfectionist or Reformer and then see which of the nine levels of Type One they are presently at—the range is from healthy to unhealthy for each type.

I find it to be a useful tool for some people, and there are many books about the Enneagram that cover just about every area of one's life. One author, Sandra Maitri, author of *Spiritual Dimensions of the Enneagram* refers to the nine types as the "Nine Faces of the Soul."

DANCE OF THE FOUR QUARTERS

Another way to work with your Personality Resistance is through integrating the archetypes of the Self. Integrating the four archetypes of the mature masculine and feminine—king/queen, warrior, magician, and lover—can be potent.

Imagine a pyramid with four sides. Each side forms a triangle. At the top of the triangle all the four points converge for the integration of the four archetypes in any person. So a mature queen is also a warrior, magician and lover. A mature king or chief is also a warrior, magician and lover.

Robert Moore and Douglas Gillette have a series of fine books on these four archetypes by the same name. Each of the four archetypes has its own triangle on the pyramid. The top point is the ideal point and the two bottom corners are the thesis and antithesis, or what Moore and Gillette call the bi-polar shadow. Like in Voice Dialogue, the centre is the aware ego process.

The lover triangle has the archetypal lover ideal at the apex, and the bipolar shadow of the addicted lover on one of the bottom corners, and the impotent lover on the other side. The aware ego process can be seen like an energy dancer in the centre that faces this direction and can draw from the lover archetype above while keeping both feet on the ground. We need to assess whether we are getting too polarized by leaning toward the addicted lover, or are leaning toward the impotent lover. We see the addicted lover in our addictive tendencies.

The king/queen triangle has the archetypal king or queen ideal at the apex, the bipolar shadow of the tyrant on one bottom corner, and the weakling on the other side. As the dynamic juggler in the centre, we face this direction and can draw from the king or queen archetype above while keeping both feet on the ground. Again, we need to assess whether we are getting too polarized by leaning toward the tyrant or the weakling.

The Magician or Shaman triangle similarly has the archetypal Magician ideal at the apex, and the bipolar shadow of the 'Detached Manipulator' on one bottom corner and the 'Denying One' on the other side. As the orchestra leader in the centre we face this direction and can draw from the Magician archetype above while keeping both feet on the ground. We need to assess whether we are getting too polarized by leaning toward the Detached Manipulator or the Denying One.

The Warrior triangle has the archetypal Warrior ideal at the apex, and the bipolar shadow of the Sadist on one bottom corner and the Masochist on the other side. As the aware ego process in the centre, we face this direction and can draw from the Warrior above while keeping both feet on the ground. We need to assess whether we are getting too polarized by leaning toward the Sadist or the Masochist.

Moore and Gillette posit that for wholeness we can put two pyramids base-to-base to form a diamond with the King at one end and the Queen at the other. Inside the man is the archetypal Queen or Anima, the partner to his inner King. Inside the woman is the archetypal King or Animus, the partner to her inner Queen.

Sidra Stone, PH.D has written an important book for women's individuation called *The Shadow King—The Invisible Force That Holds Women Back*. In the book she reveals how to transform the Inner Patriarch from an unseen enemy to a powerful ally, enabling each woman to claim her full and unique feminine power.

As the seasoned energy dancer in the centre we can dance with all these potent energies. The more we practice dancing with our personality resistance from the centre the more we heal, transform and evolve our aware ego process.

TRANSFORMING THE NEGATIVE TRIANGLE: PERFECTIONIST, INNER CRITIC & PUSHER

Often, the linchpin to our personality resistance is what I call the negative triangle. Picture a triangle with vulnerability being squashed underneath. On one side we have perfectionism or the inner perfectionist; at the top we have inner criticism or the inner critic; and on the other side we have the 'pushing' or inner pusher. The negative triangle becomes the Bermuda Triangle when we get lost in this pattern.

It gets entrenched within when we avoid feeling what we perceive as weak—inadequate, unlovable, not good enough, 'There is something wrong with me,' or 'I am a failure,' and so on. Our inner perfectionist sets the bar high so we can be an achiever or self-improver and be seen as a winner or good enough or lovable.

Then the critic whispers in our ear, "It's not good enough!" So our pusher tries harder. Our perfectionist then raises the bar higher. Our critic says it's still not good enough. You get the picture! It's only leading us to chaos and collapse.

This vicious circle is driving many people these days. It often results in unusual symptoms and addictive tendencies to manage them. Remember Isaac's Dream? If he had agreed with his inner critic or his inner doubter or the outer judges, he would never have left home and followed his dream of uncovering his Inner Treasure. It helps to listen to and acknowledge our critical or doubting voices but not to identify with them.

Part of the problem comes from living in a culture that worships the 'special one'. Hollywood is the expert in shaping our notions of this. We can get trapped in either thinking we are special or less than ordinary.

If we identify with special, like Icarus we fly straight to the sun and have nowhere to go but down into the sea of depression. If we identify with being less than ordinary then we'll be too wounded to uncover our unique gifts for meaning and purpose.

Remembering our triangle again, if we place ordinary at one corner and unique at the other corner with awareness at the top, we can acknowledge that we are ordinary in a very human sense but we are also unique. Each person is both!

THE GIFT OF DREAMWORK

Remember the dream about the busy professional in chapter three who was speeding down the freeway in a fast car? At first it feels thrilling, but as the speed increased, he worried about going too fast and tried to apply the brakes. He panicked because there were no brakes! He 'woke' up in a sweat, then realized that it was only a dream… but jumped out of bed, inhaled some strong coffee and raced onto the freeway of life.

Usually, I see busy people like this right after their crash occurs. It can be a literal or metaphorical accident—in fact it may take a few 'accidents' to get their attention! The crash might be a burnout. In his case the dream was showing his personality resistance to slowing down and living in balance.

It's the pesky Bermuda triangle syndrome again. This professional fears failure, so he ramps up his inner perfectionist. Again the inner critic says whatever they are doing is never good enough—even if they received that promotion—so the pusher pushes harder.

Many professionals are starting to crash with conditions described as burnout, Chronic Fatigue or Adrenal Fatigue. Like many mothers who are on the job all the time parenting their children, busy professionals no longer leave work at the office. The cell phone and portable office can travel anywhere they go!

We can use Voice Dialogue to work through the negative triangle of personality resistance. Imagine four triangles, with awareness at the top of each. In the first triangle we place the busy professional self or any primary self like mother in the power corner and on the opposite corner we place vulnerability. On the second triangle we place the inner critic in the power corner and on the opposite side we place vulnerability. On the third triangle we place the perfectionist in the power side and vulnerability opposite it. For the fourth triangle we place the pusher in the power side and vulnerability opposite that.

Remember that awareness is like the neutral lamp that lights up our stage. It doesn't take sides but just provides needed illumination. Now we can clearly see all five of the main characters. There is the busy professional, the inner critic, the inner perfectionist, the inner pusher and our inner child who is enlisting these selves to protect it and try to get its needs met.

Once we honour these selves and then consciously address the vulnerability underneath with our energy dancer in the centre, we can listen to what our inner child really needs and attend to these needs in a healthy way. Then the chaos rebalances for form and flow. We became rigid to protect our vulnerability. As our rigidity softens under the light of awareness, then our vulnerability can flow. We now have choice between the gas pedal and the brake. We are in control at the wheel of our life again and have choice around when it is time for activity and time for rest. Our inner perfectionist can be transformed into the voice of discernment, the inner perfectionist can set reasonable goals for evolving and our inner pusher can give us the needed energy to accomplish them.

THE ACORN'S SHELL

We could say that the acorn's shell is a metaphor for the rigid personality structure that protects the acorn from its fall to the ground from its previous home of being attached to the 'world tree.' The shell protects the vulnerability and essential blueprint inside, as the acorn is blown around on the ground by the winds of change.

At a certain point however, the shell needs to be cracked open for the acorn's blueprint or soul's code (other names are psychic fingerprint or God Seed) to unfold and root itself into the Ground of Being.

The unfolding soul sends its roots down into the ground first. Only when it is firmly rooted will a tiny shoot start to emerge and burst forth from the ground.

There are these two great directions happening simultaneously—

descent into the darkness of fertile soil for soul, and ascent toward the light for spirit. A healthy plant is neither all roots nor all shoots, but needs both.

To journey on the vertical plane we need roots and shoots. We need to deepen into soulfulness and reach upward for the clarity and light of spirit. We need to descend into the lower world and ascend into the upper world while keeping firmly rooted here, in this place.

If we come back to our image of our transformational cross again, there is the vertical plane and the horizontal plane.

If we transpose that onto a tree, we see the vertical is rooted at the bottom in the earth, receiving nourishment from the water underground, and the branches reach upward to the sky for the nourishment of light and rain.

MEANING AND PURPOSE, MUTUALITY AND PARTNERING

At the age of forty-nine, in 2003, I was living contentedly with my life partner, Sue, practicing mutuality and partnering. My private practice as a mentor and psychotherapist was getting established, and I was still a member of the men's group and co-leading soulful men's retreats. I also became the Centre Coordinator for a Sufi spiritual group and led meditation classes there.

In chapter seven we will explore giving our gifts to a meaningful need in the world for cultivating soulful living.

CHAPTER 7: SOUL OF THE WORLD: LIVING THE SOULFUL LIFE

Nature is the one sacred manuscript out of which all the others have been inspired.

—Hazrat Inayat Khan

All religions, arts, and sciences are branches of the same tree.

—Albert Einstein

Never doubt that a small group of thoughtful, committed citizens can change the world, indeed it's the only thing that ever has.

—Margaret Mead

Seven: How can we clear barriers in our thinking so we can heal, transform and evolve soulfully?

We have come a long way on our journey. If we revisit our maturation awakening path (MAP), the seventh phase is about contributing to the Soul of the World, thereby living a Soulful Life. In the first couple of chapters we looked at the Inner World of the Psyche. In chapters four and five we rested in the Home of the Soul, mystery and presence and cultivated soulful relationships through mutuality and partnering. In chapter six we began unfolding our Soul and its Gifts of Inner Treasure.

In the introduction we learned that for deep meaning and purpose (MAP) we need to give our Natural Gifts (NG) to a Meaningful Need (MN) that we see in the world. If we steward our gifts by giving them to a meaningful need in the world, the Soul of the World is increased and we cultivate a soulful life.

In the seventh stage we take a greater perspective on our life and the world. Can you imagine climbing a mountain and seeing the entirety of your life so far? Or if you were an eagle soaring above your life and your home, seeing the larger perspective and honing in on the essential details that you really need to be looking at? What are the inner gifts you were born with or that have emerged over your lifetime?

When you give your gifts to a meaningful need, then you're really participating in making the world a more soulful place and you're living a soulful life. It's no longer an egocentric 'caterpillar life' of mindless consumption. You have become, symbolically, the butterfly with its beautiful wings whose journey is about pollinating, giving your gifts to a meaningful need and spreading more beauty in the world.

The Buddhist scholar Howard Thurman suggests, "Don't ask what the world needs. Ask what makes you come alive, and go do it. Because what the world needs are people who have come alive!"

Our meaningful need might be different at each life stage. In the magic and play of childhood the boy who finds the golden key in the forest is meeting his meaningful need for discovering his naturalness in connection to nature. Without play in a natural setting he may start to suffer the symptoms of 'nature deficit disorder' and lose his natural wildness and become overly domesticated, while objectifying nature.

Regardless of what biological age we are, when we are in our youth, developing mastery and proactivity might mean completing the second half of our education to keep our first agreement, like the son does in 'Spirit in the Bottle' story. When he gives his Inner Treasure as a Gift of healing to his patients in his vocation as a doctor, then he is living a soulful life of meaning and purpose.

To enter mature adulthood, we are called to rest in mystery and presence and hunt for deeper meaning and purpose through our midlife awakening process.

At the end of the film *The Doctor*, Jack is seen living with meaning and purpose as he balances personal and impersonal energies to become caring and clear as a skillful healer with heart. His work becomes his vocation or calling. We see him serving mystery and presence while practicing mutuality and partnering as he mentors his apprentices in the art of compassionate and skillful care. By giving his Natural Gift (NG) of healing to a meaningful need (MN) seen in his patients, he becomes a Doctor who is a Healer.

His wife Anne is also discovering meaning and purpose by balancing her personal and impersonal energies so she is caring and clear. She is stewarding mystery and presence and practicing mutuality and partnering through her loving parenting, by finding understanding and forgiveness for Jack's midlife passage, and through her selfless community work.

Some of our cutting-edge filmmakers are the new mythmakers of our time and are reflecting back to us crucial messages around how out of balance we have become. Directors like James Cameron use both fictional subjective narratives as metaphors to wake us up, and cutting edge factual documentaries, designed to do the same thing.

You can tell a lot about a culture based on the movies it celebrates as a box office hit. It's a telling reflection when we pay tribute to a film with one of the highest things that popular egocentric culture values, namely a lot of money.

The highest grossing movie in the world, for all time, is the 2010 film *Avatar* by Canadian Co-Producer James Cameron. *Avatar* examines how greedy corporate interests try to destroy the local indigenous people in order to take the precious resources from their land on a distant planet called Pandora. This prophetic film skillfully points out the fact that our disconnection from nature is not just in individuals, but also in collective groups as well.

In *Avatar*, the lead couple Jake and Neytiri navigate through the hero and heroine's journey as they muster forces to defeat the greedy corporate interests that would destroy the Na'vi culture and Pandora. As a result we witness them heal, transform and evolve, soulfully blossoming into meaning and purpose, mystery and presence as lovers, warriors, and magicians. By the end of the film they are transforming and evolving into the king and queen archetype as they decide to give their lives fully to what they love and serve.

J.R.R. Tolkien first published *The Hobbit* in 1937 and followed with *The Fellowship of the Ring* in 1954, the year I was born. Tolkien wrote *The Hobbit* based on his personal experiences of World War One, and we can see his impressions of World War Two in the full series.

Mythical stories like *The Lord of the Rings* and *Avatar* invite us to look at the bigger perspective in our life and times. They both address similar themes. How are Sauron and greedy corporate interests showing up today? Will the personification of evil within us, as a sinister shadow that places shareholder dividends before common good, take over the forces of integrity within us? Will our greed triumph over our generosity? Do we get addicted to the egocentric map of money and power? Do we keep numbing out with our supernormal stimuli and addictions? Will our domination over nature be our downfall? Will we learn to embrace our indigenous soul?

Alternatively, will we surrender to the power of love and wisdom in order to remember our Inner Treasure so we can heal, transform and evolve soulfully in time? How can we transform egocentric law into the justice of love, awareness and wisdom? What is our role in this? Like Bilbo or Jake Scully we may see ourselves as ordinary and wounded, but we may also answer the call to adventure and become a wounded healer.

What is the gift in your wound? What gifts do we have and how can they serve the whole? Is it time to answer the call to adventure on our maturation awakening path?

Mythic stories are metaphors for a subjective truth. The characters are fictional, they aren't real but filmmakers like Jackson and Cameron use poetic narrative to give us a very real warning about present dangers on our Earth.

James Cameron is also the executive producer of a recent grand scale reality TV show called *Years of Living Dangerously*. It's a nine part series and stars famous actors and journalists like Harrison Ford, Jessica Alba, Don Cheadle, America Ferrera, Arnold Schwarzenegger, Mark Bitman and Thomas L. Friedman who show their concern for social justice and put their natural gifts in action by serving this meaningful need.

It's the first series of this scale that reports on real events around the world that are endangering the health of the earth, humanity and other species. Cutting-edge science is represented along with compelling subjective narrative where most viewers feel empathy and a connection with the main characters. There is a healthy blend of subjective reality and objective reality.

STAGES OF MORAL DEVELOPMENT

One of the ways we measure maturation in humans is by our evolution in moral development. There has been much research done by developmental psychologists on moral development. For example, the Swiss psychologist Jean Piaget originally posited a theory of moral development. Then, in 1958, at the University of Chicago, Lawrence Kohlberg created an adaptation of Piaget's theory and identified six identifiable development stages in a person's moral development.

Kohlberg determined that the process of moral development was principally concerned with justice and continued throughout one's lifetime. There has been critiques of the theory from several perspectives, such as how it emphasizes justice to the exclusion of other moral values, such as caring.

Kohlberg's six stages can be more generally grouped into three levels of two stages each: pre-conventional, conventional and post-conventional, following Piaget's constructivist requirements for a stage model, as described in his theory of cognitive development. It is extremely rare to regress in stages—to lose the use of higher stage abilities. Stages cannot be skipped; each provides a new and necessary perspective, more comprehensive and differentiated than its predecessors but integrated with them.

STAGE	GOAL
Pre-conventional	
Stage 1:	Obedience to authority
Stage 2:	Nice behaviour in exchange for future favours
Conventional	
Stage 3:	Live up to others' expectations
Stage 4:	Follow rules to maintain social order
Post-conventional	
Stage 5:	Adhere to social contract when it is valid
Stage 6:	Personal moral system based on abstract principles

The understanding gained in each stage is retained in later stages, but may be regarded by those in later stages as simplistic, lacking in sufficient attention to detail. Some authors describe these three general stages as egocentric, ethnocentric and world-centric.

ETHICS OF CARE

One of the founders of the ethics of care movement is American ethicist and psychologist Carol Gilligan. Gilligan was a student of Lawrence Kohlberg and developed her moral theory in contrast to her mentor's theory of stages of moral development. She disputed his concept of human maturity as it favoured boys and men over girls and women.

A *'different voice'* is a communication theory derived from Gilligan's book of the same name. The theory is a moral development, which claims that women tend to think and speak in different ways than men when they confront ethical dilemmas. This theory also suggests that the feminine ethic of care and the masculine ethic of justice are different.

Gilligan takes account of both men and women. Even though most of the experiences in her book suggest typical acts of women, she takes in consideration that women can also think in ways of 'justice' and men can think in ways of 'caring.' According to this theory, women (caring) are predominantly associated with being personal or connected, and men (justice) are predominantly associated with being impersonal.

Gilligan's model can also be expressed in four stages of moral development as Selfish, Care, Universal Care and Cosmic Care.

Similarly, James W. Fowler III, Professor of Theology and Human Development, wrote a book on moral development using a Christian lens called, *Stages of Faith: The Psychology of Human Development and the Quest for Meaning* (1981).

DANCE OF MASCULINE & FEMININE

As a wholistic mentor and psychotherapist, I sometimes help clients come to greater wholeness by fully embodying both their essential masculine and feminine qualities. In her book *Waking the Global Heart*, Anodea Judith lays out a map of the development of the archetypal feminine and masculine over the entire history of humanity.

She draws partly on the work of Jungian author Gareth Hill and his comprehensive book, *Masculine and Feminine*, to show how the feminine and masculine essence has evolved over four world epochs or stages.

Humanity's first great epoch was the stage of the static feminine, the period of the Great Mother Goddess religions. The second stage was the dynamic masculine of the warrior tribes. The third stage was and continues to be the static masculine, the age of Patriarchy. The fourth stage is the emerging dynamic feminine.

Each stage has its healthy side and its shadow side. For example, the static feminine is receptive and nurturing, yet can be smothering. The dynamic masculine can be focused and direct, yet in its shadow form rebels from all authority. The static masculine gives structure but can become rigid and domineering. The dynamic feminine can process change but can get stuck in endless processing without ever reaching a goal.

The Archetypal Feminine and Masculine is in each of us, just like how in the yin-yang symbol for wholeness we see yin within the yang and yang within the yin. For wholeness, we can learn to integrate yin and yang and all the healthy aspects of each of these four masculine and feminine archetypes.

For example, if we are to build a house, first we need to be empty to receive a vision. In the static feminine we can be as an empty receptacle that can receive a dream or vision. The dynamic masculine commits to the project and to accomplishing the goals to complete it. The static masculine uses forms, logic and rules to build a house from the foundation up. The dynamic feminine transforms the house into a home through the dance of healthy relationships and design.

LIVING WITH INTEGRITY

According to psychologist David Gruder, Ph.D., in *The New IQ—How Integrity Intelligence Serves You, Your Relationships, and Our World*, the root problem in the world today is a lack of integrity. The antidote is to cultivate integrity in our personal health, relational health and collective health. He teaches that Integrity is the wholeness that comes when we are fully authentic as individuals, compassionate and effective co-creators with others, and servants of the collective highest good. The essence of integrity is this three-dimensional alignment. We become imbalanced when we don't take care of all three of these facets of our wholeness. With a lack of integrity, we can put too much emphasis on being a self-improver, a connector or a do-gooder and neglect the other important facets of cultivating a fulfilling life.

EVOLVING SPIRITUALLY

Addictive tendencies in the seventh chakra include religion and spiritual practices, according to Anodea Judith. When our Religions neglect the truth of Science, they become archaic and don't help us to transform and evolve soulfully. When we use spiritual practices to transcend and escape the real difficulties in life, we are wrestling with the addiction of escapism. This is often referred to as "spiritual by-passing."

Not all blows in life are meaningful—some just happen. If we can make meaning out of our suffering though, it helps reduce the suffering. In my case, working with my addictive tendencies has given me a deep glimpse into the general human wound. As the wound turns into a womb and births new life, I feel grateful for all that has happened to me. Hazrat Inayat Khan also sees the opportunity in the crisis when he says, "There are experiences such as failure in business, or misfortune, or illness, or a certain blow in one's life, whether an affair of the heart or of money or a social affair, whatever it may be—there are blows which fall upon a person and a shell breaks, a new consciousness is produced. Very few will see it as an unfoldment, very few will interpret it as such, but it is so."

Evolutionary Theologian Michael Dowd argues that we need to differentiate between the subjective use of language and the objective use of language. When he uses the word God, he means Reality. He quotes Philip K. Dick as saying, "Reality is that which when you stop believing in it, it doesn't go away." He says, "All the names that

Religions use for God are subjective expressions of the truth of time, nature and mystery. They are real whether we believe in them or not." His term Reality includes evidential based science that is showing us what is really happening in the world today.

In a recent TED X talk, Dowd speaks passionately about how "Reality reconciles Science and Religion." He challenges us to evolve beyond what he calls "Religion 1.0 that believed all the literal words of what the elders told us thousands of years ago." We also need to evolve beyond "Religion 2.0 where we believed all the literal words of the scriptures written long before we had the evidential science that we have today that prove evolution is real. Religion 3.0 is about embracing God as Reality."

Dowd goes on to say that cutting edge evolutionary science and psychology "is God's or Reality's revelatory Word being revealed to us in our time…Science is humanity's collective wisdom." He sees himself as an evidential mystic and says ecology is his theology.

Dowd's view is that our best scientists agree that cataclysmic global warming is producing devastating climate change. He says, "The good news is that we have some advanced warning and know it's coming!" If we know the truth, "we have the responsibility to do something about it in time and perhaps can ensure that our grandchildren's future is protected."

Like Michael Dowd, can we get creative with the word 'God' and find a meaning that works for us? The author of Conversations with God Neil Donald Walsh imagines the letters G.O.D. as an acronym to mean Gratitude, Oneness and Destiny.

Atum's Sufi teacher, Pir Vilayat Inayat Khan (b.1916-d.2004) said, "The culmination of the soul's journey of awakening is not just to return to its original state. Instead, it is how the soul has evolved through its passage on earth…and the unique way each soul's unfoldment has contributed to the evolution of the Universe itself." Pir Vilayat taught that the goal of spirituality is to keep evolving soulfully toward greater freedom and choice in life. Can we bear to be this free?

Atum teaches that, on the path of attainment, each human needs to learn that on the one hand we are very human and ordinary, while, on the other hand, there is some aspect of the divine in each one of us. This doesn't make us special; it makes each being unique. Our goal is to honour both our humanness and our connection with divinity. Something of this 'God Seed' in each of us yearns to unfold into the world. And yet we are just frail human beings, so this unfolding won't be perfect.

When I was teaching in the Sufi group, my inner perfectionist tried to be the 'special' teacher, while underneath I felt inadequate and less than ordinary. Hal and Sidra Stone helped me to realize that I needed to balance the earthly side of me with the spiritual one. The spiritual seeker only wants to seek, not to be a finder. Today I'm enjoying a much better life balance by embracing being ordinary and unique, earthy and soulful. The tree needs roots and branches to bear fruit.

Trying to be perfect with our perfectionist is one of great traps of spiritual practice. Remember our Bermuda triangle of egocentric power? Picture a triangle again with vulnerability at the base. The inner perfectionist on one side, the inner critic is on the top, and the inner pusher is on the opposite side. If we feel inadequate, we can bypass this feeling (inner child) and engage an inner perfectionist to try to do our spiritual practices perfectly. The inner critic then says our practice isn't good enough, leading the inner pusher to push us to be more perfect. This can be an attempt to bypass our vulnerability. Instead, we need to embrace all of our selves.

Many addictive tendencies, including the addiction to religion and spiritual practices, are fueled by this dominant negative triangle of egotism. Instead, we need to learn how to witness our egotistical selves with awareness. With awareness, love and wisdom we can embrace our relative power selves and our vulnerable selves and feel compassion and forgiveness for them all. We aren't trying to get rid of our ego when on a psychospiritual path but to transform it, so it can evolve and serve the Self, Soul and Spirit. This cultivates greater wisdom, freedom and choice. We are reminded, "The ego makes a lousy master and a great servant." We need a healthy ego to deliver our inner gifts!

Shatter your ideals on the rock of truth!
—Hazrat Inayat Khan

Author and Psychotherapist Bill Plotkin, in his excellent book, *Wild Mind – A Field Guide To The Human* Psyche has the most comprehensive map that I have seen so far for practically working with the seven directions, four facets of the Self, the Soul and Spirit. He teaches that by cultivating a "3D ego" we can embrace and integrate our sub personalities. We can transform and evolve from an egocentric life to soulful living by offering our Gifts through our "soulcentric delivery system."

Clearing barriers to uncovering my inner gifts, and giving them, is a daily practice. If I feel vulnerable, then my small selves can try to rebel and take over the ship again. I need to listen to their concerns and see that their basic needs are met. Then I can enroll them into serving my soul's purpose. Aligned and united they are willing to serve the aware ego process, the captain of this ship. As the captain, I serve the king and queen of my psyche; the king and queen serve the Divine (Soul and Spirit). Then there is right order in my psyche. My role is to steward these gifts of presence so they arrive at their destination of serving those stuck in transition who need healing, transforming and evolving to live soulfully with natural aliveness, deep presence, intimacy, meaning and purpose.

SHARING OUR GIFTS, LEARNING FROM MYTHS AND STORIES

The first time I told the 'Half Boy' story was in 2002 at a soulful men's retreat. A few weeks before the retreat, my wife Sue was invited to a woman's retreat with our friend Shasta. It looked like I was to be home alone for the long weekend, and so I called Shasta's husband Brian and asked if he had plans for the weekend. He and I had met at many men's retreats with Michael Meade and Malidoma Somé and had become soulful friends, but unfortunately Michael and Malidoma had stopped doing the men's retreats in our part of the world.

I had been longing to start a soulful retreat for men locally to fill that gap, and spoke to my mentor Atum about my dream, since he led men's groups in Germany at the time. Atum believed that many men would be hesitant to journey into the soulful depths that I was envisioning, and suggested that I start small by just inviting a few men I knew from the existing soulful men's retreats. He said, like starting a fire, you want to get a good hot bed of coals before adding more wood to the fire.

Armed with this image, I called Brian and he excitedly agreed, saying he had been thinking about the same thing. We called about six other guys we knew who would be receptive and they all said yes! Our first Soultime for Men retreat was launched that spring. We have been co-facilitating these retreats together semi-annually for about twelve years now.

Over the years, like Tolkien's Bilbo Baggins, we have journeyed to the misty mountain and to the depths of the dragon's den, and back again. We have been through harrowing ordeals and great adventures, and have come home with chests full of Inner Treasure.

Brian is a wonderful friend and collaborator. He even looks like a wizard with his long grey beard! He is a masterful craftsman and violinmaker by trade but I don't think he would be offended if I referred to him as a soulful musician and wise alchemist.

Along our journey, a couple of other dedicated and courageous companions have joined our leadership team, Roq Gareau and Bob Timms. Together, we have been blessed to witness each other, and many men who have joined us on retreat, heal deep wounds, transform their stuck places and step into their inner gifts for deeper meaning and purpose. We are a weather beaten crew with a deep thirst for meaningful ritual. We have all been tempered from wrestling with our demons of lack of direction, enmeshed relationships and addictive tendencies. The demons are starting to transform into a rowdy bunch of genies that have recently been released from their bottles carrying chests of Inner Treasure!

For our soultime journeys we carry 'weapons of mass transformation' like ritual, myth, poetry, musical instruments, deep process, healing modalities and a firm belief in the work, based on our own experience.

Some of our most meaningful events have been when fathers and sons or blood brothers have come together. It's amazing for me to see fathers really witnessing their sons deeply for the first time. I'm astounded when brothers who have been at loggerheads can bury the hatchet, and not in each other's back.

I can't possibly express how great it feels to know that I have soul brothers that I can share anything with and know they will still be there for me. In fact, the darker the shadow material I share with them, the more they seem to trust me. Go figure, not exactly what most of us were taught as men!

Popular culture seems to keep men busy, conditioning them to be negatively competing with each other, working themselves to death or numbing out with any number of supernormal addictive substances. It's time for men to awaken to their deep connection to the Earth, the Self, Soul and Spirit, the animals, and each other. We can help each other embrace both head and heart. Only when we heal the split between thinking and feeling, acting and being, will we be able to become healthy lovers and husbands, consciously partnering with our partners, and becoming caring parents to our children.

After the Soultime for Men was established the next year, Brian and Shasta, Sue and I co-created a Soultime Retreat for Men & Women to celebrate conscious creative expression together. Every winter we gather a temporary tribe of friends to go to a wilderness retreat and have a whole bunch of fun exploring dreams, music, dance, poetry, art, process, ritual and the wilderness.

When we were children, we usually met new friends through mutual magic and play. Once we became adults burdened by tons of responsibility it was easy to become too serious and disconnected. We've found that by getting folks into wild places with friends, they recover the young ones inside who loved to play in the woods with their friends as children. Sometimes the hurt parts of us need to find expression first, but pretty soon the adventurous ones want to come out to play.

We have been co-facilitating these mixed Soultime Retreats also for twelve years now. At our gatherings anyone can lead something if they want to, or enjoy just being a participant, or simply enjoy the setting and participate in what feels right. One of the wonderful things about the retreats is that they are collaborative. Brian, Shasta, Sue and I facilitate the organizational aspects and create the essential container.

We take turns facilitating sessions where the whole group checks-in. Then we open it up to see if anyone has brought something they want to share in a workshop. Sometimes with larger gatherings, we may choose to split into smaller groups, depending on how many workshop facilitators come forward. Alternatively, someone can request something from someone they know has gifts in the area they are interested in. For example Brian and Shasta are amazing musicians, and therefore, are often asked to lead singing, drumming, song writing or didgeridoo healing.

I usually bring a pocket full of stories like the ones I have shared in this book. People often ask me to do storytelling for the group. In my mid-thirties, when I was suffering from midlife crisis, it would have been hard to imagine that my future self would be doing anything like this. Public speaking was my greatest fear as it is for many people!

My own reluctance to speak in a large group is an example of a personality resistance I had to heal before I could start giving some of my inner gifts. My fear was paralyzing me into living an unhappy fate. I feel blessed to have sat at the feet of master storytellers like Atum and Michael Meade. My love of storytelling became greater than my fear of speaking in groups. This has led me to living my meaningful and purposeful destiny.

Through these retreats we have been blessed to witness and encourage each other to show up with our inner gifts, and share them with the community. It's so essential to be seen and encouraged in this way. In our soulful community, we really embrace the amateur, and what we applaud is depth of heart and the courage to take a risk. I'm reminded that the word amateur comes from the word amour, for 'love'. To be an amateur is to be a lover. Courage too, comes from the Latin word *cor*, for 'heart'.

These retreats are certainly designed to bring more fun and play into our lives, but they are also for enacting deep ritual if that is summoned.

NATURAL GIFTS (NG) AND PERSONALITY RESISTANCE (PR)

There are many ways to begin uncovering your inner or Natural Gifts. Relating to your birth element or medicine animal(s) are just two of them.

There are many assessments available too. In 2012 some friends and I co-founded the Natural Gifts Society to help people uncover their Natural Gifts for deeper meaning and purpose. At the Natural Gifts Society we have an assessment that you can take that helps you uncover your five top gifts.

Go to www.naturalgiftssociety.org to learn more. Discovering your gifts and purpose is easy for some people and challenging for others. Humans generally have resistance to deep change.

In order to move forward and give our gifts to the world, this resistance needs to be listened to and overcome. There are likely valid objections that will need to be addressed first. If we can get all our selves aligned in shared leadership, our selves can serve our soul.

QUESTIONS ON MY QUEST

In the introduction and throughout the nine months of my quest of writing this book, I've been contemplating how I can dig even deeper for more Inner Treasure to heal, transform and evolve more soulfully. I've looked to my past for learning, to the present for understanding and to the future for inspiration. Here are some questions that I have been contemplating.

I share them with you as a work in progress, and in the hope that each reader will find something that resonates with their own conscience and sense of being a global and universally interconnected being.

1. What can I do in the wake of catastrophic global warming and climate change?

At an international conference of Spiritual Directors in Vancouver in 2007, Cosmologist Brian Swimme was the keynote speaker. He declared that this is the most urgent time in the history of our world. Like never before, we humans, by our sheer numbers, have become a macro power on our earth. We have become the enormous caterpillar that is devouring resources faster than is sustainable for our home, planet earth.

Later in the year, Pope Francis declared that the science of evolution, and devastating climate change are real. In a recent interview he addressed over a billion Catholics and encouraged them to take the urgency of tackling climate change seriously. He plans to address the United Nations General Assembly and convene a summit of the world's main religions in hopes of bolstering the crucial U.N. climate meeting in Paris in 2015.

Closer to home in Canada, Prime Minister Steven Harper broke Ottawa's global commitments, ignored its emission-reduction targets and made no effort to put a price on pollution.

The payback for sacrificing Canada's reputation as a responsible member of the global community? A commodity the industry can't sell in an oil-saturated world.

2. How can I take in the fact that an unprecedented number of species are going extinct?

Brian Swimme goes on to say that we are losing an alarming number of species every day. We have no idea how this will impact us, because we have yet to fully understand how interdependent we are with all other species.

The Great Web is being profoundly altered and we don't know how this will change life on earth. We don't even have language for this kind of species loss. It's being called the 'third great extinction.'

Swimme suggests this is why we stay in denial about the immensity of the problem. Think about it—if these are the most urgent pieces of news, why aren't they on the headlines of every newspaper and news report? Remember, with addiction comes denial. Brian explains that we need new language that describes the immensity of what is really going on. He is suggesting new terms like biocide and ecocide are needed.

Instead, we use misleading terms like 'climate change' and can be lured into thinking it is inconsequential because the climate changes every day. When we view the effects of massive change in climate from the perspective of those it is negatively impacting the most, climate devastation would be a better term.

3. What role does addiction have in this?

Denial is present in any addictive pattern. It's an unconscious way that we protect ourselves from the painful truth. In the recently released movie *Noah*, we see one of our earliest European ancestors, Noah, getting very drunk at the end of the film, foreshadowing our addiction to alcohol as a substitute for spirit and as a way to numb out from too much negative stress. In the *Lord of the Rings*, Bilbo could have stayed in his comfortable life of denial but we know that Sauron and Saruman would have reached the Shire sooner or later.

If the trouble hasn't found you yet, enjoy the calm before the storm, but know a wizard will be knocking on your door soon and inviting you on the call to a great adventure. Be alert—often the knock comes through unusual symptoms these days!

As a mentor and psychotherapist I see all kinds of symptoms in the form of addictive tendencies in my clients and in myself. Individually, we are a symptom of the culture we live in. James Hillman, along with Michael Ventura, in their passionate book *We've Had a Hundred Years of Psychotherapy and the World is Getting Worse* show concern about whether egocentric styles of therapy will make the needed changes.

In the cult of individualism, it becomes all about the little 'me' and 'my' therapy. Hillman and Ventura point out that we need to include our Soul and the Soul of the World in our process for deep transformation of our society and institutions.

It would be wise to ask how our therapy is helping humanity to heal, transform and evolve soulfully. As a therapist, a perspective that I find helpful is to see all of humanity, including me, as an addict who needs help. If we are all cells of this body called Earth or Nature, then we are using supernormal stimuli unconsciously to avoid reality and becoming addicted, or we are suffering from the addictive behaviour of the other cells that are addicted. Are we, like Neo in *The Matrix* ready to wake up and be willing to take the red pill to face the painful Truth that we are all part of the matrix of denial? Or will we opt for the blue pill and stay in blissful ignorance?

The choice is ours: do we keep suffering, or do we answer the call to heal, transform and evolve soulfully as a collective?

In our culture, we're constantly being bombarded with supernormal stimuli that trigger hard-wired drives and responses, distorting our choices so we turn in unhealthy directions. This often leaves us feeling burnt-out, confused, lonely and ashamed.

The First Nations people hadn't changed much in thousands of years until the modern Europeans arrived with their terrible diseases, addictive eating and drinking habits. The Indigenous People didn't stand a chance against such a violent onslaught.

I have mentioned some of the addictive tendencies linked to each chakra to invite reflection, but this is only a small representation of the many addictions prevalent at this time. We might be addicted to self-sabotage, to shame, guilt, envy, and competition or to other dysfunctional patterns of behaviour. Many of us are addicted to oil, so much so that we will tolerate projects like the Alberta Tar Sands to allow the one percent to get filthy rich, mining for dirty oil.

Recently Desmond Tutu, the great South African Anglican Archbishop, flew up to Alberta, Canada to speak truth to power. I don't think that it's any accident that the monster trucks in the film *Avatar* resemble the same kind of huge trucks found at the Alberta Tar Sands!

In this past nine months Sue and I have been attending gatherings in support of the First Nations who are standing up for our collective health and for nature. We have also been researching how our diet is fostering addictive tendencies and keeping us asleep to what is really going on.

We discovered a book called *The Paleo Solution* by Rob Wolfe. It has been a real eye opener for looking at the assumptions we were making about our diet based on faulty science and flawed spirituality.

As I switch to a simple, healthy, hunter-gatherer-forager diet I feel much more energized and have lost a couple of inches off my belly and over fifteen unnecessary pounds. Some studies suggest that soon over twenty-five percent of GDP in the US will go towards preventable health care. The addictive way we are eating is unsustainable and if it continues, it's going to render us bankrupt, or kill us.

4. How can my relationship with my wife transform and evolve more soulfully?

As I remember the 'Third' in our relationship, and Relationship as Teacher, Healer and Guide, I fall into the arms of love once again. Our bonding patterns are not so entrenched, as we both take self-responsibility for stepping out of the egotistical boxing ring. Adrenaline can be addictive for our brain and without true intimacy we may pick a fight in order to get attention. Coleman Barks' modern translation of Rumi's wisdom reminds us that, "Out beyond ideas of wrongdoing and rightdoing there is a field, I'll meet you there! When the soul lies down in that grass, the world is too full to talk about. Ideas, language, even the phrase 'each other' doesn't make any sense."

Learning about the developmental stages of relationships has helped us reflect on the predictable stages we have journeyed through as a couple, to rest into our present stage and invites us to prepare for the next stage of our soulful evolution.

We discovered an important book on addictive tendencies in relationships called *Cupid's Poison Arrow: From Habit to Harmony in Sexual Relationships* by Marina Robinson. She explains that, "We fall in love amid showers of passionate fireworks, bond for a time ... and then often get fed up with each other and grow irritable or numb. Perhaps we try to remodel our mate, seek solace online, or pursue a new love interest. Ancient sages recognized this biological snare and hinted at a way to dodge it: use lovemaking to balance one another and harmony arises naturally."

According to Robinson, apparently we are hardwired for a drive to mate with many partners to procreate and enhance the gene pool. This causes men to start unconsciously seeking a new partner to procreate with once they have ejaculated. Robinson suggests that, "In contrast to affectionate love, erotic (mating) feelings have much in common with addiction to alcohol or drugs. Intense neurochemical messages ensure that we become "hooked" on a mate, at least for a while."

If men and women can shift their focus off 'conquest' in the form of ejaculation as a supernormal stimulus, then we can enjoy pair-bonding style lovemaking. The gentle art of kareeza is about enjoying the journey of lovemaking rather than the emphasis being on the destination of ejaculation. We can learn to put an emphasis on intimate relating and caressing each other.

5. What impact has the Residential Schools had on our Aboriginal population?

In September 2013, I felt called to witness the Truth and Reconciliation Commission's event in Vancouver. It was a forum for witnessing and healing the horrific treatment of Aboriginal children who were forced to go to abusive Residential Schools in Canada from the 1950's to 1980's.

At one meeting, an inner circle of about twenty-five First Nations survivors shared the abusive treatment they had to endure in various Residential Schools as children. I sat in the next circle that surrounded them, an arms length away from a sixty-five year old First Nations man in front of me. All the survivors touched me very deeply with their painful and courageous stories; and tears started streaming down their faces and mine.

Many spoke about their fear of speaking out and were worried that it wouldn't help, or worst it would just traumatize them again by bringing back old memories they have tried so hard to suppress. Many of them have developed chronic addictions to ease their pain. Who wants to admit they were raped or beaten as a child? Many felt ashamed! When the man in front of me spoke I could hear his voice crack as the six-year-old boy inside of him emerged and started to sob. I nearly started sobbing myself at the immensity of his grief.

I staggered out of the room shaken by the realization that it was Christian authority figures that did this to them.

In another event I learned that most of the Christian sects that were involved had admitted their participation and were offering apologies. I felt angry that only the Catholics, my birth Tradition, had refused to admit their involvement or to offer sincere apologies to make amends. This seems like our version of Apartheid! Hopefully, Pope Francis will make giving a sincere apology a priority?

We can see in the recent film *Philomena*, based on a true story about Philomena Lee, that some Catholic authority figures have historically had a negative attitude toward sexuality and the body. It shows the appalling way some of the Catholic nuns in Ireland treated unwed mothers and their newborn children. Their children were taken from these mothers against their will and put up for adoption and were sold to wealthy Americans for a thousand pounds each.

Many of the world's ancient Elders or Religions (Religion 1.0 or Religion 2.0) have taught that the body, and therefore nature, was 'fallen and corrupt'. I believe this fear of their dark shadow was projected onto the world's aboriginal people and they have been suffering persecution and death for hundreds of years. Many of the World's indigenous tribes are going extinct as a result.

DOCTRINE OF DISCOVERY

Indigenous elders from all over the world gathered in July 2014 to address important issues like the *Papal Bulls*, written in the fifteenth century, that are still etched into Catholic doctrine, giving Catholics the almighty right to oppress indigenous people. The elders concluded that this is a critical time to take a stand for denouncing the *Doctrine of Discovery*, especially since recent statements by Pope Francis on the environment and human ecology: "When I look at America, also my own homeland, so many forests, all cut, that have become land… that can no longer give life. This is our sin, exploiting the Earth and not allowing her to give us what she has within her," he said.

Maybe Pope Francis is following in his namesake Saint Francis of Assisi's footsteps when he states, "If you have men who will exclude any of God's creatures from the shelter of compassion and pity, you will have men who will deal likewise with their fellow men!" St. Francis, as another David, faced down the giant Goliath of his time. Will Pope Francis find a similar courage to face this giant of an issue too?

This year, Pope Francis shocked cardinals, bishops and priests by using his annual Christmas remarks to deliver a scathing critique of the Vatican itself, the central governing body of the Catholic Church. He said the Vatican is plagued with "spiritual Alzheimer's," "existential schizophrenia," "social exhibitionism" and a lust for power—all of which have resulted in an "orchestra that plays out of tune." Saint Francis reformed Catholicism in his time and Pope Francis is doing the same these days.

HOPE FOR THE FUTURE

Recently, Sue and I went to the National Aboriginal Day celebrations in Vancouver. It was wonderful to see that First Nations people are beginning to prosper again. We could see a lot of health and possibility in the young female and male hoop dancers. The young women particularly impressed us with their passionate stance on social justice. It was heart warming to see the elders appreciating the courage and beauty of the young ones. I felt a deep kinship with the First Nations People and the Metis Canadians.

METIS NATION

One of Canada's brightest minds, John Ralston Saul, argues that Canada can best be described as a Metis Nation, heavily influenced and shaped by Aboriginal ideas. He points out that Egalitarianism, a proper balance between individual and group, and a penchant for negotiation over violence are all Aboriginal values that Canada absorbed. In his book *Fair Country: Telling Truths About Canada* he argues, "An obstacle to our progress is that Canada has an increasingly ineffective elite, a colonial non-intellectual business elite that doesn't believe in Canada. It is critical that we recognize these aspects of the country in order to rethink its future."

6. A thousand children are dying each day due to starvation or lack of clean drinking water. How can I take this in and what can I do?

When I first saw Brian Swimme, in 2006, he claimed that when he was asked why he is so passionate about what he does, he shared that over forty thousand children are dying each day. I was shocked by this statistic and felt kind of overwhelmed. Sue suggested that we could at least start supporting a child in Africa through regular monthly donations, which we began doing.

In the First Nations' tradition and in many other indigenous cultures, they had what could be considered a gift economy. Lewis Hyde has a wonderful book called *The Gift: How The Creative Spirit Transforms The World* where he articulates the origins of gift economies and how they have been debilitated by modern monetized economics. A gift economy is not about bartering—it is more the spirit of:, "I give you my gift because that's what I'm destined to do. I have faith that you'll give your gift to somebody else and if everyone does that it creates a Great Web of reciprocity."

However, as soon as you bring in a different monetary system that says the guy with the most money and power wins, and some gifts are valued more than others, it creates negative competition. Some would say this is good for the monetized economy, but how good is it for the soul? Not to mention that it's often detrimental to the welfare of the soul of the world too!

First Nations people were taken advantage of because they practice an "I-Thou" subjective experience of nature. They couldn't imagine selling nature like an object; it's against their nature and spirituality. Society's present courts of law operate on a European "I-it" objectification of valuing land as a monetary object so land claim settlements on indigenous territory are fraught with problems, while the courts force the First Nations people to prove stewardship and ownership based on European criteria. It is antithetical to their cultural tradition.

> *I have found that among its other benefits,*
> *giving liberates the soul of the giver.*
>
> —Maya Angelou

When I co-founded the non-profit Natural Gifts Society a few years ago with my friends, it was my response to this lack of soul and lack of eco in economics. I wanted to help locally in some small "ecocentric" way, while thinking globally, transforming and evolving soulfully from our consumerist oriented egocentric society. My dream was to support the indigenous notion that this creation we call "Earth" is a manifestation of the Creator's Body. When we give our unique gifts we are being creative and it is our destiny to co-create in this way. We then participate in the Trinity of Creator, Creativity and Creation.

In my first collaborative book *Awaken Your Inner Gifts*, I speak about the concept of yin and yang currencies. I mentioned that in *The Future of Money: Creating New Wealth, Work and a Wiser World*, economist Bernard Lietaer points out our present dilemma and suggests some solutions.

According to Lietaer, on the one hand Yang currencies are international currencies that are efficient but not resilient or sustainable for our environment. Yin currencies on the other hand are resilient and help foster soulful community but aren't very efficient. We need to have both efficiency and resiliency.

And so, what we are co-creating with the Natural Gifts Society is a more resilient soulful community based on giving our gifts, as seen in traditional indigenous communities.

(See our website for more information and photos at www.naturalgiftssociety.org)

Our Soultime Retreats, Soultime Express, and my volunteer storytelling for children and seniors also cultivate soulful community. My friends and I are giving our gifts for natural vitality, deep presence, intimacy, meaning and purpose, while contributing to creating more gift culture, and gift economy.

SHARING THE WEALTH

Focusing on only acquiring yang currency is efficient but creates an unbalanced and unfair hierarchy, so the rich get richer, and the poor are getting poorer. This is a greedy grab for money and power for the few, versus living with meaning and prosperity for all. This kind of domineering Capitalism is causing intense chaos and calamity in our world.

In a recent TED Talk in Vancouver, Bill and Melinda Gates modeled how to transform and evolve into a meaningful and purposeful life as very wealthy people. As one of the wealthiest men of the world, and head of Microsoft, he is donating the majority of his wealth and time to philanthropy. He and Melinda journeyed to Africa and saw thousands of children dying every day, and they were profoundly moved by what they saw. They realized that a lot of this is preventable—for example a lack of contraception, a lack of education, a lack of clean water and other simple things by our standards.

So they took action and formed the *Gates Foundation* and soon after Warren Buffett—another of the world's wealthiest men—gave half of his wealth to their foundation. In the last couple of years the Gates couple have inspired over a hundred millionaires to engage in philanthropy to bring more meaning into their lives. Rather than wait for governments or religions to do all the humanitarian work, the Gates' are challenging other wealthy people to step up to the plate and do what is right. It turns out this kind of giving fosters resiliency and relatedness.

I've worked with people who are considered to be very wealthy by our popular culture's standards. They have forgotten their Inner Treasure, and experience a quality of inner poverty, resulting in poor health, turbulent relationships or lack of meaning and purpose. They have usually traded their soul for the fool's gold Rumi speaks of. It was a bad deal! However, we don't have to be financially rich to give our gifts to make a meaningful impact. We can volunteer our gifts in some small way toward a meaningful need for a sense of avocation. We do it for the love of it!

When Brian Swimme shared his passion at the Spiritual Directors Conference he said that another name for the Big Bang is the 'Great Flaring Forth'. The universe is also transforming and evolving. We are the stardust of the universe and we are the universe evolving. He refers to our collective story as the Great Story. For the first time in history, We are the Universe being able to reflect on itself. To transform and evolve, all of the world religions will need to update their story with this Universal Story or Big Story.

When a star explodes, it creates out of that explosion. Each time that we transform we explode into a greater consciousness for further evolution. The tiny acorn needs to crack open to give the precious gifts that are inside.

In each acorn there is the potential for a whole forest of Oak Trees if nature and our True Nature is honoured!

7. How can I transform and evolve more soulfully?

When I left the Catholic Church and Christianity at age ten it was because it didn't make much sense to my rational mind and emerging worldview. If someone had asked me if I was a religious person then, I would have said no. I do not believe in the literal, judgmental old man in the sky, or the devil with horns tempting me. I would probably have said I was an atheist or maybe an agnostic if I knew what that meant back then.

I recently heard an insightful talk by author and scientist Rupert Sheldrake that I found inspiring. He said many scientists are kept in the closet around their spirituality for fear of not being taken seriously. He also rejected the kind of Christianity he was brought up with, experimented with mind-altering drugs and explored eastern spirituality. He eventually went to India and met Bebe Griffiths and had a life changing experience when he witnessed the inclusion of Hindu chanting in the service at Bede's Monastery. When he asked Bede about this he said, "Catholic means universal." True Catholics embrace everything.

Sheldrake found that this inclusive understanding allowed him to become an "anatheist, someone who is returning to God." He now practices praying and going to Church. An *atheist* is someone who doesn't believe in God. A *theist* is someone who believes in God. Anatheism allows us to return to 'Reality,' embracing the wisdom of all Traditions. We can transform to evolve soulfully beyond rigid god ideals that don't accord with what Mystery and Presence and the best science is revealing.

Pantheism holds that the divine is synonymous with the universe. Monotheism is the belief in one personal and transcendent God. Panentheism embraces the transcendent and immanence by positing that a monotheistic God, polytheistic gods, or an eternal animating force interpenetrates every part of nature and timelessly extends beyond it. Many mystical traditions like Universal Sufism embrace the transcendent and the immanent aspects of divinity. Hazrat Inayat Khan teaches that "God is in all things; still more God is in all beings."

Michael Dowd calls himself an evidential mystic. I like this term as it embraces Science, Nature, Time and Mystery as Reality.

Upon reflection, reconnecting with the profound beauty and majesty of the wilderness was a very healing mystical, ecospiritual experience for me. Of course, I have benefited enormously from the 'miracles' of modern science and now enjoy embracing the incredible gifts from Mystery, Nature, Time and Science.

I imagine that there are at least three levels of consciousness we can be aware of, the gross, subtle and causal realms, each can be experienced at the individual and the collective level. Each night, we rest into the loving arms of Mystery and Presence (the causal) as we enter deep sleep. During the dreamtime we journey through (the subtle) realm. In this realm we can meet facets of our Self, inner guides and work though our inner psychospiritual issues. In the morning we wake into the subtle realm of ego, persona and shadow, then (the gross) realm of our body and senses. If we practice becoming more aware we can experience all three levels of gross, subtle and causal realms while awake.

For example, as you read this page you are using the sense of sight. Your senses operate in the gross realm of your body. For 'insight,' ask yourself, who is reading? Is it your judging self? If so, this is a sub personality, a subtle part of your inner world of psyche. Who is noticing your inner judge? Awareness notices your inner judge without judging it. We can say that awareness is prior to your personality and senses. In that sense it is a pre-sense or presence.

Mystery and Presence are always present but when we are

identified with our senses or seeing through a sub personality we tend to forget other perspectives. All we need to do is to re-member and fall backwards into the arms of Mystery and Presence to compassionately witness how a part of us is caught in judgment.

I imagine this as the dance from me to my evolving aware ego process. When I'm identified with a *little me*, then my perspective is very limited. If I can transform and evolve into my aware ego process then my perspectives evolve so I can draw from the Inner Treasure of Self, Soul and Spirit.

With this larger perspective I can contribute soulfully to the, we, of my conscious partnerships with others. If we become more conscious, then we contribute to the aware ego process of humanity that is transforming and evolving. Subjectively, this is a great dance of Love, Lover and Beloved within the Great Body! Objectively, this is Reality's evolution.

THE WEDDING DAY REMEMBERED

One of my favourite ways to celebrate Remembrance Day is to walk along the water's edge to the park overlooking the ocean where Sue and I were married all those years ago. Arriving at the park, I sit on my familiar park bench. The view from this beautiful place is stunning!

I notice the silhouette of Cyprus and Grouse Mountains on the North Shore, I can see West Vancouver across the water. From where I sit, there is a beautiful view of the sun setting behind Bowen Island. My thoughts begin to drift northwest in the direction of our dear friends Brian and Shasta and how they generously arranged all the music for our wedding. My soul friend Brian was my best man. These friends are a true inspiration in how they are constantly giving their Inner Treasure, their Natural Gifts of music, encouragement and facilitation to meet the meaningful needs of soulful expression in our community. They are wonderful examples of elders who live with meaning and purpose while resting in deep mystery and presence.

As memories flood me with warm feelings from that special day I notice my heart soften and start expanding. Then I stand and walk over to the cliff where our wedding service was performed and look out over the ocean. It seemed odd that the platform that we had our wedding ceremony on was torn down so soon after the wedding and a chain link fence was erected in its place. I'm glad it didn't collapse in the middle of the ceremony, like in one of those bizarre wedding blooper shows!

My practice is then to imagine the wedding ceremony again, like I have done so many times before. It's my way of remembering how beautiful that day was and all the wonderful people who were there. It was a profound moment of wholeness! Whenever I'm feeling a bit blue or wanting to make a shift in my life, it helps to come here and renew my vows, as a soulful ritual of contemplating how I can transform and evolve next.

As I look around I imagine seeing so many of our friends, family and teachers that were here to witness and bless our union. There is Atum O'Kane and David Roomy, two of the deep mentors for my soul, and there are many more of our soul friends gathered.

Even the animals showed up for the wedding! There were dogs and many birds. An eagle perched in the branches above us. Some crows made their presence known to everyone through their loud voices. Seagulls wafted in the breeze overhead calling out to the mystery of the sea. A pair of Great Blue Herons danced gracefully in midair just as we completed the service.

One of our friends is a leader of the Sufi Whirling Dervishes and he exclaimed that the ritual reminded him of the *Conference of the Birds*. This is a famous Sufi story where thirty birds feel lost and go in search of their king, the Simurg. A wise bird guides them through seven challenging valleys where many birds were nearly lost. Finally they make it to the top of the mountain and are about to approach the palace of their king. They are disappointed to find out that there is no palace or king, only a small round lake. The thirty birds circle the lake and curiously peer into its waters. They are surprised to see a reflection of their own image. All thirty of them are standing in a circle of wholeness. It turns out Simurg means thirty birds. Then the overhead sun reaches its zenith and their image is shattered by the brilliant Light of the One Sun.

I picture Sue across from me, and looking deeply into her eyes I begin to softly sing our wedding vows to her, "All I ask of you, is forever to remember me as loving you. Ishq Allah Maboud Allah!" Then I turn to the imagined group of our community and sing the same words to them. Finally, I sing it a third time to the glory of Nature. I love this place!

The Celts and John O'Donahue in *Anam Cara* speak about the 'sacred thin places', and I'm sure this place is one of the portals to the soul of the world. At least it is for me!

Sue and I wanted to have as many spiritual traditions represented as possible—for an interspiritual perspective. We have friends from many different Traditions and ones that are spiritual but not religious (SBNR), and folks who don't think of themselves as spiritual at all. We enlisted a Unitarian Minister and two Sufi Ministers to perform the service. We had chant leaders from the First Nations, Hindu, Sufi, Jewish and Buddhist Traditions leading everyone in devotional songs in the park.

My best man Brian wore a brightly coloured African outfit. I wore a cool East Indian bridegroom's outfit and my bride wore a stunning white satin dress. It looked like the United Nations and truly reflected the diversity of Canada's multiculturalism.

As we shared our vows and exchanged our rings, we placed our hands on our hearts and turned to face our soulful community. Bowing to them, they showered us with rose pedals as we danced down the path of Love between them.

MYSTERY AND PRESENCE

At the age of fifty-six, in 2010, I was happily married, practicing mutuality and partnering with Sue. I felt blessed to be experiencing deep meaning and purpose in my vocation as a mentor and psychotherapist. I had become a certified Raphaelite Work Practitioner, Voice Dialogue Facilitator, Clear Your Beliefs Practitioner, President of the Process Counselling Society and was still leading soulful men's retreats biannually. With this sense of fulfillment, I felt called to leave a legacy and give back to the community through philanthropy, so I co-founded the Natural Gifts Society, to contribute to the soul of the world.

Now in my sixtieth year, I'm contemplating what the next change might be that I need to make in order to heal, transform and evolve soulfully. One new venture is writing these books! At times a sense of inadequacy would arise whenever I would share my vulnerability. Then I would remember the words of Leonard Cohen from his poem, *Anthem* to, "Ring the bells that still can ring, forget your perfect offering, there is a crack in everything, that's how the light gets in." I hear my inner guide whisper, "Just relax into the arms of mystery and presence."

With all this meaningful activity, my personal vitality began to suffer, so my focus for these last nine months has been to improve my personal vitality through conscious movement and a healthier diet. As a result, I am feeling a better balance of natural vitality, deep presence, intimacy, meaning and purpose.

My stepson recently turned thirty-five and shared with me that he too went through an early midlife crisis a few years ago when his restaurant business collapsed. With the financial pressure soon afterward his relationship of five years broke apart. He decided to try to find his birth father for support and eventually found him but then he was really disappointed when his birth father didn't respond to his bid for connection. He ended up feeling depressed for a time but then he focused on improving his health. Eventually he found his passion, meaning and purpose through coaching others in improving their health. About a year ago he met his beloved partner who shares the same passion as he does as a fitness trainer and is feeling grateful to be in a loving partnership. His midlife crisis has also transformed into a midlife awakening process.

He wholeheartedly thanked me for being a loving father figure in his life. I was deeply touched when he honoured me for teaching him to live from his values with integrity. Now he feels really good about his life. It was an incredibly meaningful moment for me and reminded me that I too would like to wholeheartedly thank my mentors for teaching me to live from my deepest values with integrity.

Brother David Steindl-Rast reminds us that to be happy we need to be grateful. Most people think that when we get what we want, then we will be grateful. He disagrees, teaching that this attitude only fuels more wanting. Instead, we can be grateful for what we have now, and this gratitude fosters true happiness.

"We have thousands of opportunities every day to be grateful: for having good weather, to have slept well last night, to be able to get up, to be healthy, to have enough to eat…. There's opportunity upon opportunity to be grateful; that's what life is."

In another talk, he says that we sometimes get too hung up on the weather, thinking or saying, "This weather is good weather or bad weather!" Instead, he suggests that we greet each weather pattern as if it were unique. The same goes with other parts of our life. How do we celebrate each other's uniqueness each day?

The great Sufi master Hazrat Inayat Khan taught that, "A mystic, in the full sense of the word, must have balance. He or she must be as wise in worldly matters as in spiritual things." He says, "The soul comes to a stage of realization where the whole of life becomes to him or her one sublime vision of the immanence of God."

Integration of the opposites is essential in his message. If the Heart had wings, he says one side is compassion and the other side is truth. If we only side with truth then we may hurt the ones we love. If we only side with compassion then we may not speak the truth when we need to. Wisdom knows how to speak the truth with compassion.

In the Appendix, you will find practices for exploring the maturation awakening path, to heal, transform and evolve more soulfully in your health, relationships and vocation.

BELOVED DANCE

by Dave Wali Waugh

Some people dance by the sway of their bodies,
Some people dance with their hands on the skin of a drum.
Some people dance with the breath in their flute,
Some people dance with their long-necked lute.
Some people dance with the drum in their ear,
Some people dance with their fear.
Some people dance with their rage,
Some people dance right out of the cage.
Some people dance by holding a hand,
Some people dance by making a stand.
Some people dance by the beat of their heart,
Sadly, for some people, their dance may never start.
All I know is,

Before we die, we need to dance.

APPENDIX: THE MATURATION AWAKENING PATH

"The unexamined life is not worth living."

—Plato

7 days for practicing the maturation awakening path of wholistic awakening yoga

INTRODUCTION:

We can see maturation in the healthy, mature Oak Tree that bears the fruit of its gifts as acorns, giving them freely to the world. Within each acorn is a blueprint for another oak tree, and so on. We could say that a tiny acorn carries exponential potential.

We also see maturation in the caterpillar that transforms and evolves into the beautiful butterfly. Symbolically it has evolved from being a ravenous consumer to a pollinator of beauty.

We see mature humans who are uncovering their gifts and giving them to a meaningful need while staying healthy in body, emotion, mind, soul, relationships and vocation. This is natural for some people but for the rest of us healing, transformation and evolution happens through conscious practice.

If we bite into an apple that's unripe, it is bitter to the taste. When the apple is ripe it is said to be mature and it tastes good.

Some people are still at a stage of development that could be called immature or unripe. I don't mean this as a judgment but as an observation. We usually don't expect a child to get a job to support the family, as they simply aren't mature enough for that level of responsibility. Some adults are advanced in terms of years of age, but are immature in their personal, relational or vocational wellness.

For example, if we are too sedentary we may not have enough physical vitality to accomplish our goals. With awareness, we are able to awaken to the situation, then heal, transform and evolve into greater health for increased physical vitality.

The science of physicality, psychology and spirituality are proving that there are certain practices we can do to help us mature. We can't rely on our will power alone. Supernormal stimulus can powerfully cause us to stray from our intentions. It is helpful to transform our unhealthy habits into healthy daily habits. When someone engages in this consciously, I like to think of it as answering the call to a maturation awakening path.

Maturation is defined in the Merriam-Webster online dictionary as:

- A: the process of becoming mature
- B: the emergence of personal and behavioural characteristics through growth processes
- C: the final stages of differentiation of cells, tissues, or organs.

When I speak of awakening I mean healing, transforming and

evolving either, physically, emotionally, mentally, soulfully, spiritually, relationally and vocationally.

There are also different levels of consciousness we can awaken to. For example, each night we go to sleep and enter the dream state, from which we can shift to a deeper state beyond dreaming, where there are no dreams. When we wake in the morning normally we say we are awake.

There are at least three levels of consciousness that we experience each twenty-four hour period—deep sleep, dreaming and waking.

During the day, when we are awake, we may not be aware of our addictive tendencies on this ordinary level. We could say that we are caught in a dream or spell. When we awaken to our habitual pattern we could say that we are experiencing a greater level of awakening.

Through meditative practices, we can awaken to other levels of consciousness that are similar to the states of dreaming and deep sleep except they are happening while we are awake. This helps us heal, transform and evolve into greater states of consciousness.

States come and go, however. If we stabilize in a greater level of consciousness, then we become awakened to a new phase or stage of our development.

As mentioned earlier, I imagine this as a shift from the 'little me' to my aware ego process that can access my Self, Soul and Spirit. With this greater perspective I can contribute to cultivating conscious relationships with individuals and the collective: from identifying with the 'little me' to shifting into my aware ego process, and from a limited sense of 'we' to the collective aware ego process. I call this a *path* because there is a direction toward healing barriers to cultivating natural vitality, conscious relationships, meaning and purpose.

These three facets of life appear to me to be essential: personal health, relational health and contributing to the world in some meaningful way for a sense of purpose.

INTEGRATIVE PSYCHOLOGY

Ken Wilber has an uncanny ability to compile large amounts of research into an integrative model that transcends and includes multiple perspectives. If we take a circle and place a peace sign in the centre, we create three sections for the trinity of Goodness, Truth and Beauty. This includes our individual, subjective experiences (the beautiful and the good) and objective experiences (the true).

BEAUTY, TRUTH, GOODNESS

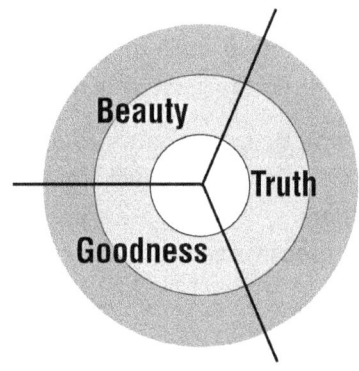

Source: The Integral Operating System by Ken Wilber, 2005

Wilber demonstrated that the three basic perspectives of inquiry could be organized into: I (Subjective, Beauty), We (Subjective, Goodness), and It (Objective, Truth). Each domain is unique and has its own language, values, focus and ways of knowing.

Wilber took these domains and created his four-quadrant Integral Model of I, We, It and Its, that included the singular and the plural and created 'a space' for each unique domain. Table I summarizes some of the elements of his model. The upper left quadrant signifies the interior subjective or 'I' perspective of what the subjective 'I' finds beautiful. 'Beauty is in the eye or 'I' of the beholder.'

INTEGRAL SPIRITUALITY

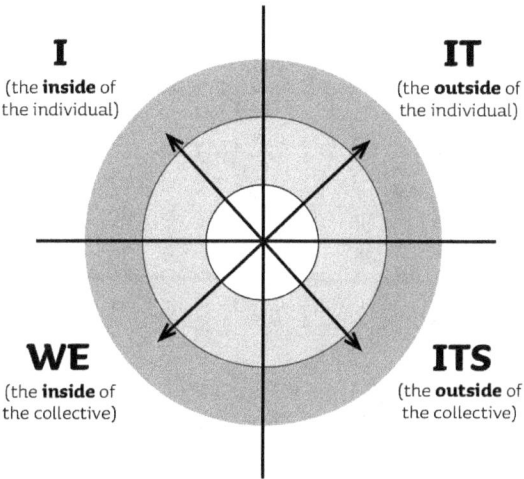

Source: The Integral Operating System by Ken Wilber, 2005

The interior portion of our Inner Gifts MAP (Meaning and Purpose = TN+EQ+NG-PR (True Nature plus Essential Qualities plus Natural Gifts minus Personality Resistance)—refers to this upper left domain. This is where our Inner World of Psyche resides.

Then, the upper right quadrant is the singular objective perspective of our cells, organs and body. 'Objective Science' resides here.

The lower left in the Integral Model is where the 'We' of relationships resides. Finally, the lower right is the 'Its' of cultural systems, for example, organizations and countries.

In our map for manifesting more meaningful and purposeful work, our Meaningful Need (MN) that we need to give our Natural Gifts (NG) to, resides in either of the lower quadrants, or both. MAP = TN + EQ + NG – PR + MN.

If we look at our circle with the four quadrants again, the MAP (Maturation Awakening Path) is the whole circle that grows like rings on a tree as we transform and evolve.

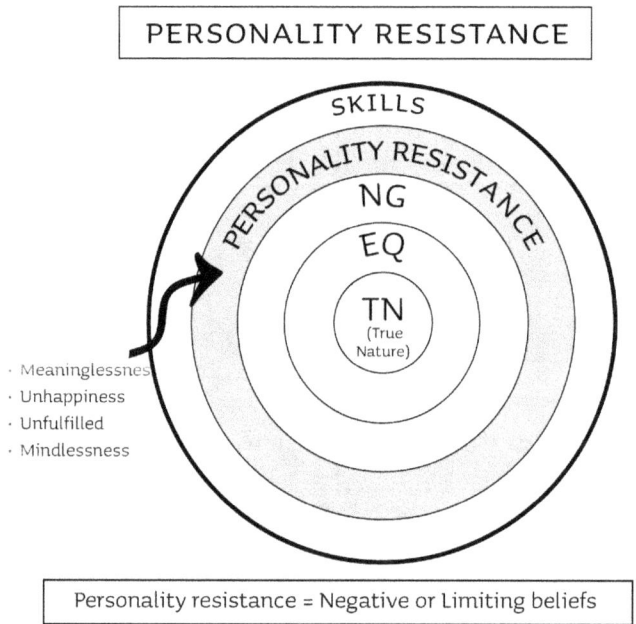

Personality resistance = Negative or Limiting beliefs

Let's start outside the circle, moving in.

Skills are something that we can acquire. We can learn to drill a hole. We can learn to use a word processing system. So, skills are really helpful tools.

But then we get to the *Personality Resistance* layer, and like the shell of the acorn, this can be an extremely hard layer to break through. People often find it difficult to go inside and discover some of the deeper, subtler levels inside themselves.

In this diagram we can see the *Personality Resistance* is dense as represented by the darker colour. When we are blocked on this level it is hard to access our inner resources or outer resources.

To overcome this resistance we need to drop below, becoming aware of our *Natural Gifts*, right into the source of human experience, spaciousness that is formless. And then out of the formlessness come our *Essential Qualities*, which are really gifts from our *True Nature*.

If we use an example of a teacher discovering her Natural Gift of teaching, she may choose to meditate, going into spaciousness, and then the *Essential Quality* of patience could arise.

We can all agree that the *Essential Quality* of patience would be very helpful for a teacher to embody.

When we are aware that *Essential Qualities* are gifts from our *True Nature* for us, we can ask questions such as, "What do I need today? Patience? Compassion? Peace?"

Those *Essential Qualities* are available to us—if we just seek, then the solutions are usually right next to our problems. This sometimes occurs in nature—right next to the poisonous plant often grows the plant that is the antidote to the poison.

When the *Personality Resistance* has been cleared, the person can access their inner resources and connect them to a *Meaningful Need* in the community.

For integrative development it is important to have healthy physicality, psychology, spirituality, relationships, vocation, organizational structures and groups. Each of the domains can transform and evolve.

When we discover our Natural Gifts, it is important to keep our body healthy and give our gifts to transform our self, our relationships and our society. If we have physical barriers to manifesting our gifts or giving them, we need to take care of our foundation. Our body is like the temple for our Inner Treasure, these precious gifts.

In the rest of the Appendix I will offer an Inner Compass Multidimensional Awakening Practice (ICMAP) to transform our limited ego into an evolving centre, so we encourage evolution in all three of these facets of life.

Someone can stray from the path and that happens occasionally and is expected. If the path were working for us, we would simply return to the path. Perhaps the detour is an important learning step for our journey. Other possibilities are that we need a better compass or some guidance for our journey.

Being on a path with practices doesn't mean we are trying to be perfect or that the practices have to be done perfectly. Adopting practices simply means that we're exploring a path to evolve consciously. These practices can be used by anyone from any tradition or someone that doesn't follow any tradition. Feel free to adapt them to suit you and take what works, and leave the rest.

These practices are not meant to take the place of appropriate professional assistance. If you are working with a coach, doctor, trainer, spiritual guide or a therapist, it is wise to inform them of what you are exploring to enlist their support.

In order to embark on a quest it is helpful to know what your questions are. Earlier I mentioned that there are universal questions that often arise when someone is undergoing a major life transition like:

Who am I really? Who am I becoming? What is love? What do I love to do? What is meaningful? What is my soul's purpose? Who is going with me?

There are also specific questions we can contemplate around clearing our barriers to living with deeper aliveness, intimacy, meaning and purpose. Each day of the week we will be exploring one of the following questions:

- How can we clear our barriers to living with deeper physical vitality?
- How can we clear our barriers to living with deeper emotional vitality?
- How can we clear barriers to accomplishing our goals in life?
- How can we clear barriers to living with deeper intimacy for greater relational vitality?
- How can we clear barriers to uncovering our inner resources?

- How can we clear barriers to uncovering and giving our inner gifts so we can live with deeper meaning and purpose for greater vocational vitality?
- How can we clear barriers in our thinking so we can heal, transform and evolve soulfully?

In pursuing these questions, we will be exploring the seven major chakras (energy centres) and also some of the minor ones.

Seven is also a useful number for us to divide our practices into—I call it the Practice Calendar, and we conveniently have seven days in a week and seven elements for practicing the maturation awakening path.

WHOLISTIC AWAKENING YOGA

It is difficult to use language to describe spiritual experience because we need to consider Formlessness and Form when we speak about Ultimate Reality. The best we can do is use metaphors to represent that, which can only be experienced directly. In the East we see five major schools of yoga or paths to cultivate maturation: Hatha, Raja, Jhana, Bhakti and Karma.

Hatha yoga is the path of developing our physical vitality. Raja yoga is the path of contemplation and meditation for developing presence. Jhana yoga is the path of developing intellectual vitality. Bhakti yoga is the path of devotion and relational vitality. Karma yoga is the path of actively helping to improve the lives of others for vocational vitality. In fact, different traditions highlight one or more of these paths. Each person has a unique typology and one of these paths may suite their typology more than the others.

I imagine drawing from each of these paths for a creative way (wholistic awakening yoga) to cultivate natural vitality, deep presence, intimacy, meaning and purpose. There are four essential questions that can help us contemplate each of these paths. 1. How can I become more physically vital? 2. Who or what am I really? 3. Who or what do

I love? 4. How can I give my unique gifts to a meaningful need in the world for a sense of meaning and purpose, so as contribute to the soul of the world?

SEVEN DIRECTIONS

Many spiritual traditions emphasize the ascending path to spirit—this is wonderful for transcendence, but we also need to honour the immanence. We need to fully incarnate—this is the path of descending into soulfulness. We are the microcosm of the macrocosm, yet we live mostly in what Michael Meade calls the mesocosm (middle world).

To heal, transform and evolve soulfully, we will need to embrace all realms, the full spectrum of our evolving wholeness. We can do this by consciously cultivating our evolving centre.

ELEMENTS OF AWAKENING AND ATTAINMENT

I encountered the elements again through another Sufi Teacher, Himayat Inayati PhD., founder of the Raphaelite Work Healing and, at the time, the leader of the Sufi Healing Order. I trained with Himayat for seven years in order to become a Certified Raphaelite Work Practitioner. There is a strong emphasis in this training on working with the seven major energy centres and also the minor energy centres for healing and transformation.

The African teacher Malidoma Somé has also had considerable influence on my thinking about initiation and the elemental realm. His orientation to the elements is rooted in the Dagara Tradition of Burkina Faso. The elements in the West-African Dagara Medicine Wheel are earth, water, fire, mineral and nature.

The First Nations Medicine Wheel also uses the elements to position us on a kind of human map and compass for greater orientation and direction in life.

Trying to integrate all these perspectives is challenging, but I have included some of the essential concepts from all of them in the soulful map I am offering.

MEDICINE WHEEL

Looking at a circle again as a symbol of wholeness, we can see the First Peoples' use of a medicine wheel as a kind of human map and compass for direction in life.

Some Traditions, like the Algonquin People of Ontario, make their medicine wheel multidimensional, honouring the seven directions. These are the directions of the upper world, the lower world, the middle world of the four cardinal directions and the inner world. Our evolving centre is located in the centre of the wheel and embraces all of the directions.

The Algonquin people honour the Great Mystery and call their spirituality "the way of the heart." The heart is also the centre of our seven major chakras.

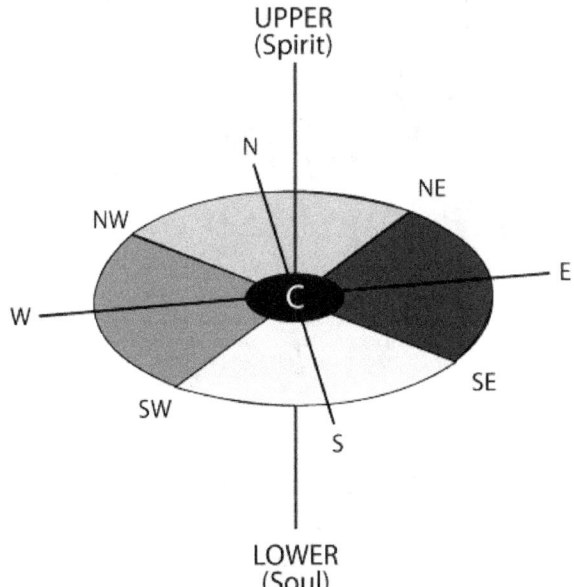

Most people these days try to live exclusively in the middle world of day-to-day life. When this is all there is to life, we have identified with our limited small selves perspective and there is a danger of ending up living in a flat land of meaninglessness and lack of purposeful direction.

For transformation and evolution we need to connect with the upper world of spirit and the lower world of soul while integrating all the directions in the centre. Then, once we uncover our Inner Treasure, we emerge out again into the four cardinal directions with a soulful path of co-creating a world of beauty. That is, until we fall out of right-relationship, and we get called to another trip around the wheel.

In the Algonquin medicine wheel, our childhood and springtime are in the East, our time of youth and summer are in the South, adulthood and fall are in the West, and elderhood and winter are in the North.

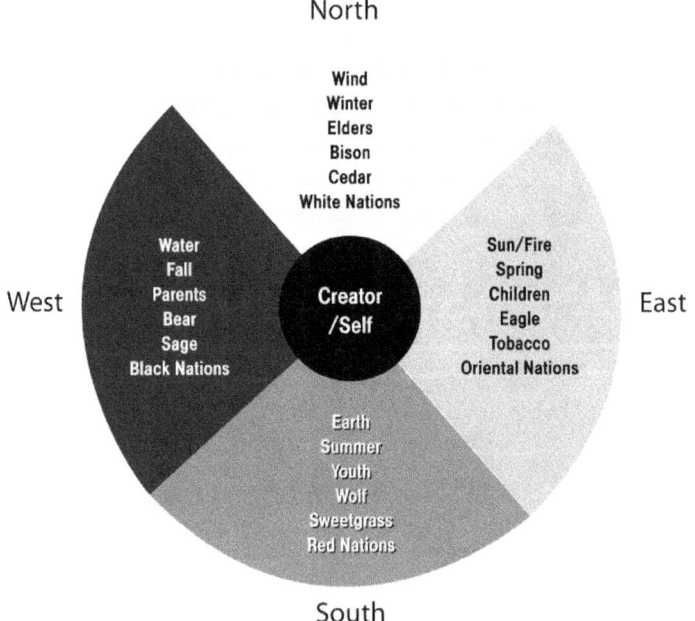

With the intention of inviting conscious healing, transformation and evolution our ICMAP (Inner Compass Multidimensional Awakening Practice) can be differentiated into four facets that you can practice for evolving wholeness.

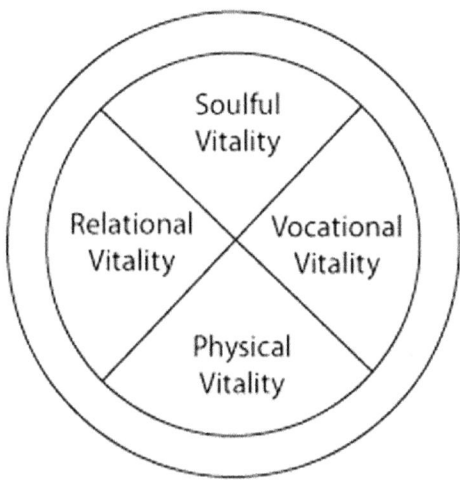

Here is another version of this:

MAP1: Movement and Physicality
MAP2: Mystery and Presence
MAP3: Mutuality and Partnering
MAP4: Meaning and Purpose

In this body map, all the words that I use start with the letter 'p', as in *path*. Each day I will begin with a step from Tibetan Buddhist teacher Ed Bastian's seven steps for Interspiritual Meditation. So, let's begin our practice week.

DAY 1—MONDAY: PRACTICE THE PATH

Yesterday I was clever so I wanted to change the world. Today I am wise so I am changing myself.

—Rumi

MAP 1: MOVEMENT AND PHYSICALITY: MAGIC AND PLAY

How can we clear our barriers to living with deeper physical vitality?

1. Motivation and Intention: "May all beings become healthy and happy in body, mind and spirit. May I become healthy and happy in body, mind and spirit!"

"Physical, mental, and spiritual health are intertwined, and meditation nurtures sustainable health and happiness. We begin meditating with determination and confidence that it will help us to heal the innermost causes of illness and suffering. We rest into an InterSpiritual Consciousness for universal healing."

Today is Monday on our practice calendar and the element of the first chakra is earth. From the moment we wake and rise out of bed in the morning our bodies are moving. Did you get enough sleep? Do you feel rested? To practice the path, the focus is on cultivating a healthy body to honour the temple of our physicality and the place we live.

Is your living space supportive of your health and wellness? When washing your body, imagine using the water as a purification practice to let go of any negative impressions from the day before, so you can start this day fresh. Feel gratitude for the gift of the earth of this physical body and the gift of water for drinking, cleaning and cooking. Take care of your basic needs for fresh air, clean water, elimination, healthy food and safety today.

In one study on depression it was shown that physical exercise, especially varied exercise in nature, was far more effective than medication for getting long-term results.

Our bodies love to move and to rest. Depending on your learning style and typology, there are many movement practices for you to choose from. Tai Chi, Qi Gung, Sufi Whirling, Dance, Yoga, Walking, Cross Country Skiing, Gardening, Chasing Swallows and playing in the forest, just to name a few.

Remember how you loved to play when you were a child and make some room for that playful child in your life to recover the magic and play of childhood. To make movement a practice, simply add motivation, intention, dedication and a contemplative, mindful focus to the practice.

We are focusing primarily on the first chakra and the subtle energy centres in this area, getting our roots, yet aligning with all of the rest of the seven major chakras (energy centres).

In walking meditation, you can set an intention to be present in the presence as you walk. Focus on your breath, and body using the phrase "present" on the in-breath and "in the presence," on the out-breath. When a distracting thought comes up, just notice it without judgment and return to your breath and the practice of repeating the phrase.

You can explore further by dropping the phrase and just focus on your breath or you could reverse the phrase saying "present" on the out breath and "in the presence" on the in breath. Since this is a body-oriented practice you could practice noticing one of your bodily senses, for example, hearing, what sounds do you hear as you walk? Put all your attention on the sense of hearing!

Then you can consciously shift to another sense and focus your attention there. Feel gratitude for the gifts of your body and senses.

The old expression says, 'You are what you eat.' For physical vitality it is important to practice eating in a healthy mindful way. It helps to be aware of using food as a way to self-soothe or as a reward.

Contemplate which self in you is the one who is eating? Is it the reward eater, or the celebratory eater, or the lonely eater? Honouring the spirit of the animal or plant that gave its life so we may live helps us connect to the soul of the world through eating.

It also reminds us to choose the healthiest food possible. Imagine your body is a temple and you are offering this food to the divine within.

Suggested Reading & Viewing:

- Woodman, Marion. *Addiction to Perfection – The Still Unravished Bride: A Psychological Study*, Inner City Books. 1982.
- *Fed Up*—documentary film, 2014
- *The Perfect Human Diet*— documentary film, 2014
- Wolfe, Robb. *The Paleo Solution*, Victory Belt Publishing, 2010.
- Sanfilippo, Diane. *Practical Paleo*, Victory Belt Publishing, 2012.
- Gokhale, Esther. *8 Steps to a Pain-Free Back*, Pendo Press, 2008.

DAY 2—TUESDAY: PRACTICE THE PATH: MASTERY AND PROACTIVITY

How can we clear our barriers to living with deeper emotional vitality?

2. Gratitude: "May I Be Grateful to Life's Many Gifts."

"With gratitude we invoke and honour our teachers, mentors, and great spiritual role models. We invite these great beings to remain present and pray that their example and presence will guide us. We focus on the blessings of friends, family, and the environment that nurture and sustain us."

Today is Tuesday on our practice calendar. The second chakra is the water centre and is located in the genital region. Here we have process on the ascending path and passion on the descending path. Are your emotions stuck or flowing? E-motions want to flow. Are you passionate and grateful about your life, your work and your primary relationships?

Reflect back on your life and see if you can identify trauma and addictive tendencies. Record them in your journal. Interview family members, especially the 'black sheep of the family'. See if you can identify areas of trauma that may be holding implicit memories.

ADDICTIVE TENDENCIES

Anodea Judith, in her comprehensive book *Eastern Body, Western Mind* suggests that certain addictions are related to particular chakras (energy centres):

- Chakra 7—Religion, Spiritual Practices

- Chakra 6—Hallucinogens, Marijuana
- Chakra 5—Opiates, Marijuana
- Chakra 4—Tobacco (Smoking), Sugar, Love, Marijuana
- Chakra 3—Amphetamines, Cocaine, Caffeine, Work, Anger
- Chakra 2—Alcohol, Sex, Heroin
- Chakra 1—Foods, Gambling, Shopping, Work

Perhaps explore some healing bodywork to heal stuck emotions. Be present to your feelings with compassion for how you were wounded. Learn to recognize other addictive tendencies like, power over others, self-sabotage, shame, guilt and so on.

Get support for any addictive tendencies.

Suggested Reading:

- *Cupid's Poisoned Arrow: From Habit to Harmony in Sexual Relationships* by Marina Robinson
- Rosenburg, Marshall B. *Nonviolent Communication: A Language of Life*, Google Books, 2003.
- Gottfried, Dr. Sarah. *The Hormone Cure: Reclaim Balance, Sleep, Sex Drive and Vitality*, Scribner, 2013.

DAY 3—WEDNESDAY: PRACTICE THE PATH: MASTERY AND PROACTIVITY

How can we clear barriers to accomplishing our goals in life?

3. "May I Be Awake & Transformed."

"Focusing on the highest ideal for our life, we acknowledge and confess our shortcomings and promise to patiently persevere in our personal transformation. We vow to remove our inner obstacles and negativities. Without guilt, we forgive others and ourselves as we offer our lives in service to our highest goals."

Today is Wednesday on our practice calendar. The third chakra is the fire centre in the solar plexus. In this centre, we need the power in the ascending line to focus our attention where we want it to go. In the descending line, we need to harness our proactivity to align with and accomplish our goals. Do you know what your inner gifts are? Are you out of balance between activity and rest?

Who are the allies, mentors and elders for your path? What goals do you need to set to accomplish your dreams? Make your goals tangible and measurable. You can use the seven elements as a map to manifest your goals.

Start with the nature element in your seventh chakra to connect with your True Nature and nature, vowing to participate in the soul of the world. Move down to your third eye into the mineral element to remember your Gifts and purpose. Descend into the fifth chakra and the ether element in your throat to praise the Source of your Inner Gifts. Then descend into the air element of your heart and fourth chakra to contemplate who you will lovingly partner with today.

Decide what part of your vision you are willing to commit to and use the fire element of power and proactivity in the third chakra to manifest your goals. Use the water element in your second chakra to process your passion, and finally move into your first chakra to earth your goal by landing it physically in this place of completion. Then pause, celebrate completion and feel gratitude by sending a prayer of thanks in praise of the Creator (or whatever Name works for you).

Whenever we set a goal for ourselves then personality resistance (PR) to the change is likely close behind. One part of us wants to press on the gas pedal to move ahead and another part fears change so slams on the brakes. Each part may have valid perspectives. It's helpful to listen to each side from the centre and then take their perspectives into consideration before making a firm commitment. The idealist offers a vision of possibility. The doubting or cautionary voice may help us be more realistic. Voice Dialogue is a practical method to more conscious decision-making.

Practice: Focus your attention on your breath. If your mind wanders, like training a puppy patiently and lovingly, bring your attention back to your breath. For some people it helps to count one on the in breath and two on the out breath and continue up to ten, then repeat at one again and so on. If a thought arises, ask yourself, "What voice or sub personality is this?" Then return to the breath or counting.

It helps to set a timer and the only goal is to sit for the time allotted and to be present and mindful as best you can. Reflect on the message or voices that appeared and record in your journal.

You can practice Voice Dialogue with a self that emerged from your process through journaling. As the facilitator you can dialogue with this self to try to understand how it is presently serving you and what need of yours might not be getting met. Be curious about what the opposite self would be and then dialogue with it. Then come back to the centre and read what both selves wrote. With greater awareness then you can decide the best course of action to get your needs met.

Examples of some common pairs of opposites are:

- Control - Release
- Power - Vulnerability
- Rational – Emotional
- Perfectionist – Imperfect
- Pleaser – Selfish or Rebel
- Inner Critic – Inner Teacher
- Pusher – Beach Bum
- Extrovert – Introvert
- Serious – Playful
- Independent – Needy
- Responsible – Lazy or Irresponsible

Suggested Reading:

- Stone, Hal, and Sidra Stone. *Embracing Our Selves; The Voice Dialogue Training Manual.* Mill Valley: New World Library, Naturaj, 1998.

DAY 4—THURSDAY: PRACTICE THE PATH: MYSTERY AND PRESENCE

MAP 3 – MUTUALITY AND PARTNERING

How can we clear barriers to living with deeper intimacy for greater relational vitality?

4."May I be Loving & Compassionate."

"We set our intention on love and compassion—the transforming energy for health and happiness of all. We vow to help all beings be free from the causes of their suffering."

Today is Thursday on our practice calendar. We have arrived at the fourth chakra now and are in the air element located in the heart. In the centre, we awaken to a healing presence, this is our evolving centre. In the left centre we bring healing presence and purification to our inner parts, and in the right centre we remember soulful partnering. These are the left and right centres for transformation, like the wings of the heart or the wings of the butterfly.

Resting in the Deep Heart we experience the Home of Our Soul, Our True Nature, Mystery and Presence, Reality, the Source of Love and Wisdom (Whatever Name that works for you.) Here are some possible contemplations.

- Who are your soul guides?

- Who are your soul friends?
- Who do you need to forgive and let go of from the past?
- Are your relationships intimate or soulful?
- What are your practices for resting in the Home of Your Soul, your True Nature, Mystery and Presence?
- Identify your attachment style.
- Cultivate the Third Presence for soulful relationships.
- Create a multi-generational family tree or genogram and list traumas and addictive tendencies.

Mystery and Presence Practice: Notice your breath without trying to change it. Focus your attention in the centre of your chest and allow your chest to soften and open. Rest in your deep Heart, the Ground of Being, your True Nature; the Home of your Soul.

Bring your attention to your physical heart, allow this area to soften and open. Bring compassion to any parts of you that are suffering. Then bring your attention to your right breast, allow this area to soften and open. Rest in the deep field of mystery and presence.

Come back to the centre of your chest again. Rest in presence. Notice the two wings of your Great Heart, purification on the left extending down to your fingers on your left hand, and partnering on the right, also extending right down to your fingers on your right hand.

Open your arms wide like the wings of the butterfly, or an eagle, and feel the expansiveness of the wings of the Great Heart! Then bring them back together in prayer posture in the centre of your chest. Share gratitude for whatever came. Finally, dedicate this practice to the benefit of all beings, or whoever needs it most.

MUTUALITY AND PARTNERING PRACTICE:

Partnering practice for couples is essential to honour the high dream and work through the low dream, in Process language. This means working through positive and negative bonding patterns in Voice Dialogue.

Balance your hemispheres with awareness—right and left, thinking and feeling, impersonal and personal, power and vulnerability. Centre in your heart for healing presence and feel compassion for all the parts of your personality and all the parts of your partner's personality.

PRACTICE:

Make good use of your inner warrior by protecting each other's vulnerability and dedicating time for your inner lovers! Beforehand, agree on a neutral time-out signal if either person feels overwhelmed or needs a break. Prepare by planning a time that works for both you and your partner. Put it on the calendar and stick to the time. Arrive ready to focus all your attention on the process.

Depending on your typology designate a place for the Third, your Relationship as Teacher, Healer and Guide. You could create a shrine based on the elements. You could place a whiteboard or something to write on later in this place. Draw a line across the middle separating the top from the bottom. Or you could use an empty chair.

You could have both of your names written at the top of the whiteboard. For example, *Dave and Sue*. You could name the Third as a combination of your names, such as Dasu and Suave. You could also use Divine pairs, like Rama and Sita, Shiva and Shakti or Abba and Sophia, etc. This Third represents the Sacred Love that brought the two of you together.

It helps to use a timer. You could spin a pen to see who goes first. The pointy end of the pen points to the sender and the other person will be the receiver.

Sit comfortably close to and facing your partner. Close your eyes.

Take a minute or two for each person to centre within himself or herself, becoming whole within yourselves to the best of your ability at this time. Close your eyes and embrace the opposites within yourself with awareness. Remember you have two eyes and a third eye that can see the opposites with awareness. If your inner critic or judge is active, just make note of it with awareness. See if you can feel compassion for this part of you that is trying to protect your vulnerability.

When the timer sounds gently open your eyes and hold your partner's hands. Gaze softly into each other's left eye, this is the receptive side that connects with your brain's right hemisphere (the left side of your body corresponds to the right hemisphere of your brain and vice versa). Feel the warmth of your partners loving touch. Allow their healing presence and gaze to soften your heart. The sender shares one essential quality they appreciate in their partner.

Keep it simple, for example; "I appreciated your loving support when you held my hand at the doctor's office yesterday!" The receiver takes the appreciation in fully and while still gazing into their partner's left eye, says simply, "Thank you!" The receiver also repeats back the essence of what they understood their partner to say.

Then switch partners. The sender becomes the receiver, and the receiver becomes the sender. For example, "I appreciated your thoughtfulness this morning, when you made me a cup of tea!"

At the end of the first round, you could write the essential qualities on the bottom half of the whiteboard, such as, 'Loving support and thoughtfulness.' (You can take as many rounds as you like.) Embrace and hold each other for enough time to co-regulate.

When you feel deeply connected, turn and sit shoulder to shoulder and face the whiteboard. Now that you are facing the Third Presence, love in the form of these particular essential qualities, i.e. loving support and thoughtfulness etc. Place a challenge on the whiteboard above the line—for example, 'Who will pick up the groceries on Saturday?'

Working as partners shoulder-to-shoulder, then face-to-face, share how you feel about this activity. Finally, brainstorm options and action steps to take. If either of you gets too defensive, then you may need to call a time out to self-regulate before continuing. It's best to come back to the process as soon as you feel safe to do so.

It helps to determine what developmental stage your relationship is in and what change needs to happen to transform and evolve to your next soulful stage of relating? See the Couple's Institute for information on stages of relationship.

Reading together and doing exercises from a book on cultivating conscious relationships can be a very intimate practice.

Suggested Reading:

- Rowan, John. *Healing the Male Psyche—Therapy as Initiation*, Routledge, 1997
- Luke, Helen. *Kaleidoscope—The Way of Women*, Parabola Books, 1992
- Barks, Coleman. *The Essential Rumi*, Harper San Francisco. 1995.
- Oliver, Mary. *Wild Geese*, Bloodaxe Books Ltd. 2004
- Zimmerman, Jack and McCandless, Jacqueline. *Flesh and Spirit*, Bramble Books, 1998.

DAY 5—FRIDAY: PRACTICE THE PATH, MUTUALITY AND PARTNERING

How can we clear barriers to uncovering our inner resources?

5. Mindfulness: "May I Be Centred and Mindful Through Breathing."

"Mindfully, we concentrate on our breathing. This calms, clears and focuses our mind. Thought, memories, and feelings are observed and released. We focus on our breath, drawing it into the heart-centre of our being. Opening ourselves to the reciprocity of universal love, healing, and wisdom we establish the tranquil focus for deep meditation."

Today is Friday on our practice calendar. The fifth chakra located in the throat is the ether element where we experience prayer, on the ascending path and praise on the descending path. By prayer, I don't mean just mechanically uttering phrases learned by rote. What would a conversation between Lover and Beloved sound like? Maybe it would take the form of song or poetry? What would it be like to speak to the divine as if you were best friends? What would you talk about?

Allow yourself the freedom to include all of yourself, even the parts of you that you feel ashamed of. Of course, if your God image is a judgmental parent, you might not feel safe to do that. Perhaps, like your own parents, you might hide parts of yourself that they would disapprove of.

I invite you to wonder about your God image. Is it serving you or keeping you in a parent-child, bonding pattern with a parental authority figure? Is it possible to transform and evolve your God image to one that loves you unconditionally?

The Sufi way of meditation is referred to as remembrance practice.

Our small selves have forgotten our Self, Soul and connection to the Source, Spirit, Home of the Soul, Mystery and Presence, Reality, and so on. When we re-member our connection to the Source, we feel part of the Oneness again.

REMEMBRANCE PRACTICE

Sit comfortably and bow your head slightly to the left in the direction of your human heart, to begin. Say a prayer that is meaningful to you. Then say the phrase, 'Honouring my inner world of psyche' as you gently move your head from left to right in a semi-circle arriving in stillness at a zenith point straight above your crown chakra at the top of your head. Then, consciously sigh, releasing your breath and anything you want to release, to the Source all around you.

Then bow your head again, this time into the centre of your chest saying, 'Resting in the Home of my Soul'. Then sigh again, releasing your breath fully into the Home of your Soul. Rest with your head bowed into the temple of your Great Heart. Say, 'Resting in being True Nature'. Express a deep sigh again. Let go fully and rest in Presence. When you are ready, slowly raise your head to eye level, exhaling, and say as you are rising, 'Remembering the Gifts of my Unfolding Soul'. Sigh again.

Sitting still with head facing forward say, 'Present in the Presence'. Experiment with saying it on the in-breath and the out-breath, then just rest in silence. Pause for as long as you like. Notice your state and any Essential Qualities that are present like peace, compassion, forgiveness, light, joy, and so on.

Now switch the phrase slightly to, 'Presents in the Presence'. Alternate this on the *in* breath and the *out* breath. Then rest and notice again if there are presents, like Inner Gifts that are given to you as a present.

Take a moment for thankfulness for any Inner Gifts that you have received from the Source. Share praise in gratitude to the Source of the Gifts. Dedicate the fruit of your practice to those who need it most.

COUPLES OR GROUP PRACTICE

Couples could do this practice together; then share the gazing practice mentioned on Thursday. When it is the senders turn, then share briefly what Essential Qualities have emerged in them. The receiver again just says, 'Thank you!' Then they switch turns. This fosters Mutuality And Partnering.

To practice awakening the essential Gifts of Presence in a group, I first lead a group meditation, then have participants pair and share some of their experience. It helps to use a timer and ring a bell when it is time to switch and time to wrap-up. Then, I invite the group to rest in Presence and invite whoever feels called to share with the group, the essence of their experience. If they would like some essential reflection, I invite them to raise their hand. Then I open it up to the group to whoever wants to give them an essential reflection. When they do, then the person calls on them with a nod. The person gives them a reflection naming the Essential Qualities they witnessed. The first person again just says 'Thank-you!' and breathing in deeply receives the offering fully.

At the end we say a prayer for the benefit of anyone in the world who could use this essence the most, to receive it as a Gift. It feels wonderful to be seen for our soul's essence rather than only the various personas we are normally identified with.

We can even practice in simple moments like when brushing our teeth. Look into your own eyes for a moment and acknowledge the divine being that is seeing you.

Rumi gives us another hint as to where the Inner Treasure is to be found:

> *I am so small I can barely be seen.*
> *How can this great love be inside of me?*
> *Look at your eyes, they are small but they*
> *See enormous things.*
>
> —*Rumi (Translation: Robert Bly)*

DAY 6—SATURDAY: PRACTICE THE PATH: MEANING AND PURPOSE

How can we clear barriers to uncovering and giving our inner gifts so we can live with deeper meaning and purpose for greater vocational vitality?

MAP2 (Mystery And Presence)
MAP4 (Meaning And Purpose)

6. Meditation: "May I Become Wise through Meditation."

"Meditation and contemplation are taught in many ways by many traditions. With sincere respect and appreciation for others and dedication to our own practice, we silently engage in our own meditation. Alone or in community we deepen our own wisdom as well as our InterSpiritual communion with other diverse experiences of the "sacred."

Today is Saturday on our practice calendar and the element is mineral at the sixth chakra, located in our third eye area. Today we get clear on our Inner Gifts, our purpose and the meaningful need our Gifts serve in the world with the ICMAP (Inner Compass Multidimensional Awakening Practice.)

If you recall our map for manifesting a life of meaning and purpose is Meaning and Purpose (MAP) = True Nature (TN) + Essential Qualities (EQ) + Natural Gifts (NG) − Personality Resistance (PR) + Meaningful Need (MN)

INNER COMPASS MULTIDIMENSIONAL AWAKENING PRACTICE (ICMAP):

In this body map practice, all the words that I use start with the letter 'p', as in path. The practice and journey is moving mindfully from your left foot, up through your central channel, to your seventh energy centre at the top of your head, then back down through your central channel, to your first energy centre at your perineum and into your right foot for walking your path.

Find a posture that is comfortable yet alert. Close your eyes gently. Begin by focusing your attention in the centre of your chest. I invite you to place one hand on the centre of your chest and the other on your belly. Choose whichever hand feels most natural to you. Feel the warmth of your touch. This helps you centre and integrate. Notice your breath. Allow presence to arise from the centre of your chest. Presence or pre-sense is prior to your senses. This is like the centre of your compass. The centre is directionless. Say the phrase, 'Present in the Presence.' Pause and be aware.

Next connect your compass needle, your attention, into your left foot. Your left foot represents practice. Be present and aware of the minor energy centres in your left foot. Mindfully explore the sensations in your left leg: your foot, to your ankle, to your calf, knee and then your thigh. At the top of your left thigh is another subtle energy centre. Be present to this centre and notice if your left leg softens and opens.

Bring your attention to your first major energy centre in your perineum region between your anus and genitals. This is the centre of physicality on the ascending path and place on the descending path. Be present to this centre and see if it softens and opens. Imagine sending your roots down into the ground.

Send your attention to your right foot and notice the subtle energy centres and sensations in your right foot. Your right foot represents your path. See if your right foot softens and opens with presence. Move your attention mindfully up the inside of your right leg noticing your ankle, calf, knee and then your thigh. At the top of your right thigh is another subtle energy centre. Be present to this centre and notice if your right leg softens and opens. This subtle centre in the right thigh represents play. Bring your attention to your first major energy centre again. This is the earth centre, the centre for physicality and place. Feel gratitude for your six bodily senses here. This lower third of your body represents magic and play.

Notice the gift of sensation. Feel sensation in your body. Notice the gift of touch. Feel your seat touching the chair or floor. Notice the gift of taste. Notice the gift of smell. Notice the gift of seeing. Notice the gift of hearing. Notice sound and also notice the silence. Awareness is a pre-sense, prior to the senses. Pause and be aware.

Next bring your attention to your second major energy centre just below your belly button. This is the water centre, the centre of your emotions and sexuality. On the ascending path this centre represents process and on the descending path passion. Be present to this centre and allow your emotions to be as they are without judgment. See if there is flow. E-motions want to flow.

Move your attention to the third major energy centre located in your solar plexus region. This is the fire centre and represents mastery and proactivity, power on the ascending path and proactivity on the descending path. This centre gives us the power to focus our attention where we want it to go and the proactivity to set our goals and accomplish them. If you notice a thought, just be aware of it and focus on your third energy centre again.

Focus and bring the arrow of your attention to the centre of your chest again. Rest in the heart of presence.

(Pause)

Stay here for as long as you like. If you made a recording you may want to pause it here and just rest in mystery and presence, the Home of your Soul.

(Pause)

Move your attention to the left side of your chest. This is the location of your human heart. Gently breathe into this subtle energy centre. Imagine that it is like a rose that may be closed. With the light of your awareness caress the rose until it warms and starts opening. This centre represents purification on our soulful map.

Bring your left hand to your heart centre. In the centre of your left palm is another subtle energy centre that represents parts. Each finger represents different parts, voices or sub personalities inside of us. The left thumb represents our persona. The pointer finger represents the part that protects us, or the protector. The middle finger represents the part of our personality that is primary. The ring finger represents our practitioner. The golden ring (on the ring finger) symbolically represents deep peace, or any other Essential Quality you may need. The baby finger represents our powerless vulnerable self or inner child. (You may have your own list of selves.) When we embrace the opposites we experience deep peace.

REMEMBRANCE PRACTICE

This phase of the practice guides you through the fourth, fifth, sixth and seventh major energy centres.

Sit comfortably and bow your head slightly to the left in the direction of your human heart to begin. Say a prayer that is meaningful to you. Then say the phrase, 'Honouring my inner world of psyche' as you gently move your head from left to right in a semi-circle arriving at a zenith point straight above your crown chakra at the top of your head. Then consciously sigh, releasing your breath and anything you want to release, to the Source all around you.

Then bow your head again, this time into the centre of your chest saying, 'Resting in the Home of my Soul.' Then sigh, again releasing your breath fully into the Home of your Soul. Rest with your head bowed into the temple of your Great Heart. Then say, 'Resting in being True Nature.' Sigh. Let go fully and rest in Presence. Pause. When you are ready, slowly raise your head to eye level, exhaling while saying as you are rising, "Remembering the Gifts of my Unfolding Soul."

Now sigh!

(Pause)

Sitting still with head faced forward say, 'Present in the Presence'. Experiment with saying it on the in breath and the out breath, then just rest in silence. Notice your state and any Essential Qualities that are present like peace, compassion, forgiveness, light, joy, and so on.

Now switch the phrase slightly to, 'Presents in the Presence.' Alternate this on the in breath and the out breath. Then rest and notice again if there are presents, like Essential Qualities or Natural Gifts present. Prayer is the focus for the ascending path of the fifth chakra and praise is the focus for the path of the descending path in the fifth chakra. Presents—as in gifts—are the focus for the ascending path of the sixth chakra. What are your presents, your inner gifts of presence? Praise is the focus for the descending path of the fifth chakra. Feel gratitude to the Source for your inner or Natural Gifts!

Bring your attention to your seventh chakra, the crown and the pinnacle of the ascending path representing greater perspective. Picture the Earth from space. Feel the immensity of the Cosmos. Rest in Clear Mind as spacious pure awareness.

(Pause)

Contemplate, "What is the Source of these Inner Gifts?"

(Pause)

Say, "May I steward these Gifts, giving them to a meaningful need in the world." Then feel the pull downward into full participation with your inner gifts into the descending path of the seventh chakra.

In your descending sixth energy centre, contemplate an image or insight into your purpose for today. Inquire, "What is my psychic fingerprint? What is my unfolding soul's purpose?"

Feel gratitude and give praise to the Source in the descending path of the fifth chakra for any Inner Gifts or sense of your unfolding soul's purpose.

Move further down into the descending path of the fourth chakra located in the right breast. There is a subtle energy centre here that responds to your presence. Imagine there is another rose on this side of your chest. It may be closed, yet it begins to open, as the warmth of your breath and presence caress it. This is the centre for partnering. In this centre we partner with presence and our parts.

(Pause)

Send your attention down your right arm; there is a subtle energy centre in your right palm. This is the centre for your soulful plan. Bring your right hand to the centre of your chest. The right thumb represents philanthropy. What is your plan to give your gifts to a meaningful need today? The right pointer finger represents our Planet Earth; the right middle finger represents people; the right ring finger represents partner(s); and the baby finger represents parenting. Imagine giving your gifts of presence to all these areas.

Now I invite you to spread both your arms wide like the majestic Oak Tree or wings of the butterfly. Imagine giving your gifts to a meaningful need to increase the soul of the world and giving your presence to your loved ones for wholeness.

Then bring your hands together in prayer posture in the centre of your chest, the fourth energy centre of presence and say: "May I serve soulfully with love, wisdom and compassion for natural vitality, deep presence, intimacy, meaning and purpose."

Now move your attention to the third energy centre and contemplate what tangible measurable goals can you proactively set for your manifesting your purpose today. Write them down.

Move your attention to your second chakra and feel your passion for your purpose and vow to process skillfully with yourself and others to manifest your purpose and soulful life today.

Descending to the first energy centre, imagine planting the seeds of your purpose in the ideal place while honouring your physicality.

Be present to your left thigh and then to your right thigh and notice your right thigh energy centre for play.

Move your attention to your left foot, to remember to practice and then to your right foot to remember the path.

Finally, gently open your eyes and notice the state you are in. Feel gratitude for whatever you were aware of. Move your body in some novel way, enjoying being soulfully embodied.

Think or say out loud: "May I be present in the presence giving my gifts to a meaningful need today for the joy of living with natural vitality, deep presence, intimacy, meaning and purpose!"

I like to finish with an inspirational quote:

May you experience each day as a sacred gift woven around the heart of wonder!

—John O'Donohue

This is the main practice that I typically do on a daily basis, along with some breathing practice, singing and movement practice. My intention is to cultivate greater personal, relational and vocational vitality.

Here is a chart of the energy points and corresponding p's. Begin the practice with the left foot in the ascending line and end with path on the descending line.

MAP 2 & 4 Energy Centres:

Energy Centre	**Element**	**Location**	**Ascending**	**Descending**
7th Major	Nature	Crown	Perspective	Participation
6th Major	Mineral	Third Eye	Presents	Purpose
5th Major	Ether	Throat	Prayer	Praise
4th Minor	Air	Right Little Finger		Parenting
4th Minor	Air	Right Ring Finger		Partner(s)
4th Minor	Air	Right Middle Finger		People
4th Minor	Air	Right Pointer Finger		Planet

4th Minor	Air	Right Thumb		Philanthropy
4th Minor	Air	Right Palm		Plan
4th Minor	Air	Right Breast		Partnering
4th Minor	Air	Left ring finger's ring		Peace
4th Minor	Air	Left little finger		Powerless one
4th Minor	Air	Left Ring Finger		Practitioner
4th Minor	Air	Left Middle Finger		Primary
4th Minor	Air	Left Pointer Finger		Protector
4th Minor	Air	Left Thumb		Persona
4th Minor	Air	Left Palm		Parts
4th Minor	Air	Left Breast		Purification
4th Major	Air	Heart Centre	Presence	Presence
3rd Major	Fire	Solar Plexus	Power	Proactivity
2nd Major	Water	Genital Area	Process	Passion
1st Major	Earth	Perineum	Physicality	Place
1st Minor	Earth	Right Thigh	Play	Play
1st Minor	Earth	Right Foot	Path	Path
1st Minor	Earth	Left Thigh	Present	Present
1st Minor	Earth	Left Foot	Practice	Practice

I encourage you to make it your own by applying the practices from your own Tradition, or if you are spiritual but not religious (SBNR), you can adapt the practice, as you like. I don't see myself as a spiritual teacher, but rather as a wholistic mentor and psychospiritual facilitator.

Consult a spiritual teacher if you need specific spiritual guidance in your tradition.

Suggested Reading:

- Meade, Michael. *Fate And Destiny: The two Agreements of the Soul*, Greenfire Press, 2010
- Judith, Anodea and Lion Goodman. *Creating on Purpose—The Spiritual Technology of Manifesting Through The Chakras*, Sounds True, 2012
- Riso, Don Richard and Russ Hudson. *The Wisdom of the Enneagram—The Complete Guide to Psychological And Spiritual Growth For The Nine Personality Types*, Google Books 1999.
- Some, Malidoma. *The Healing Wisdom of Africa: Finding Life Purpose Through Nature, Ritual, and Community*, Jeremy P. Tarcher/Putnam, 1998
- Millman, Dan. *The Four Purposes of Life*, An H. J. Kramer book published in a joint venture with New World Library, 2011.

DAY 7—SUNDAY: PRACTICE THE PATH MAPS 2 & 4: MYSTERY AND PRESENCE, MEANING AND PURPOSE

How can we clear barriers in our thinking so we can heal, transform and evolve soulfully?

Today is Sunday and we are in the nature element on our practice calendar. The focus today is on gaining a larger perspective, then choosing to participate fully in the descending journey of cultivating a soulful life in the world.

INTERSPIRITUAL MEDITATION & MADALA

As I've shared before, my root teacher for cultivating soul is Sufi Teacher Thomas Atum O'Kane. Recently I have also been training with Buddhist teacher and educator Ed Bastian PH.D, who discovered that when he was teaching in an alternative school, each child responded best to the kind of learning that took their unique learning style into account. He teaches that this applies to spiritual practice too. He has developed a mandala process to help people apply this teaching to finding out what their unique spiritual style is.

> "God respects me when I work,
> but He (She) loves me when I sing."
>
> —Rabindranath Tagore

MAP 2: MYSTERY AND PRESENCE

This first practice is applicable to those who want to add an InterSpiritual perspective to their existing spiritual tradition or for those who think of themselves as the SBNR (spiritual but not religious). This InterSpiritual Meditation and Seven-Step Process was created by

Buddhist Teacher Ed Bastian PH.D. See *www.interspiritualmeditation.org* for Ed's basic framework and classes. Feel free to customize it for your own learning style and typology.

Ed's second book, *Mandala*, is helpful in determining your unique learning style. You could record these words and then play them back to yourself until you have memorized the sequence. I encourage you to make it your own by integrating the practices from your own Tradition or if you are spiritual but not religious (SBNR), you can adapt the practice, as you like. Consult a spiritual teacher if you need specific spiritual guidance. The great Jewish Rabbi Zalman Schachter-Shalomi used to say, "May I have a Jewish soul, a Sufi heart, a Buddhist mind and Christian hands…"

In this interspiritual spirit I like to add a chant with each of the seven steps to represent seven of the world's spiritual traditions.

INTERSPIRITUAL MEDITATION MAP: SEVEN STAGES

This contemplative process is shared by people from many perspectives and traditions. It can be practiced alone and in community with others. We gather in the language of silence and experience our inter-connectedness. We don't impose on others our own personal beliefs, rituals, or the names for our absolute truths, deities, or God.

We celebrate the wise and compassionate practices of all traditions and the profound unity within our diversity. We are of one heart. In silence, each of us engages in our own prayers, words, and visualizations for each of the seven steps. The sound of a bell leads us from one to the next.

1. Motivation and Intention: May all beings become healthy and happy in body, mind and spirit. May I become healthy and happy in body, mind and spirit!

Physical, mental, and spiritual health are intertwined, and meditation nurtures sustainable health and happiness. We begin meditating with determination and confidence that it will help us to heal the innermost causes of illness and suffering. We rest into an InterSpiritual Consciousness for universal healing.

2. Gratitude: "May I Be Grateful to Life's Many Gifts."

With gratitude we invoke and honour our teachers, mentors, and great spiritual role models. We invite these great beings to remain present and pray that their example and presence will guide us. We focus on the blessings of friends, family, and the environment that nurture and sustain us.

3. "May I Be Awake & Transformed."

Focusing on the highest ideal for our life, we acknowledge and confess our shortcomings and promise to patiently persevere in our personal transformation. We vow to remove our inner obstacles and negativities. Without guilt, we forgive others and ourselves as we offer our lives in service to our highest goals.

4. "May I be Loving & Compassionate."

We set our intention on love and compassion—the transforming energy for health and happiness of all. We vow to help all beings be free from the causes of their suffering.

5. "Mindfulness: "May I Be Centred and Mindful through Breathing."

Mindfully, we concentrate on our breathing. This calms, clears and focuses our mind. Thought, memories, and feelings are observed and released. We focus on our breath, drawing it into the heart-centre of our being. Opening ourselves to the reciprocity of universal love, healing, and wisdom we establish the tranquil focus for deep meditation.

6. Meditation: "May I Become Wise through Meditation."

Meditation and contemplation are taught in many ways by many traditions. With sincere respect and appreciation for others and dedication to our own practice, we silently engage in our own meditation. Alone or in community we deepen our own wisdom as well as our InterSpiritual communion with other diverse experiences of the "sacred."

7. "May I serve all beings with Compassion, Peace, and Wisdom."

Visualizing our family, friends, colleagues, antagonists, and all beings through out the world we rededicate ourselves to becoming servants of peace, justice, and environmental health. May this meditation help us to engage together in the world with passion, patience, kindness, and wisdom.

SOULFUL DIALOGUE WITH NATURE

This practice can help you experience a subjective dimension with nature and heal a sense of separation. Find a tree you are drawn to. On the horizontal plane, if we had a slice of the tree's diameter, we could see the tree has rings that show its biological age and evolution over time. If we create a circle around the tree we create a compass or medicine wheel with our tree rooted in the centre. If you stand with your back resting into the tree you can feel rooted and still. Close your eyes and focus your attention in the centre of your chest. There is a heart centre of the tree and a Heart centre in you.

You can imagine that in your Heart centre there is the centre of a compass, this is the Home of your Soul, Mystery and Presence, the directionless place. From this centre of Presence open your eyes and see what direction you are facing. With your back still supported by the tree, are you facing East, South, North or West? This orients you to where you are now. You are here, rooted in this place, facing this direction. Is this the direction you want to travel?

In the Algonquin Medicine wheel I mentioned earlier the seven directions are honoured. There is the upper world for the Creator, Great Spirit, Great Mystery; and the lower world, our unique soul, our psychic fingerprint, our god seed, the place for our roots, where our medicine grows. The four cardinal directions of creation give us the main points of our human compass. The direction within is where we rest in our heart centre; our evolving centre, the place where all these directions intersect and where we rest in our True Nature. This is the place where the true freedom to choose our direction in life emerges.

A Medicine Wheel can be used in many ways depending on the particular tradition. In the Algonquin Medicine wheel, in the East is the child, in the South is the youth, in the West is the adult and in the North is the elder. One way to use the wheel is for integrating all these four parts of your Self. The elder is someone who can rest in mystery and presence, while reflecting on the gifts of magic and play in their childhood, the gifts of mastery and proactivity of their youth and the gifts of meaning and purpose of their adulthood. When they interact consciously with others they are practicing mutuality and partnering.

When I apply the essence of this wisdom to Voice Dialogue, I have a model and process for facilitating a dialogue with all these inner parts or sub-personalities and the Self. If its not convenient to do this outdoors, with an actual tree, then you could draw a large circle on the floor or on a piece of paper. You could also use objects to form a circle. Grab a handful of seeds or other symbolic objects of different kinds. We will be exploring your inner garden. You could put an acorn in the centre, or some other seed, to represent your evolving aware ego process, your evolving centre, the centre that can integrate and dance with all the directions.

When you are ready sit in the centre and ask your self, "Who am I in this moment?" Perhaps the first thought that comes to you is, "I am a mother or a father!" If this is true, take an object, for example one of the seeds, and place it in the circle, intuitively choose the right direction and proximity for the weight this self carries in your life. Now you have separated one of your sub-personalities out from your centre.

Take a moment and feel the difference between this self and you. You can be aware of the object and the self that the object represents. This awareness gives you more space inside.

If you judge the object, the self or yourself, this is another self. Let's call it the judge, if it judges others, and the critic if it criticizes you. We usually have both outer judge and inner critic. Take another seed (or two if there are two voices) and place it or them in the circle, again in the direction and proximity of the weight it carries in your life. Once you have placed it there, now you have two or three seeds or selves placed in your inner garden. Notice that you can be aware of the seeds or selves and you are still in the centre. Feel how much space you have inside now. You may start to feel more relaxed as you get some space from these primary selves.

To continue with the garden metaphor, you are really the assistant gardener in your inner world of psyche. Your True Nature, the Mystery, is the Master Gardener. If you identify with any self/seed it's like you think you are one of your plants.

Soulful gardeners will tell you that they can communicate with their plants and likewise we can communicate with our selves. So I invite you to dialogue with the voice/seed that you most identify with in this moment, let's say your inner mother. Ask your inner mother to tell you about herself.

Then move to sit in her position and speak as her facing the centre. You could use a journal and let her choose the colour of the pen she writes with. Perhaps she uses a paintbrush? Allow your creativity to be spontaneous.

Once she finishes, go back to the centre and sit facing her and read what she wrote to you. This is a moment of differentiation between you and her. Feel the difference between you and her.

Continue your dialogue with her or choose another self in the same manner. You could work with a dream this way. For example if Isaac from the story, the Treasure, was doing this process he could sit in the centre and then place a seed for his dream ego in the circle. Then he could go and sit in that place and tell the dream from his dream ego's perspective.

Then Isaac could sit in the centre and reflect on what was said by his dream ego. Then he could place a seed in the circle to represent his inner wise guide. In the same way he could sit in the guides place and share the dream from this perspective. He then goes back to the centre and reflects on what his inner dream guide said to him. You could ask the guide what your gifts are for living a soulful life of presence, meaning and purpose?

It is best to end the process in the centre aware ego process. Reflect on what you have learned, and feel gratitude for any insights. Ask yourself, "Who am I becoming?"

JOURNALING

This same Voice Dialogue process can be done in a journal too.

Sit in the centre of a couch. Let your facilitator voice ask to speak to a self. It is safer to start with a self that protects you and is a primary self. Move to one side of the couch, pick up a pen with your dominant hand and write from that self's perspective. Then come back to the centre and reflect on what it said.

As the facilitator you can keep dialoguing with this self to learn how it operates in your life and what its beliefs are. When you are ready explore the opposite side, you could use your non-dominant hand for a disowned self. Similarly, dialogue with this self.

When you are complete, read what each self wrote. From the centre your aware ego process can choose more freely how to act on what was revealed. If you judge a self, that is simply another self, facilitate the judge. If you are afraid, again it is another self.

Check in with the protection self to see if it is all right to embrace this fear at this time. If the material gets too overwhelming, then it's best to seek guidance from a professional skilled in Voice Dialogue.

End in the middle. Ask yourself again, "Who am I becoming?"

EVOLUTION THROUGH SPIRAL DYNAMICS

For a compelling look at how individuals and groups evolve, "Spiral Dynamics" is a theory of human development introduced in the 1996 book *Spiral Dynamics* by Don Beck and Chris Cowan. The book was based on the 1970s theories of psychologist Clare W. Graves.

Spiral Dynamics argues that human nature is not fixed: humans are able, when forced by life conditions, to adapt to their environment by constructing new, more complex, conceptual models of the world that allow them to handle the new problems. Each new model transcends and includes all previous models.

According to Beck and Cowan, these conceptual models are organized around so-called vmemes (pronounced "v memes") — systems of core values or collective intelligences, applicable to both individuals and entire cultures.

Graves's original theory uses a double helix model to show the interrelatedness of an individual's perception of life conditions with their inner neuronal systems, producing a level of psychological existence. This double helix of two interacting forces is referred to as a spiral in Spiral Dynamics.

An ascending colour system was added in the 1970s as a graphic element in training materials used by Cowan and Beck. These are (from lowest to highest):

1. Beige (Semi-Stone Age, dominated by nature and basic survival instincts)
2. Purple (Tribal animistic, magical, spiritistic),
3. Red (Exploitative, harsh authoritarianism)
4. Blue (Purposeful and patriotic, conforming to group norms)
5. Orange (Entrepreneurial, Personal success orientation)
6. Green (Communitarian, Sensitive, humanistic)

7. Yellow (Systemic—this is the first vMeme of the second tier in which there is a quantum shift in the capacity to take multiple perspectives in life)
8. Turquoise (Holistic, Focused on a global holism/integralism, attuned to the delicate balance of interlocking life forces).

Within the model, individuals and cultures do not fall clearly in any single category (colour). Each person/culture embodies a mixture of the value patterns, with varying degrees of intensity in each. Spiral Dynamics claims not to be a linear or hierarchical model.

There are also transitional stages where the predominant vMeme is shown in capital letters and the less influential vMeme in lowercase—for example, BLUE/orange is thus the exiting phase of a predominantly BLUE coloured world view, mixed with emergent orange.

A corporation, for example, might cling to the bedrock of BLUE, while the information economy forces entirely new ways of doing business. Many illustrious corporations thus end up on the rocks as the next wave of change reveals their incapacity to adapt to new economic circumstances.

According to Spiral Dynamics, there are infinite stages of progress and regression over time, dependent upon the life circumstances of the person or culture, which are constantly in flux. Attaining higher stages of development is not synonymous with attaining a 'better' or 'more correct' values system.

All stages co-exist in both healthy and unhealthy states, meaning any stage of development can lead to undesirable outcomes with respect to the health of the human and social environment.

Each person and group is operating at a particular developmental stage of evolution. It helps to honour the stage the person or group is presently at, while inviting curiosity as to what the next developmental stage of soulful evolution offers. For more information, go to *http://en.wikipedia.org/wiki/Spiral_Dynamics*

EVOLUTIONARY LEADERSHIP

Humanity clearly needs leaders who can take multiple perspectives in life. Using the language of memes for comparison, imagine each meme is like wearing a particular pair of coloured glasses. Through a blue lens our perception is coloured blue, and so on. Even within each religion there are different memes or levels of consciousness. Each meme sees Ultimate Reality differently. Like the story of the blind men in the dark trying to describe an elephant by touch, each one has only a partial perspective. This is how major polarizations around the science versus soul debate occur. To evolve soulfully, imagine trying on different pairs of coloured glasses and reflect on how each of these different perspectives and memes live within you.

As mentioned earlier, in *Thank-God for Evolution*, Rev. Michael Dowd teaches, "Reality reconciles Science and Religion." His favorite name for God is Reality. Rather than polarize between either science or soul he invites us to embrace both science and soul.

Cosmologist Brian Swimme suggests there are three ways we can evolve soulfully into deeper maturation: by transforming our consciousness, speaking truth to power and through social innovation. When we contribute to increasing more soul in the world we can feel a sense of joy or fulfillment.

> *"Without Art, we should have no notion of the sacred; without Science, we should always worship false gods."*
>
> *- W. H. Auden*

SUGGESTED READING

- Bastian, Edward. *InterSpiritual Meditation—A Seven-Step Process from the World's Spiritual Traditions*, Spiritual Paths Publishing, 2010

- Bastian, Edward. *Mandala*, Spiritual Paths Publishing, 2014

- Dowd, Michael. *Thank God for Evolution*, The Penguin Group, 2007.

- Moore, Thomas. *The Soul's Religion*, HarperCollins, 2002.

- Plotkin, Bill. *Wild Mind—A Field Guide To The Human Psyche*, New World Library, 2013.

- Kahn, Pir Vilayat Inayat. *Awakening: A Sufi Experience*. New York: Jeremy Tarcher, 2000.

ACKNOWLEDGEMENTS

I wish to wholeheartedly thank my many clients who continue to inspire me with their courage and dedication to transforming their life. Big hugs and thank-you...through creative expression.

My sincere appreciation also goes to my deep soul friend Roq Gareau who helped give me perspective and rolled up his sleeves in the final editing process when I needed it the most.

Many thanks to my wife Sue and friends Annemarie, Vince and Eric for giving your time so generously to help with proofreading and editing.

Big hugs and thank-you to my dear companions at the Natural Gifts Society, Michael Talbot Kelly, Anne-Marie Konas, Rebecca and Peter Cheung, who were all incredibly supportive and inspiring.

ABOUT THE AUTHOR

DAVE WALI WAUGH, RPC

Dave loves to inspire people of all ages to awaken to and live their Natural Gifts through the arts of storytelling and wholistic process.

As a Wholistic Mentor And Psychotherapist and Natural Gifts Mentor, he is passionate about designing wholistic programs and facilitating processes that assist his clients to heal, transform and evolve soulfully.

He finds it very fulfilling to journey with someone who is stuck in a major life transition or with someone who is simply curious about evolving and witness them gradually awaken to a renewed sense of natural vitality, deep presence, intimacy, meaning and purpose.

Dave is the Director of Elements Counselling and the Current President of the Process Counselling Society in Vancouver BC. He is also Co-Founder and Vice-President of the Natural Gifts Society.

Dave can be reached at 604-488-9203 (mobile), or 604-739-6053 (office), or at www.evolvingsoulfully.com and www.davewaugh.net on the internet.

www.ingramcontent.com/pod-product-compliance
Lightning Source LLC
Chambersburg PA
CBHW071900290426
44110CB00013B/1216